Developing New Products and Services

Developing New Products and Services

Learning, Differentiation, and Innovation

G. Lawrence Sanders

With contributions by
Ron Huefner
Sung Jin
Yong Jin Kim
Lorena Mathien
Barbara Sherman
Xiao Tang
Chul Woo Yoo

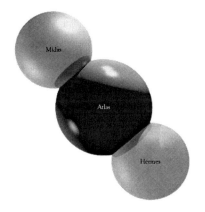

First published in 2011 by
Business Expert Press, LLC
222 East 46th Street, New York, NY 10017
www.businessexpertpress.com

ISBN-13: 978-1-60649-241-3 (paperback)

ISBN-13: 978-1-60649-242-0 (e-book)

DOI 10.4128/9781606492420

A publication in the Business Expert Press Marketing Research collection

Collection ISSN: Forthcoming (print)
Collection ISSN: Forthcoming (electronic)

Cover design by Jonathan Pennell
Interior design by Scribe Inc.

First edition: September 2011

10 9 8 7 6 5 4 3 2 1

Printed in the United States of America.

This book is dedicated to my mother Phyllis Sanders. She is a constant source of inspiration in my life.

Abstract

The focus of the book is on the up-front activities and ideas for new product and service development. A central theme of this book is that there is, or should be, a constant struggle going on in every organization, business, and system between delivering feature-rich versions of products and services using extravagant engineering and delivering low-cost versions of products and services using frugal engineering. Delivering innovative products is accomplished by an endless cycle of business planning, creative and innovative insight, and learning-about and learning-by-doing activities.

A number of powerful concepts and tools are presented in the book to facilitate new product development. For example, three templates are presented that facilitate new product and service development. The FAD (features, attributes, and design) template is used to identify the features and attributes that can be used for product and service differentiation. The Ten–Ten planning process contains two templates: an Organizational and Industry Analysis template and the Business Plan Overview template. These two templates coupled with the FAD template can be used to develop a full-blown business plan. Entrepreneurship, technology and product life cycles, product and service versioning, product line optimization, creativity, lock-in real options, business valuation, and project management topics are also covered.

Keywords

Developing new products services, NPD, product design, learning, differentiation, price discrimination, product features, innovation, business planning, organizational analysis, diffusion, entrepreneurship, technology and product life cycles, product and service versioning, product demand, product line optimization, creativity, lock-in real options, business valuation and project management

Contents

For PowerPoint slides and other supplemental materials that accompany this book, please visit www.glsanders.wordpress.com.

Preface

A central theme of this book is that there is, or should be, a constant struggle going on in every organization, business, and system. The struggle is fueled by the dynamic tension that exists between delivering Midas feature-rich versions of products and services using extravagant engineering and delivering low-cost Hermes versions of products and services using frugal engineering (see Figure 1). Midas versions are high-end products for nonprice-sensitive consumers. Hermes versions are for price-sensitive consumers. The results of this dynamic tension between Midas versioning and Hermes versioning are Atlas products and services. Atlas products and services are designed for mainstream consumers. Atlas products and services incorporate the product design features that will attract the broadest customer base and will also be profitable. The driving force behind the development of Midas, Atlas, and Hermes versions is driven by the implicit creative genius that everyone possess and most businesses should possess as they engage in continuous learning-about and learn-by-doing activities.

Anyone can learn how to be creative and innovative. Just work hard by learning about the problem, and then try to solve the problem by

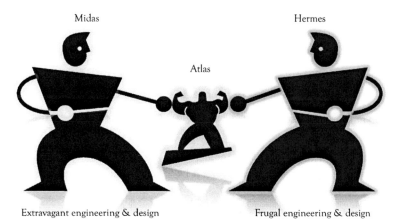

Midas

Hermes

Atlas

Extravagant engineering & design

Frugal engineering & design

Figure 1. Dynamic tension between Midas design and Hermes design.

making or doing something. Not all systems and businesses can be creative and innovative. Some companies can work hard and they can learn about a problem but they cannot build and do things because they have lost the ability to do so. They have lost the ability to learn-by-doing.

The Dueling Mantras

Our primary mantra for a business is "differentiate through innovation or perish." This is accomplished primarily through extravagant engineering and design and the construction of Midas versions. This is not an easy path to follow, because there is a natural tendency toward inertia and resting on one's laurels.[1] It is our assertion that creative and innovative business planning driven by learning-about and learning-by-doing leads to sustainable businesses. Our focus will be on the upfront activities and ideas for product and service differentiation that result in competitive products and services. They include the endless cycle of business planning, creative and innovative insight, learning-about, and learning-by-doing.

The *second mantra* of the entrepreneur is to "strive to reduce costs." This is accomplished primarily through frugal engineering and design and the construction of Hermes versions. Some organizations have been overly enthusiastic in embracing this mantra. In some businesses, learning-by-doing has been abandoned in an attempt to dramatically cut costs and increase margins in the wake of intense international competition. But this has had a negative impact on the ability of many organizations to innovate, because many companies have lost the ability to exploit new knowledge and information when it becomes available. Many organizations have lost what is referred to as absorptive capacity. Absorptive capacity is the ability of a firm to "recognize the value of new information, assimilate it, and apply it to commercial ends."[2] It is the ability to apply previously gained knowledge and insight to understanding how new information and knowledge can be applied. Developing absorptive capacity is synonymous with developing insight. Insight is the ability to perceive complex situations, problems and opportunities clearly and deeply. Andy Grove, a past founder and CEO of Intel, pegs the current situation perfectly:

Silicon Valley is a community with a strong tradition of engineering, and engineers are a peculiar breed. They are eager to solve whatever problems they encounter. If profit margins are the problem, we go to work on margins, with exquisite focus. Each company, ruggedly individualistic, does its best to expand efficiently and improve its own profitability. However, our pursuit of our individual businesses, which often involves transferring manufacturing and a great deal of engineering out of the country, has hindered our ability to bring innovations to scale at home. Without scaling, we don't just lose jobs—we lose our hold on new technologies. Losing the ability to scale will ultimately damage our capacity to innovate.[3]

The USA is losing the ability to compete in high-tech fields in part because it has abandoned learning-by-doing. Basic research and applied research involving broad-based collaboration by government, academia, and business are essential for solving societal problems and in providing a base for technology-based businesses.[4] Basic research involves understating the fundamental principles and dynamics of physics, chemistry, biology, and cybernetics to name a few. Applied research involves translating the principles and dynamics of basic research into commercial applications. The U.S. government up to about 1990 distributed about the same amount of funds to both basic and applied research projects. In recent years, the gap between basic research funding and applied research funding has been widening. The U.S. government has provided less money for applied research.[5]

Outsourcing has also reduced the level of applied research. New product development is essentially applied research. New product development is facilitated when an organization has core competencies in research and development (R&D), product design, and manufacturing. Everyone is beginning to realize that there is a synergistic interplay between R&D, product design, marketing, and manufacturing. New product development is put at risk when these activities are outsourced, off-shored, or both. Entire industries are affected as the knowledge is not readily available for solving problems and realizing new opportunities essentially because it is embedded elsewhere.

Learning-by-Doing as the Basis for Competitiveness and Sustainability

Learning-by-doing means that the organization makes and builds things, conducts experiments, and builds prototypes. This includes the manufacturing process. The loss of absorptive capacity insight can often be traced to outsourcing. Outsourcing typically occurs when products and service margins are under severe market pressure, and organizations are forced to increase productivity by turning to locations where labor costs are substantially lower. This can have serious consequences. If the organization loses its absorptive capacity, then the organization may not be able to understand and recognize when an emerging technology is important. In essence, the organization does not have the ability to acquire know-how, expertise and skills because it has lost the ability to learn-by-doing and learn-about emerging ideas and technologies. Grove's solution to recapturing creative and innovative mojo is to reduce costs by also increasing the scale of operations. The essence of his idea is that if an organization can produce more, it will also be able to take advantage of learning effects and to cover the fixed costs of production. Intel is committed to product differentiation, scale and cost reduction, in-house manufacturing, and in-house design. Long-term sustainability is inextricably linked to the synergistic interplay of design, manufacturing, and market awareness.

There is a revolution taking place in all businesses. Additive and desktop manufacturing, open-source software, and the do-it-yourself movement are fueling this revolution. Products and components can be conceptualized, designed, and built using 3D printers. These printers use a process that is similar to building up layers of plastic and composite materials to build products and parts and to prototype ideas. A do-it-yourselfer can assemble such a printer for under $1,000. A commercial printer can be obtained in the $10–$20K range. The products produced from these printers can be used to produce commercial products and for prototyping. Large-scale 3D printers are being developed to produce products and components the size of aircraft wings. There is also a revolution taking place in the development of services. Cloud computing, applications development tools, and open-source software

are having a profound impact on the delivery of software-related services and applications. Software start-ups and prototypes can be constructed without investing in large-scale hardware infrastructure. The software itself can be cobbled together with a variety of development tools and open-source software. Competition can come from any size of company from anywhere in the world. All that is needed is an idea, hard work, and experimentation.

The Big *Aha* and Learning-by-doing

As we shall see throughout the book, the magic sauce of innovation involves learning and experimentation. Weaving together the little *ahas* through a continuous learning process is the basis of interesting ideas and innovation. As illustrated in Figure 2, learning-about and learning-by-doing are the drivers of innovation and new product development.

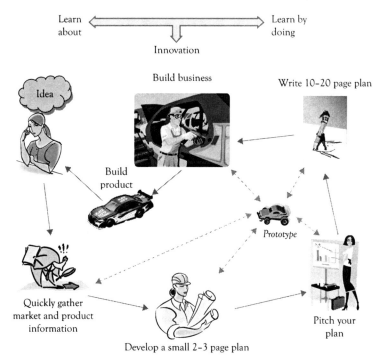

Figure 2. Learning about and learning by doing drive innovation and new product development.

This process involves the continuous mixing together of collaboration, searching for ideas, and then making things. As noted in chapter 6, the little *ahas* eventually lead to the big *aha* and the big *aha* is not necessarily the solution to the original problem. The big *aha* is simply illuminating, insightful, and innovative. Peter Sims suggests the placing of little bets to explore possibilities and engage in innovation.[6] Little bets are essentially low-risk investments with a chance of failure that incorporate the development and testing of ideas. Placing little bets leads to little *ahas* and eventually to the big *aha*. Placing little bets are actually investments in what are referred to as real options, and that topic will be covered in depth in chapter 14.

There are of course other important issues in the execution of a successful business, including the development of an efficient supply chain and the development of a strong brand. The supply chain and developing a brand are discussed throughout the book, but they deserve more attention and detail and the reader is encouraged to learn-about these topics by reading and attending professional development programs. As noted in chapter 8, organizations need above-average performance in terms of product and service innovation, the supply chain, and branding in order to survive.

Book Chapters

This book is concerned primarily with the early stages of conceptualizing new ideas that can enhance existing business models and subsequently lead to the creation of new businesses (see Figure 3). The material in this book has been in development over the last 10 years in a course on technology management and development. One purpose of the course is to understand how technologies unfold and how they guide the strategic direction of contemporary business. The course involves reading and discussing over a dozen cases a wide variety of successful, emerging, and unsuccessful businesses. The cases used in the course are usually matched to chapter topics. The case studies and class dialog coupled with the reading of the book chapters are part of the learning-about process. The learn-by-doing part of the course involves the development of a business plan for a start-up company.

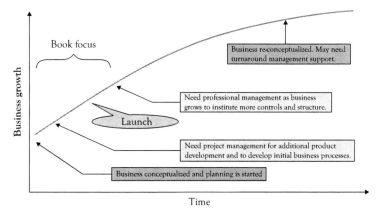

Figure 3. The focus of this book is on early stages of product
development.

Chapters

Chapter 1: Understanding Entrepreneurship, Diffusion, and R&D in the Context of Monopolistic Competition

The first chapter introduces the fundamental concepts related to understanding innovation, diffusion, technology life cycles, R&D, and entrepreneurship within the context of monopolistic competition. The importance of learning-about and learning-by-doing for developing innovative products and services is discussed.

Chapter 2: Fundamental Concepts of Product and Price Differentiation

Chapter 2 illustrates the importance of product and price differentiation and how they relate to a consumer's willingness-to-pay and to price sensitivities. The chapter also describes first-, second-, and third-degree price discrimination strategies and how they can be implemented.

Chapter 3: Differentiation in Action

Chapter 3 illustrates why product differentiation and price discrimination can generate additional revenues. The chapter focuses on the use of versioning to aid in product differentiation. A spreadsheet is dashboard presented that can be used to assist in product versioning. The importance of complementary and substitute goods and their impact on revenues is also examined.

Chapter 4: Role of Dynamic Tension in Constructing Versioning and Product Differentiation Curves

Chapter 4 illustrates a model for constructing product differentiation curves that draws on the dynamic tension that exists between developing high-end Midas products and low-end Hermes products. The results of this dynamic tension between Midas versioning and Hermes versioning are Atlas products and services. Atlas products and services are designed for mainstream consumers.

Chapter 5: Examples of Product Differentiation and Versioning Curves

This chapter shows a variety of product differentiation and versioning strategies that have been used by businesses. Some businesses focus on versioning at the high end, some businesses focus on price-sensitive consumers, and some businesses try to offer products across the entire demand curve.

Chapter 6: Facilitating Creativity and Innovation

Chapter 6 discusses the concepts of creativity and innovation. Fostering creativity and innovative activity can be accomplished by dialog and discussion, learning-about, encouragement, time, solitude, experimentation, construction, and by having a supportive environment.

Chapter 7: Conceptualizing Products and Services Using the FAD Template

This chapter introduces the FAD (features, attributes, and design) template. The FAD template is used to identify the features and attributes that can be used for product and service differentiation. The FAD template incorporates concepts from meaning-driven design (MDD), user-driven design (UDD), and technology-driven design (TDD) and also uses a classification scheme that can be used to ascertain whether attributes and features are increasing or declining in importance.

Chapter 8: Strategic Planning Approaches for Product
Differentiation and Innovation

Chapter 8 presents a brief overview of the more popular approaches for
strategic planning. This chapter also sets the stage for the Ten–Ten planning process, a simplified yet robust approach to planning that will be
detailed in chapter 9.

Chapter 9: The Ten–Ten Planning Process: Crafting a Business Story

This chapter details the Ten–Ten planning process. The Ten–Ten planning
process contains two templates: an Organizational and Industry Analysis
template and the Business Plan Overview template. The idea behind the
Ten–Ten approach is that once you have gathered some background data
related to the industry and the organization, you should be able to complete the two very quickly. The chapter also describes how the Business
Plan Overview template and the Industry and Organizational template in
conjunction with the FAD template can be used to develop an executive
summary for the business plan.

Chapter 10: Lock-In and Revenue Growth

Chapter 10 discusses the importance of lock-in from the producer's perspective in achieving revenue goals through network effects. The chapter
also highlights how buyers try to avoid lock-in in order to maintain flexibility and avoid switching costs.

Chapter 11: Valuing the Business

The entrepreneur, the entrepreneur's friends and family, investors, and
banks are interested in how much a business is worth. This chapter discusses several approaches for valuing a business and presents several examples of how they can be applied.

Chapter 12: Developing a Business Plan

Chapter 12 presents a detailed approach for constructing a business plan.
The expanded business plan provides additional focus by adding details

on the what, why, how, when, and for whom a product or service will be produced. The FAD template, the Organizational and Industry Analysis template, the Business Plan Overview template and the executive summary are used as the basis for developing a full-scale business plan. A variety of issues are also discussed including the plan format, the writing style, investors, and legal issues. This chapter also discusses how to pitch the plan to interested parties.

Chapter 13: Project Management for New Products and Services Development

This chapter presents an overview of the essential tools and techniques for project management. Once the initial business model has been created, the hard work begins. In most situations, everything is new and needs to be built up from scratch. The entire supply chain has to be built and tested to insure that orders for products and services can be accepted, filled, and supported. Project management is a critical tool in the never-ending process of business growth and renewal. It allows the entrepreneur to minimize and mitigate inherent risks and increase the potential for the successful launch of the enterprise and the ensuing business renewal.

Chapter 14: Re-priming the Business Using Real Options Concepts

This chapter is about business renewal. It does not matter how innovative or how much money the current business is making. There is a life cycle for products and technologies, and eventually the business will decline unless it can find new opportunities. This chapter focuses on how real options concepts can be used as the foundation for continually reinventing the business.

Chapter 15: Wrap-Up

This chapter discusses the importance of being entrepreneurial in renewal. If a business does not make little and big tweaks to products and services, it will become a business footnote. The ideas presented in this book will not guarantee success, but they can be used to confront and also to ignore the competition by identifying and creating opportunities that supersede the competition.

Acknowledgments

I would first like to thank the series editor Naresh Malhotra. His guidance and comments dramatically improved the content and delivery of the material.

I would also like to thank colleagues Bill Hamlen, Ken Kim, Alan Dick, and Yong Li for providing guidance and reviewing book chapters related to their expertise. I would also like to thank Larry Meile from Boston College for reading early drafts of several chapters. His comments helped to focus the theme of the book. Elisabeth Beccue was very instrumental in her deft copy editing during the final phase of the book. Thanks are also extended to Keith Randolph, my source of engineering insight, for listening to my ideas and providing feedback.

It was clear after working on the book for over a year that the complexity and breadth of topics would require assistance if the book was to be completed in a reasonable time. Special thanks are extended to the following individuals who contributed in many ways to the content and structure of the book:

- Ron Huefner assisted with preparing the chapter on firm value. Ron actually took my initial draft of the chapter and completely rewrote it. He also read the first draft of the book and provided invaluable editorial comments.
- Sung Jin assisted with preparing the chapters on lock-in and creativity. Sung also assisted with a variety of editing activities to get the book ready for production.
- Yong Jin Kim assisted with preparing the chapter on real options.
- Lorena Mathien assisted with preparing the chapter on project management.
- Barbara Sherman assisted with preparing the chapter on the FAD template.
- Xiao Tang assisted with preparing the chapters on strategic planning, the Ten–Ten planning process, and the chapter

on the development of the business plan. Xiao also assisted with a variety of editing activities to get the book ready for production.

- Chul Woo Yoo assisted with preparing the chapter on product and price differentiation and also assisted with preparing the chapter illustrating how the concepts can be applied.

Thanks to my spouse Jody and my son Sean for listening to my recount of the numerous business plans developed by the students and for serving as a sounding board for several ideas.

David Parker, publisher and founder of Business Expert Press, was always available to listen to my concerns and to help solve what I believed were difficult problems. Cindy Durand, Production Liaison at Business Expert Press, was very understanding and always available to solve the various technical issues and move the book through the production process. Thanks are also extended to Kumararaja and the production staff at Exeter Premedia Services for their excellent work on the book.

I would like thank Scott Isenberg, the Principal and Consultant for Counselpub Publishing Services, for believing in the project and helping me prepare the proposal for Business Expert Press.

Finally, I would like to thank the nearly 1,000 students who pushed me to reach further and further to formulate and develop the course content.

CHAPTER 1

Understanding Entrepreneurship, Diffusion, and R&D in the Context of Monopolistic Competition

I always like to start class with a pop quiz. It is a good way to get the old gray matter going and stirs up a bit of angst and loathing. There are only three matching questions and they all relate to the dominant types of markets: (1) perfectly competitive markets, (2) perfectly monopolistic markets, and (3) the market hybrid referred to as monopolistic competition.

Question 1: Match the market types with their definition

1. Perfectly competitive market	a. Many sellers trading a similar product to many buyers
2. Monopoly market	b. One seller trading a similar product to many buyers
3. Monopolistic competition market	c. Many sellers trading a slightly differentiated product to many buyers

If you matched 1 with a, 2 with b, and 3 with c, give yourself one point.

Question 2: Now match the types of markets with their percentages of total activity

1. Perfectly competitive market	a. Less than 1%
2. Monopoly market	b. Less than 1%
3. Monopolistic competition market	c. Over 99%

If you matched 1 with a, 2 with b, and 3 with c, give yourself one point.

Question 3: Now match the type of market that is easiest to enter

1. Perfectly competitive market	a. Somewhat easy to enter
2. Monopoly market	b. Very difficult to enter
3. Monopolistic competition market	c. Very easy to enter

If you matched 1 with a, 2 with b, and 3 with c, give yourself one point.

Give yourself a passing grade if you get above a zero.[1] Based on the description of the three types of markets, this brief questionnaire illustrates that the best place, and perhaps the only place for entrepreneurs to compete is in markets characterized by monopolistic completion.

Monopolistic Competition

Edward Chamberlin published the foundations of monopolistic competition in his 1933 book entitled *The Theory of Monopolistic Competition*. It is considered by some economists to have the same stature as John Maynard Keynes's *General Theory* in revolutionizing economic thought in the 20th century.[2] The idea behind monopolistic competition is simple in form and powerful in practice.

Monopolistic competition involves many buyers, many sellers, and easy exit and entry, with slightly differentiated products. The sellers in these markets sell products that are closely related, but not identical. They have features that differentiate them from the competition. Usually, the buyers and sellers also have good information on the attributes of the products and the prices of the products in the marketplace. Indeed, most products and services are sold in markets characterized by monopolistic competition. The list includes jewelry, movie production, food, entertainment, many electronic gadgets and components, some durable goods, books, crafts, soda, houses, cars, consulting businesses, software, game consoles, restaurants, bars, and so forth.

A monopolist is a price setter and a business competing in a perfectly competitive market is a price taker. Most businesses strive to be price setters within a certain range of prices by offering a product that is closely related, but not exactly identical to other products in the market. The key strategy for competing in markets characterized by monopolistic competition is to offer products that are differentiated. The products are sort of quasi-substitutes, but they still resemble the original product or service. For example, Apple developed the iPod to compete with existing MP3 players.

According to standard economic theory, a purely competitive market has many buyers and sellers and each individual firm is a price taker. In essence, consumers and producers determine the market price for a product or service. In perfectly competitive markets, there are many sellers and buyers, and entry into and out of the market is easy. In a perfectly competitive market, companies sell their products at prevailing market prices where marginal revenue equals marginal cost. In actuality, every business would like to control the market, set the price, and be a monopolist. All businesses should strive to compete as a monopolist, even if it is in the short term. The goal is to rake in lots of money in the short term because your company is the only seller of a slightly differentiated product or service.[3] This will be short term (unless you have an exclusive patent on a product, own a large oil field, or have exclusive rights to providing cable or utility services) because successful products will always attract the competition. The only way to compete in contemporary markets is to become a serial entrepreneur, to constantly refine and reposition your products, and to function as a near-monopolist in the short term.

The Importance of Being Entrepreneurial and Being a Short-Term Monopolist

The notion of the entrepreneurial enterprise as a monopolist is not new. Indeed, it has a long tradition and history. Kirzner[4] noted in 1973 that entrepreneurship may be a step to monopoly power. It is possible to acquire market power by adding unique features or services that are not offered by the competition. When the unique features of a product are combined with a well-thought-out production and distribution process and an understanding of the competitive environment, the results are usually positive. This knowledge and the unique knowledge resources are of course transitory, but in the short run they can provide for near-monopoly power.

Entrepreneurship is currently being viewed as a set of skills that are part of a rational and logical process for identifying and creating opportunities.[5] The process and the skills have been likened to learning how to read, write, calculate, and conduct scientific reasoning. Being a successful entrepreneur requires insight and knowledge of problem solving, strategic planning, new product development, project management, and portfolio management among others. An important reason for participating in the entrepreneurial process is that it involves a significant amount of making and building things. This, in turn, leads to learning-by-doing and the creation of new unforeseen opportunities because you have been participating in the entrepreneurial process. Participation in entrepreneurial activity leads to the creation of opportunities in the form of products and services that were not even conceptualized or anticipated in the beginning. The entrepreneurial process actually creates new markets via innovation and product differentiation. Our definition of entrepreneurship focuses on a continuous process for creating new and enhanced products and services.

> *Entrepreneurship* is a risky endeavor involving the continuous creation and re-creation of a new enterprise, a new product, or a new idea.

The origin of the word *entrepreneur* can be traced to Old French. Entrepreneurs were individuals who undertook risky endeavors such as theatrical productions. Risk is an inherent part of entrepreneurship. If there is no risk involved and there is still money to be made, then the endeavor is probably a gift.

The Entrepreneur Should Design Products and Services for Continuous Product Differentiation and Innovation

Developments in economics, marketing, operations management, and information technology have now brought the vision of customization and personalization to reality.[6] Consumers want products and services tailored to their personal needs, but they also want products that are standardized, mass produced, and inexpensive. It is possible to assemble products and services using standardized processes and standardized modular components and still achieve product differentiation. Autos, global positioning systems (GPSs), tax software, operating systems, refrigerators, and so forth are all designed so that features and performance can be easily added and subtracted. The key principle in designing products and services is to design for flexibility and to continuously improve those products and services. This is the essence of a product differentiation strategy and the only way to survive under monopolistic competition.

Entrepreneurship Can Be Found in Large and Small Companies

Large companies can be entrepreneurial, but as a company scales up it is difficult to maintain entrepreneurial momentum. For example, several promising employees left Google for the relatively entrepreneurial environment of Facebook.[7] This is a natural phenomenon in high-tech enclaves such as Silicon Valley, but there was reason for concern because Google had grown to 23,000+ employees. Google was being viewed as slow and lumbering, too bureaucratic, and too slow to respond to the innovative possibilities of emerging technologies. Google has taken several steps to retain entrepreneurial talent by permitting them to work independently and letting them recruit individuals with relevant skills.

It does not matter if a firm is a gigantic monolithic multinational or a small start-up company manufacturing kazoos or even a mom and pop organization designing and launching Web services. The objective is the same: design products and services that are new and unique, easily differentiable, and adaptable to the needs of consumers. Entrepreneurial guru, blogger, and author Guy Kawasaki describes the situation perfectly:

> A great company anticipates what a customer needs—even before she knows she wants it ... the key to driving the competition crazy is outinnovating, outservicing, and outpricing ... Create a great product or service, put it out there, see who falls in love with it ...[8]

The Kingpins of Product Differentiation and Entrepreneurial Innovation Activity

Two companies with very large sales revenues are led by entrepreneurs. Jeff Bezos, founder and CEO of Amazon.com, and Steve Jobs, the former CEO of Apple, are serial entrepreneurs and the kingpins of the differentiation strategy. Many businesses give lip service to the notion of satisfying customers' wants. Bezos means it. He is a maker of markets, a veritable doer and inventor. Amazon did not have skills in developing electronic books or selling cloud computing, so Bezos embarked on a mission to develop competencies in electronic books and cloud computing. His goal was to satisfy customer needs for books anywhere and computing anywhere at any time at an attractive low price. Bezos even enlisted a Harvard MBA to craft a business plan for the cloud computing initiative. Here is the essence of the Bezos approach for developing new businesses:

- The business should be capable of generating significant returns.
- The business should be able to scale substantially.
- The business should address an underserved market.
- The market should be highly differentiated.
- The opportunity should be in an area where a company is well-positioned to provide a new service.

Steve Jobs was always an experimenter and a doer. Although some of Apple's products, such as the Newton, the Lisa, and Apple TV, might be considered failures, he bounced back numerous times and introduced dazzlingly exceptional products that have and still are dominating the market. He is a superb example of an experimenter who sometimes failed in the marketplace, but learned from his mistakes and achieved subsequent success. This is the hallmark of the serial entrepreneur.

Our view of innovation does not require an expensive research lab, but it can. It does not demand a large team of physicists, chemists, engineers, and software developers, but it can. It does not need lots of money, even though it helps. Innovation, as always, just demands hard work and constant attention to searching for new ideas and building things, and is often accompanied by failure. Success is the result of a never-ending process of trial and error and being entrepreneurial.

Radical and Incremental Innovation

The two primary categories of innovation are radical and incremental. Radical innovation tends to replace existing ideas, products, services, or processes. They are innovations that are very different or even revolutionary and they replace existing ideas, products, services, or processes and perhaps lead to markets that were previously nonexistent. Radical innovation can lead to massive changes in an industry and to what is referred to as creative destruction in the marketplace. The internet, the horseless carriage, GPSs, and digital encoding of music and video technology were radical innovations resulting in the development of new markets.

Incremental innovations involve smaller improvements in ideas, products, services, and processes. They are like adding unique features to a product or service. But even incremental improvements can have a radical effect on the marketplace. For example, consider the incremental improvements in wireless phones that eventually lead to the development of Apple's iPhone and to the numerous smartphone offerings.

Product and Technology Life Cycles

Life cycles are a very useful way to understand how products and technology evolve over time. They are very useful in tracking product and process differentiation. They can be used to understand the evolution, growth, and decline of ideas and phenomena in the physical world, the plant and animal kingdom, and technology. The most commonly used life cycles in business are the technology life cycles and the product life cycles. They are used to track the diffusion of technologies and products.

Diffusion is the acceptance, adoption, and awareness of a technology or a product by individuals. The technology and product life cycles are essentially the same, except the product life cycle is focused on selling products while the technology life cycle is focused on innovation. The technology and product life cycles consists of four phases that follow the classic S-curve and they consist of awareness of the technology, technological growth, technological maturity, and a decline of interest in the technology (see Figure 1.1). Figure 1.2 illustrates a snapshot of where we believe several technologies belong in the life cycle in 2011.

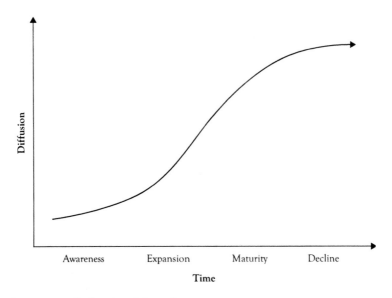

Figure 1.1. Technology life cycle.

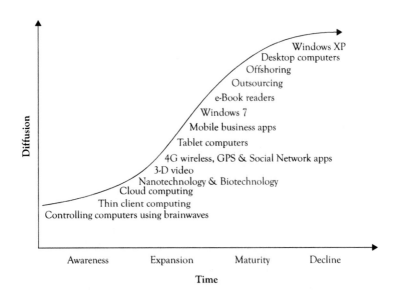

Figure 1.2. Technology life cycle profile in 2011.

Diffusion of a Technology Usually Lags Performance

There are a number of factors that influence the diffusion of products and technology. These factors include whether the technology solves an important problem, how well the public or target market understands the technology, the value versus cost calculation made by consumers, how well the product or technology has been marketed, the effectiveness of the social network in communicating the benefits of the technology, the effectiveness of the supply chain in delivering quality products in a timely manner, and finally, how well the technology performs. Performance is the most important factor influencing diffusion, but it can be trumped by any of these factors. There were nearly a quarter of a million patents granted by the U.S. Patent Office in 2010. There have been nearly 5.2 million patents granted since 1963.[9] The point is that technology development never stops.

The diffusion and subsequent awareness of a product usually lags increases in product performance (see Figure 1.3). This is in part related to Moore's law. The essence of Moore's law is that the performance of products increases over time, whereas the cost of the product stays the same or decreases. This increase in performance is a function of technological developments and, of course, the learning curve. The idea behind

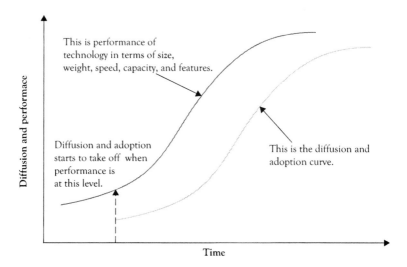

Figure 1.3. Diffusion lags performance.

the learning curve is that a company or an individual gets better at doing something the more they do it. Moore originally stated the idea in the context of computer-processing power (see Figure 1.4).

Moore is widely known for "Moore's Law," in which he predicted that the number of components the industry would be able to place on a computer chip would double every year. In 1975, he updated his prediction to once every 2 years. It has become the guiding principle for the semiconductor industry to deliver ever-more-powerful chips while decreasing the cost of electronics.[10]

Over time, individual firms and the industry become more efficient and the products have better features. The net result is that product performance increases, production capabilities increase, and the cost of production decreases. Increases in product performance are coupled with improvements in manufacturing efficiency and attract more customers. Research and development (R&D) and learning curve effects drive all this.[11] One of the most important outcomes of the learning curve is that it provides short-term cost advantages to those firms that achieve large market share and additionally creates barriers to market entry. The essence of Moore's law is that organizations learn by doing. They begin to break down tasks, tasks become specialized, and some tasks are automated. These organizations also begin to develop complementary competencies that are the foundation for new innovations and products.

Discontinuities, Chasms, and Hype in the Diffusion Process

Some technologies and products fail very quickly because they are simply not effective. Others do not fail initially because of the hype surrounding the product. But they eventually flop because existing customers become disillusioned and communicate their dissatisfaction in a variety of informal and formal communication networks. There are also instances where a product is very useful, yet fails because of inadequate marketing and a problematic supply chain. In all of these instances, the traditional S-curve is not suitable for understanding and illustrating discontinuities in the diffusion and awareness of a new product or emerging technology.

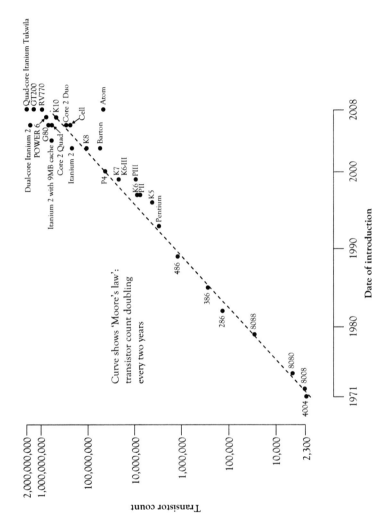

Figure 1.4. Transistor count and Moore's law.

A very popular approach to understanding growth and diffusion of technologies and products is Gartner's Hype Cycle.[12] It is an adaptation of the technology life cycle and attempts to deal with discontinuities in adoption. One of the more interesting features of Gartner's Hype Cycle is that it takes into account the unbridled and almost euphoric optimism that accompanies the introduction of some technologies and, of course, the inevitable precipitous decline of the next-best thing (see Figure 1.5). The Hype Cycle consists of five phases: (1) the Technology Trigger, (2) the Peak of Inflated Expectations, (3) the Trough of Disillusionment, (4) the Slope of Enlightenment, and (5) the Plateau of Productivity.

Another approach to handling the very difficult cross-over between awareness of the technology and massive adoption was developed by Geoffrey Moore.[13] He uses a bell curve to model technology and adds a couple of cracks or discontinuities in the curve to illustrate the difficult diffusion issues that need to be dealt with when selling high-technology products. He notes that there is a large chasm that has to be crossed when a technology transitions from emerging and glitchy technology to productive, easy-to-use, and readily applicable to solving problems. The early adopters of an emerging technology are usually more willing to put up

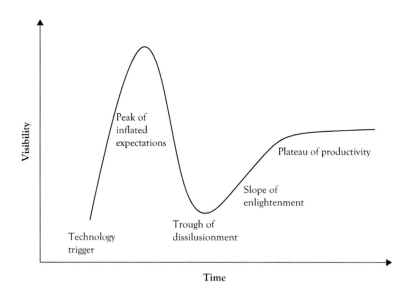

Figure 1.5. Gartner Hype Cycle.

with the glitches than the masses. Technologies and products that are not capable of making the transition fade into the chasm.

The Bridge Model of Technology Life Cycle

We have adapted the Hype Cycle model and the chasm approaches and integrated them into the traditional S-curve that is used to model the technological life cycle. As illustrated in Figure 1.6, there is often a crisis of adoption as a technology begins to transition from awareness to expansion. There is a major bridge to be crossed where attention to design and marketing and performance are critical. It is the *Bridge of Hope.* If the performance of the technology is inadequate or the technology falls off of the public's radar, then there is a diffusion crisis, and the technology can fall into the chasm and become irrelevant. It is possible to crawl out of the chasm with better product design, an influx of resources, and better marketing, but it is a difficult climb out of the abyss. The climb out of the abyss is over the *Bridge of Adversity.* Companies that have invested in emerging technologies are forever hopeful that they can cross the abyss from relative obscurity to

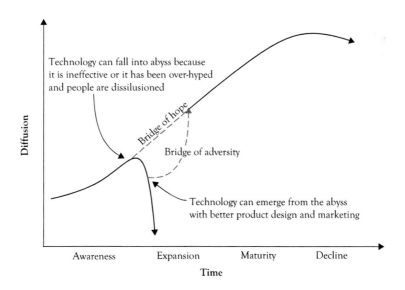

Figure 1.6. Crossing the bridge of hope and climbing the bridge of adversity.

expansion and reap the monetary rewards derived from the expansion of the marketplace.

Technologies Do Not Necessarily Fall Into the Abyss: They Become Embedded in New Technology

In some ways, technological change is similar to evolutionary change. Some technologies are simply eclipsed by other technologies and fade or die away, such as in the case of the horse and buggy giving way to the Model T and analog TVs succumbing to digital TVs. Sometimes, technologies evolve through subtle differentiation such as the case with cell phones, GPS devices, and operating systems. There are instances where major mutations take place when two different technologies are combined such as in the case of the merging of GPS, cell phones, MP3 players, and Web 2.0 social networking.

In many instances, technology does not just die out or become obsolete, it just becomes part and parcel of a new technology. One of the early partitioning and time-sharing and operating systems, IBM's VM370, was developed in the 1960s and 1970s. The concepts developed for the VM370 operating systems are the foundation for many existing operating systems, including UNIX, Linux, and all of Microsoft's products, as well as the current crop of the so-called virtual machine applications. The cloud-computing concept is actually an extension of the IBM's VM370 architecture. Thin client computing, where a significant part of the processing is done on a central server, was touted as the next big technology in the early 1990s. It faded for a while and then has reemerged as an important concept with the emergence of cloud computing.

There is Power in Numbers: Network Effects and Metcalfe's Law

Metcalfe's law states that the value or utility of a network is proportional to the number of user's of the network. At one time, Metcalfe indicated that utility was a square function (utility = n^2). For example, a phone network with 10 people has a utility of 100 and a network with 1,000 people has a utility value of 10,000. He has since scaled that back and the utility of a network is based on a log function (utility = $n \times \log(n)$).[14] The log model is presented in Figure 1.7. Thus, for a 100-user network, this would translate to utility = $100 \times 2 = 200$ or 200 utility units. The equation is not the important issue. It is the idea that if you have more people using a phone, a fax, railroad, a Web 2.0 application or whatever, your network will become more attractive and attract even more users. Consider the choice to go with a local cable TV network or a satellite TV network. If individuals take into account what network other people are choosing, then there is a network externality or a network effect that influences the decision.

In the economics literature, a network effect typically refers to a change in the positive benefit that a consumer receives from a good, when the number of consumers of the good increases.[15] Network effects are not limited to phone, wireless, and telecommunications networks. They can also include the following:

- Transportation networks such as roads, railroads, and flight paths.
- Communication systems such as the postal service, express mail services, and pony express.

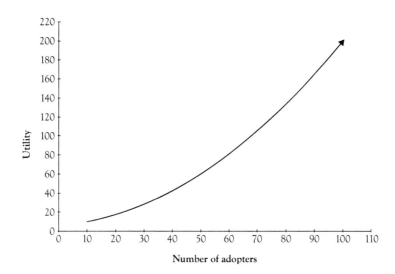

Figure 1.7. The size of the network increases the value of the network.

- Communication media such as books, printed materials, schools, and universities, because they disseminate ideas and knowledge and those ideas have greater utility.
- Social networks involving a social structure between individuals or organizations with similar interests. They include political, cultural, religious, sports clubs, social clubs, volunteer groups, family, friends, industry trade groups, and market segments. Facebook, Twitter, and Web 2.0 social-networking applications.

Economists also talk about network failures. That is a situation where the technology or network selected is not the best technology, thus leading consumers and business down a path that is not optimum. In reality, consumers are often very aware of the trade-offs in performance that exists between competing technologies. Take the case of the success of the VHS recording format over the Beta format. The success of VHS is often touted as an example of network failure. The picture quality of the VHS format was, in fact, reasonably close to the quality of the Beta format.[16] In addition, the VHS tapes had a greater capacity and cost less than the Beta tapes. It was not a failure of the market to recognize the superiority of Beta; it was rather that consumers revealed their preferences for certain features by purchasing the VHS format.

The best of all worlds is when the stars are aligned properly and an organization can realize network effects and take advantage of Moore's law by increasing the performance of a product while reducing or maintain costs. The net result is to spur hypergrowth in the diffusion and sales of a product or service.

The Role of R&D Process in Innovation

The objectives of R&D are to develop existing and new core competencies, to further existing and new products, and to develop existing and new business processes through invention and innovation.[17] The R&D process is the engine that drives product and process differentiation.

Innovation is typically defined as the ideas, the products, the services, or processes that are perceived as being new and different and they have been implemented or even commercialized.

Research and development are usually thrown together as one concept, but in reality they are somewhat distinct processes.[18] Research is typically considered to be science-oriented whereas development is the mechanism for translating the science into commercial products and services. Basic science can be thought of as the engine for pushing new discoveries and ideas into society. This is in contrast to the concept of market pull. Market pull is essentially the process of translating the basic science into products and services in order to satisfy customer needs, wants, and demands. The interaction between science push and market pull creates a very powerful feedback loop that spurs on the development and diffusion of new products and services.[19]

As noted earlier, the diffusion and awareness of technologies typically follows an S-curve. In the early stages of the S-curve, there are very few people aware of the technology. Market research is not important at this stage because there are few untapped wants because of the lack of awareness. As a technology matures and begins to take off, there is a propagation of awareness with increased insight of the possibilities of a technology.[20] It is at this stage that market research becomes viable. It is also at this stage that many similar products begin to emerge because of the surfacing of a kind of group *aha* because of the interconnectedness of businesses and research groups. This group *aha* occurs because market research by producers and product development laboratories leads to the same conclusions about consumer wants. Once consumers begin to use products and have had the opportunity to experience a product, they also begin to identify areas of deficiencies in the product and areas where a feature might be added. And this is where market research is very effective because market researchers are very adept at identifying changes in consumer wants.

As the market matures, the demand for the products also begins to decline with the emergence of substitute products and technological obsolescence. It is then necessary to re-prime the pump and reload science. This is done by working with new science and new technologies in

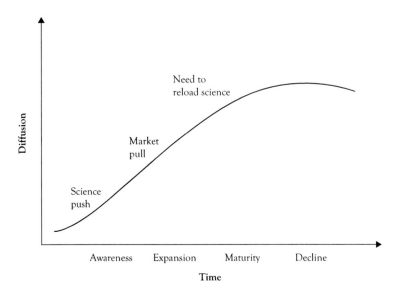

Figure 1.8. Push, pull, and reload.

order to identify new opportunities for developing products and services. Figure 1.8 illustrates the concepts of science push and market pull and how they relate to diffusion and awareness.

Push, Pull, and Reload can go on Forever

Some individuals believe that there is a limit on the ability of innovative activities to bring new products to the market. This suggests that differentiation cannot go on forever. This line of reasoning is similar to the idea attributed to someone in the U.S. patent office that: "Everything that can be invented has been invented." There is good news, however, from the patent office. Research has shown that companies can keep innovating and still contribute to the bottom line because it appears that, in general, there are no diminishing returns to scale for R&D expenditures.[21] In essence, continued investment in R&D yields rewards, revenues, and profits. Even though a particular technology may have a performance limit, advances in R&D and in basic science along with customer pull will start the process anew. Moore's law continues to work for Intel because they continuously re-prime the pump. They have gone from focusing on the clock rate of their CPU, which is constrained by thermodynamic considerations, to exploring multiple CPU cores and restructuring the overall microarchitecture of their chips.

R&D for Start-Ups and Small Businesses

For the entrepreneur, there is significant overlap related to research, product development, and the actual production of products and services. Many organizations are just too small to become involved in basic research and they have to rely on combining existing and emerging technologies in creative ways. Entrepreneurs view R&D as interdependent processes that are intertwined and not very distinct. For the entrepreneur, research and product development includes:

- generating an idea for a product or services;
- gathering and synthesizing information on the idea;
- designing the product or services;
- developing a prototype of the product or service;
- developing a production process for the product or service;
- producing the product or service.

Our focus in this book is primarily on the first four steps including idea generation, gathering information, preliminary design, and prototyping. From the standpoint of the entrepreneur, these steps are the essence of R&D. Steps 5 and 6 are part of product engineering and they will not be discussed in depth.

Search and the Role of Learning-About in Developing Ideas for New Products and Services

In addition to generating new knowledge, conducting R&D leads to smarter organizations because the knowledge these organizations already have helped understand new information when it becomes available. The best way to conduct R&D and to improve the organizational innovation and creativity is to learn-by-doing and to engage in search activity. In this section, we will discuss searching for ideas first and we will discuss learning-by-doing later.

Learning-about, or the search process, involves reading magazines, books, and technical articles, attending schools, observing the competition, one-on-one discussion, interacting with customers, and attending symposia and conferences. It involves acquiring knowledge and integrating and synthesizing that knowledge. This is the first step in developing individual and organizational knowledge structures. Learning-about in its basic form is search and synthesis. It is too expensive in terms of time and resources for organizations to build every product and service that is conceived. Many companies therefore learn-about an idea by reading, interacting with experts, and also by attending symposia and conferences related to an emerging technology. The goal is to gain insight and understand the potential of an emerging technology or a new idea.

It is our thesis that book learning, lectures, and even homework are usually beneficial. This is essentially the learning-about process. Search plays a key part in the learning-about process. This is particularly true when an organization searches outside the organization for ideas related to product innovation. Search can be classified in terms of the breadth and depth of the search.[22] The breadth of the search refers to the number of outside sources used and consulted. The depth of search refers to the intensity of the relationship between the searcher and the external sources. Table 1.1 lists potential sources of external information that can be used by entrepreneurs and product developers when engaging in an innovative activity.

As illustrated in Figure 1.9 (adapted from Laursen and Salter[23]), it appears that the breadth of search is important for incremental improvements innovation and that both breadth and depth of search are important for new and radical innovation. In terms of the breadth of the search, it appears that the sweet spot is about eleven sources plus or minus two sources (see Figure 1.10, adapted from Laursen and Salter[24]). This is a rather useful finding upon further reflection. When searching for new information, it is often difficult to determine how much information to gather and the number of sources for collecting information in order to avoid information overload. The point is that you have to seek out a variety of sources of information in order to improve the chances of introducing a successful innovation.

Table 1.1. External sources of information[25]

Sources of information from the market
Suppliers of equipment, materials, components, or software
Clients or customers
Competitors
Consultants
Commercial laboratories/R&D enterprises
Sources of information from institutions
Universities or other higher education institutes
Government research organizations
Other public sectors, e.g., business links and government offices
Private research institutes
Sources of information from the profession
Professional conferences and meetings
Trade associations
Technical/trade press and computer databases
Fairs and exhibitions
Sources from specialized places
Technical standards
Health and safety standards and regulations
Environmental standards and regulations

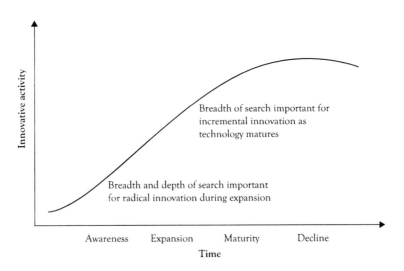

Figure 1.9. Breadth and depth of search and innovative activity.

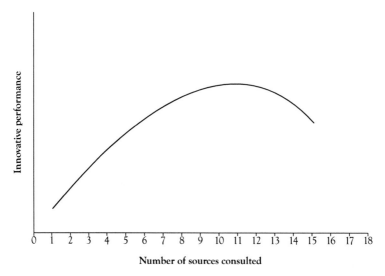

Figure 1.10. Breadth of search and innovative performance.

Building Things and the Role of Learn-By-Doing in Developing Ideas for New Products and Services

Learning-by-doing means that the organization or entrepreneur makes and builds things, conducts experiments, and builds prototypes. R&D is essentially learning by doing. Individuals and organizations benefit from learning-by-doing because it builds up absorptive capacity.[26] Absorptive capacity is the result of having already developed knowledge and insight in a particular domain, for example, in medicine, baseball, networking, or memory chips. Having absorptive capacity means that prior knowledge facilitates the learning of new knowledge. Developing absorptive capacity is synonymous with developing insight. It gives an individual or an organization the ability to understand, assimilate, transfer, and exploit new knowledge and new information as it becomes available and then to apply it to solving problems and developing commercially viable products. Learning-by-doing is essentially design and development.

The key activity for innovative activity is the learning-by-doing process. Learning-by-doing means that you make and build things, try experiments, and construct prototypes. Sometimes, there is a facilitator, such as a teacher, a project manager, colleagues, a fellow student, a book, or a YouTube video, to get you started on the path to creativity.

Roger Shank is a well-known expert on artificial intelligence, learning, and knowledge. He has been on a crusade to change the way kids are taught. He wants children to learn by doing and engage in more experimentation and reflection and spend less time on being tested on the so-called "body of knowledge that everyone must know."[27]

> If you want to learn to throw a football, drive a car, build a mouse trap, design a building, cook a stir fry, or be a management consultant, you must have a go at doing it. Throughout history, youths have been apprenticed to masters in order to learn a trade ... Parents usually teach children in this way. They don't give a series of lectures to their children to prepare them to walk, talk, climb, run, play a game, or learn how to behave. They just let their children do these things. If he throws poorly, he simply tries again. Parents tolerate sitting in the passenger seat while their teenager tries out the driver's seat for the first time. It's nerve-racking, but parents put up with it, because they know there's no better way.... When it comes to school, however, instead of allowing students to learn by doing, we create courses of instruction to tell students about the theory of the task without concentrating on the doing of the task. It's not easy to see how to apply apprenticeship to mass education. So in its place, we lecture.

R&D is essentially learning-by-doing. Individuals and organizations benefit from learning-by-doing in the context of R&D because it builds up absorptive capacity.[28] Absorptive capacity is simply a function of having previously developed knowledge structures in a particular domain (e.g., domain knowledge in medicine, baseball, networking, or memory chips). It gives an individual or an organization the ability to understand, assimilate, transfer, and exploit new knowledge and information and then to apply it to solving problems and developing commercially viable products.

The Role of the Supply Chain and the Brand in Product Differentiation

Differentiation should be the engine driving the business, but businesses must also attend to improving the *supply chain* and the *brand* in order to succeed. Improving the supply chain and improving the brand image are also methods for product differentiation. They contribute to the unique bundle of perceptions that customers have towards a business.

The supply chain is the connected activities related to the creation of a product or service up through the delivery of the product to the customer. It includes the upstream suppliers as well as downstream activities such as wholesalers and distribution warehouses and after sales support.[29] Key activities for improving the supply chain are to reduce transaction costs to improve business processes. Consumers often perceive efficient and responsive supply chains as an attribute or a product feature.

The brand is the image of a product or service in the marketplace. Consumers essentially perceive the brand as being a feature of the product and, in many instances, it is viewed as the avatar for the product. Images and visions are immediately invoked when mentioning Apple, or Amazon, Google, Wal-Mart, and Disney. Our focus in this book will be on the process of innovation and differentiation, but we also recognize that successful companies must attend to improving the supply chain and developing a strong brand.

Conclusion

In this chapter, we have introduced many of the fundamental concepts related to understanding differentiation and the diffusion of innovations within the context of monopolistic competition. The key points are the following:

- Monopolistic competition involves many buyers and sellers of products that are closely related, but not identical where entry and exit are easy. It is the dominant form of competition.
- Entrepreneurship is the best method for competing in monopolistically competitive environments. Entrepreneurship involves engaging in a risky endeavor with continuous

creation and re-creation of a new enterprise, a new product, or a new idea.

- Radical innovation tends to replace existing ideas, products, services, and processes. Incremental innovations involve smaller improvements in ideas, products, services, and processes.
- Technology life cycles and the product life cycles are used to understand the diffusion of technologies and products.
- Diffusion is the acceptance, adoption, and awareness of a technology or a product by individuals.
- The diffusion of a technology usually lags the performance of a technology and this can be understood using Moore and Metcalf's laws.
- The Bridge model is a useful way to understand discontinuities in the technology life cycle where problems can occur.
- R&D activities are present in large and small organizations, they are just implemented differently.
- Learning-about involves searching, reading, inquiry, and synthesis. Learning-by-doing involves making and building things. Learning-about and learning-by-doing are the foundation of R&D.
- Developing a strong supply chain and a strong brand through marketing are critical for delivering differentiated products and services.

This chapter has illustrated the foundational concepts for competing in the current marketplace. Subsequent chapters will build on this foundation and present additional details on how to accomplish differentiation and innovation through product and services versioning.

CHAPTER 2

Fundamental Concepts of Product and Price Differentiation

One of the key concepts for the entrepreneur to understand is that product differentiation permits them to change their price according to what consumers believe they can afford. Some consumers are very price-sensitive and others are not so price-sensitive, and this can change by the type of product being purchased and by the buying context. The price that a consumer is willing to pay is called the reservation price or the willingness-to-pay price and it is somewhat unique across individuals. If you can determine the willingness-to-pay price for a product, then you may be able to charge different prices according to the willingness-to-pay. This is, of course, a form of price discrimination, or in more polite terms, price differentiation. The terms price discrimination and price differentiation will be used interchangeably throughout this discussion.

Hal Varian[1] has identified three approaches to price discrimination. They are personalized pricing, versioning, and group pricing. The ideas will be briefly introduced and then examined in greater depth in a later chapter.

The Demand Curve

The typical demand curve has the price on the *y*-axis and the quantity demanded on the *x*-axis and is downward-sloping. A demand curve can be represented as a linear mathematical formula with quantity or price as the dependent variable. A demand curve is a very useful diagram for describing the relationship between the price level and the quantity demanded at each price level. In general, as the price of a product increases, the demand for the good decreases. Similarly, as the price of a product decreases, the demand for the good increases. The next section of the chapter discusses how the demand curve can be used to identify the optimal price and quantity for selling just one version of a product.

First-Degree Price Discrimination: Personalized Pricing

First-degree price discrimination has been around ever since people began bartering and exchanging goods.[2] It is simply an attempt to charge different prices to different customers for the same product. Figure 2.1 presents an example of an aggregate demand curve for a cord of wood in a small town. In an ideal world, from the producer's perspective, one producer could identify each consumer's willingness-to-pay function and set prices accordingly (cf. Varian 1996). Let us assume that one company owns all of the timber in the area and is therefore a monopoly. Instead of charging $40 to each consumer, the monopolist charges a different price to each consumer depending on their ability and willingness to pay for the cord of wood. This is essentially personalized pricing, where the selling price is customized for each buyer. This is a good strategy for a monopolist because they can generate more revenue than just picking a single price point. Each consumer is thus charged a different price for the same product.

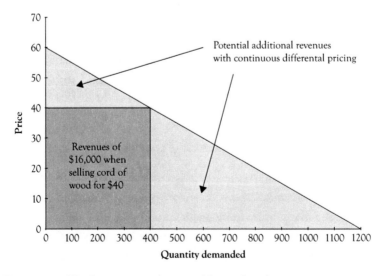

Figure 2.1. Need a way to capture additional revenue.

This strategy is also known as perfect price discrimination. Personalized pricing is very difficult to implement in practice for four reasons. First, it is difficult to identify the willingness-to-pay functions for each consumer. Second, customers often get upset when they find out that another consumer has paid less for a product or service than they have paid. The third reason that personalized pricing causes problems is that perfect price discrimination can lead to arbitrage, where opportunistic buyers purchase the product at a discounted price in one market and then sell it at a profit in another market. The fourth and final reason that it is difficult to implement is that, in certain instances, it is illegal. This issue will be dealt with at the end of the chapter.

Though personalized pricing is difficult to implement, it can be accomplished and is in fact embraced by some companies. Amazon, for example, presents their customers with personalized product recommendations using past search and buying behavior, and large supermarkets use their scanner data to configure promotions tailored to their customers.

Personalized pricing requires the effective measurement of consumer preferences. The supplier must in some way conduct market research to determine individualized pricing strategies. This can be accomplished by using technology to analyze historical buying patterns. Online retailers, such as Amazon, can very easily analyze transactions using historical data. Offline retailers have to collect and sort the data from a variety of sources unless their customers participate in a rewards program or a customer discount program that incorporates a mechanism for gathering customer transaction information. Amazon has participated in many of types of personalized marketing and pricing schemes because they have the infrastructure in place to gather and analyze behavior. Companies such as Amazon use some form of collaborative filtering to determine product recommendations for books, videos, and many other products.

Collaborative Filtering

There are many ways to implement collaborative filtering. Collaborative filtering goes something like this. John likes audio books by David Sedaris. Other people who have bought audio books by David Sedaris also bought books by George Carlin. Therefore, the so-called *recommender system* at Amazon or at Audible books would make a recommendation to John that he should buy a book by George Carlin. Collaborative filtering systems can also include rating systems; in fact, Amazon and a number of other online retailers will try very hard to get you to help them by asking you to rate a product you have just bought. They will use the ratings to develop an entire web of recommendations to many of their customers and to retarget you with similar products. Here is another example of collaborative filtering in action: John bought and gave his new Kindle e-book reader a five star rating. He and many other buyers of the Amazon Kindle also bought a leather case. The *recommender system* will subsequently recommend a leather case to everyone who subsequently buys the Kindle.

Collaborative filtering can also involve price differentiation and price personalization. If the person who buys the Kindle does not buy the leather case at the same time, then the *recommender system* will send an email indicating that the leather case is on sale or wait until the Kindle customer logs back onto the system and then presents the customer with a discounted price on the leather case.

Auctions are also a form of personalized pricing. Theoretically, an auction participant will bid up to their reservation price or their willingness-to-pay level for a product. Figure 2.2 illustrates that the revenue generated by offering a product at a single price of $30 will generate

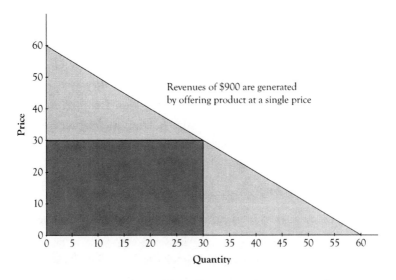

Figure 2.2. Revenues derived by selling a product at a single price.

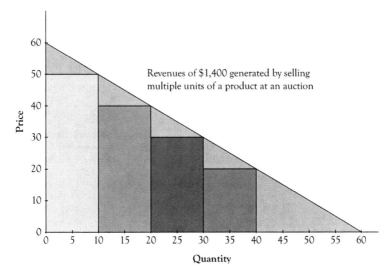

Figure 2.3. Auctions can be used for personalized pricing.

$900 in revenues. As illustrated in Figure 2.3, the use of an auction could theoretically generate revenues of $1,400. Auctions permit sellers to price discriminate according to the customers' willingness-to-pay. Some individuals will bid $10 or $20 and others will bid $30, or $40 or more. As a result, a seller could theoretically generate additional revenues of $500 by offering multiple units of a product at an auction. The next chapter will illustrate in detail how this revenue is generated using versioning.

Developing personalized pricing is an idealized goal for producers because the potential opportunities for revenue generation are exceptional. However, because it is difficult to accomplish in practice, producers often turn toward *second-* and *third-*degree price discrimination to generate additional revenues.

Second-Degree Price Discrimination: Versioning

As noted by Varian and Shapiro in 1998, the idea behind versioning is to engage in differential pricing by offering different versions of a product. Figure 2.4 illustrates the versioning concept. Ideally, the different versions should be perceived as having different levels of quality. We also maintain that the number of versions should be related to the number of distinct

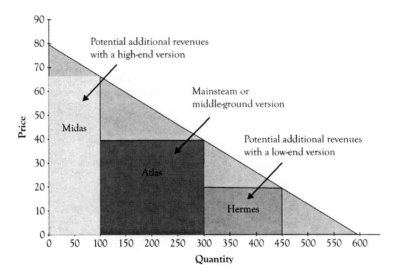

Figure 2.4. Second-degree price discrimination.

market segments. In many instances, it is difficult to identify the optimum number of market segments, and it is also difficult to develop products for each market segment. Goldilocks pricing is a rule of thumb that suggests that you should start out with three price levels. The idea behind Goldilocks pricing is that 1 product is too few, 10 products too many, and 3 is just the right amount.[3] There is evidence that having too many choices places a significant cognitive and emotional burden on the ability of individuals to make decisions.[4] It is my experience that somewhere between two and four versions should be offered. A subsequent chapter will illustrate how Goldilocks pricing has been implicitly or explicitly implemented by a variety of companies. The key to versioning is to try to anticipate customer's needs and then to try and develop organizational competencies for delivering those products and services.

As noted earlier and illustrated in the next chapter, versioning also leads to increased revenues and profits. You will leave money on the table if you do not have a high-end product for consumers who are not price-sensitive. In addition, you will not sell any product to customers who are very price-sensitive. There are several additional compelling reasons for versioning. By having several products, you can experiment and watch economic behavior as consumers will focus on the features and products that are most desirable. This sort of experimentation is the basis of monopolistic competition and the mechanism that allows the entrepreneur to successfully compete. Product versions can be generated in a variety of ways, including distinct product features, product design, and product promotions such as product rebates and product availability, for example, when the product is delivered.

In this book, we will refer to three foundational versions of products. The high-end product is referred to as a Midas version and it is targeted toward nonprice-sensitive consumers. Midas products are extravagantly engineered and contain advanced features and attributes. Hermes products are targeted toward price-sensitive consumers and are frugally engineered and designed with basic features. Atlas products are designed for the middle ground or the mainstream. They not only have basic features, but also have several advanced features, and are priced between Midas and Hermes versions. More details on the motivation behind the three versions will be presented throughout the book.

An example of versioning is found in the airline industry. Airline companies usually provide two or three levels of seats, such as economy class seats, business class seats, and first-class seats. The first-class tickets are the most expensive and they offer customers the highest quality service. Consumers who are willing to pay for the extra services will purchase the first-class ticket. On the other hand, customers who purchase the economy-class ticket receive a lower level of service. But they are not willing to pay for the extra services and features offered to the first-class and business-class customers. As illustrated in the hypothetical example in Figure 2.5, if an airline offers only an economy ticket at a set price of $300, then the revenues generated would be $36,000. However, as illustrated in Figure 2.6, if the airline offers an economy ticket at $300, a business-class ticket for $600, and first-class tickets for $800, then the company could potentially generate additional revenues of $22,000.

Bundling is a special type of versioning that often involves information content that is in a digital format. Online and offline newspapers, encyclopedias, and magazines are examples of information bundles. Software in addition to having versions is also bundled. Examples include the so-called office bundles containing word processing, presentation, and spreadsheet software and the tax software bundles that

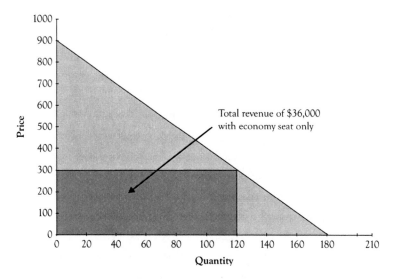

Figure 2.5. Revenues generated by only offering economy seats.

include electronic filing, state filing, as well as additional tax preparation features.

Bundling strategies frequently appear in markets for informational goods. As you can imagine, the marginal cost of information goods is theoretically close to zero. Let us imagine four consumers who are interested in buying two computer games such as the Football Madness game and the Soccer is My Life game. Suppose also that the four customers (Bob, Carol, Ted, and Alice) are willing to pay $18, $10, $8, and $2, respectively, for Football Madness. Suppose also that Bob, Carol, Ted, and Alice have different reservation prices for the Soccer is My Life game. Bob would pay $3 for the game, Carol would pay $16, Ted would pay $17, and Alice would pay $19 for the soccer game. If the retail cost of both games is $16, then none of these individuals would buy both games. In this case, Bob would only buy Football Madness and Carol, and Ted and Alice would only buy Soccer is My Life. In this scenario, the seller would only obtain $64 in revenues (4 × $16). However, if the seller bundles the two titles together and sells the total package for $20, then the seller could generate $80 in revenues. The bundled product price is under what each individual was willing to pay for the two games (Bob: $21, Carol: $26, Ted: $25, and Alice: $21). In this case, the seller is better off and the four consumers are

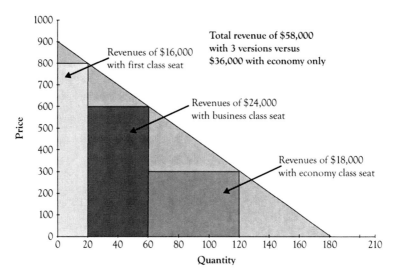

Figure 2.6. Versioning airline seats generates additional revenue.

happy because of the bundling strategy. Bundling is particularly useful with digital goods because the cost to reproduce digital copies is trivial.

Third-degree Price Discrimination: Group Pricing

Groups are the collection of customers with some common character-istics. The idea behind group pricing is to establish different prices for different groups or customer segments. Usually, the groups are segmented because one group is price-sensitive and the members of the group have a lower-willingness-to-pay function. Examples of such groups include retired seniors versus the nonretired, business travelers versus tourists, and students versus the general public. These groups are targeted by using senior discounts, student discounts, rewards programs, frequent-flyer programs, and buying clubs.

For example, statistical software companies, such as SAS and SPSS, sell their product to students at a much lower price than they do to commercial businesses because the student customer segment is price-sensitive and not willing to pay the high price for the statistical software. Statistical software is usually very expensive costing over $1,000, but often the student edition is around $100. By charging a lower price, companies can extract revenues from segments that are price-sensitive and not willing to pay for the product. As illustrated in the Figure 2.7, a hypothetical company offering statistical software could generate $5,000,000 in revenues by selling their software to individuals and businesses at a price of $1,000. However, if the statistical software company also sells a nonsupported version to students through academic institutions, then they could theoretically generate an additional $2,000,000 in revenues (see Figure 2.8).

One objective of having products for price-sensitive groups, such as students, is to acquire them as customers by trying to get them locked-in to using a product. They may eventually become customers for high-end products and services. In addition, it is better to have them as paying customers, rather have them engaged in copying the software. Group pricing is a common form of price discrimination, which is illustrated in Figure 2.9.

As noted by Phillips, there is not a clear line that distinguishes versioning from group pricing.[5] Indeed, most approaches contain elements of group pricing and versioning. The Midas, Atlas, and Hermes categories are also product versions, but they are also targeted at Midas, Atlas, and

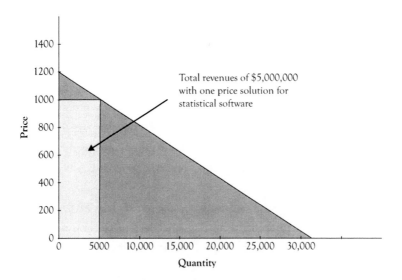

Figure 2.7. Revenues generated by set price for statistical software.

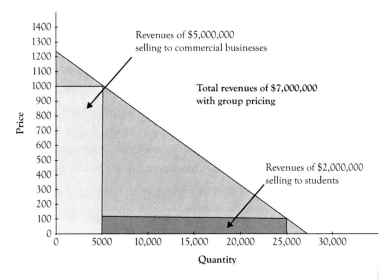

Figure 2.8. Group pricing and additional revenues.

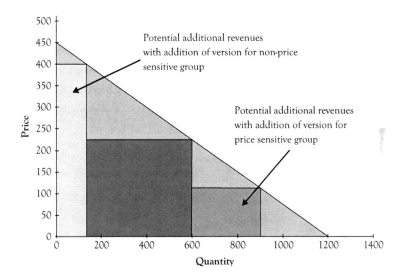

Figure 2.9. Third-degree price discrimination: group pricing.

Hermes groups according to their price sensitivities and their willingness-to-pay. As noted above, additional details on the motivation behind the three versions and the willingness-to-pay segments will be presented in later chapters.

Legal Issues Related to Price Discrimination and Product Differentiation

Price discrimination has a negative connotation because monopolies and oligopolies sometimes use their market power to unfair advantage and engage in predatory pricing schemes. Predatory pricing, however, is rare in markets characterized by monopolistic competition because there are many sellers and the products are largely substitutable, even if only slightly differentiated. In some ways, price discrimination is the rule rather than the exception in contemporary commerce transactions. Here are several relevant guidelines on price discrimination from the FTC (Federal Trade Commission):

> A seller charging competing buyers different prices for the same "commodity" or discriminating in the provision of "allowances"— compensation for advertising and other services—may be violating the Robinson-Patman Act. This kind of price discrimination may give favored customers an edge in the market that has nothing to do with their superior efficiency. Price discriminations are generally lawful, particularly if they reflect the different costs of dealing with different buyers or are the result of a seller's attempts to meet a competitor's offering.

> … There are two legal defenses to these types of alleged Robinson-Patman violations: (1) the price difference is justified by different costs in manufacture, sale, or delivery (e.g., volume discounts), or (2) the price concession was given in good faith to meet a competitor's price.[6]

> … Can prices ever be "too low?" The short answer is yes, but not very often. Generally, low prices benefit consumers. Consumers are harmed only if below-cost pricing allows a dominant competitor to knock its rivals out of the market and then raise prices to above-market levels for a substantial time. A firm's independent decision to reduce prices to a level below its own costs does not necessarily injure competition, and, in fact, may simply reflect particularly vigorous competition. Instances of a large firm using

low prices to drive smaller competitors out of the market in hopes of raising prices after they leave are rare. This strategy can only be successful if the short-run losses from pricing below cost will be made up for by much higher prices over a longer period of time after competitors leave the market. Although the FTC examines claims of predatory pricing carefully, courts, including the Supreme Court, have been skeptical of such claims ...[7]

There is a significant amount of latitude in the way that firms can use price discrimination, yet still remain on the right side of the law. Here are a few guidelines, derived from the FTC pronouncements, which can be used to assist in determining whether versioning strategies and group pricing strategies are legal.

Guideline 1: You may be able to legally charge different prices for a product (price discrimination) if you differentiate your product, by way of features and services.

Guideline 2: You may be able to legally charge different prices for a product (price discrimination) to different groups if you can demonstrate that there are different price sensitivities between the groups.

Guideline 3: You may be able to legally charge different prices for a product if the price discrimination reflects the costs of dealing with different buyers or it reflects an attempt to meet a competitor's offering.

In general, a versioning strategy may be legal if a product is differentiated by way of features and services. It can be inferred that a practice is probably not price discrimination if you can segment people into different income groups according to their price sensitivities and their willingness-to-pay. Groups such as seniors and youth are price-sensitive. It is sometimes *ok* to charge differential prices to groups that are underrepresented in a market. For example, women are often charged less when they attend happy hour. The key to avoiding charges of predatory practices is to set the price above the marginal cost to produce the product. Selling a product at a price that is lower than the variable costs to produce the product can lead to charges of *dumping*. This strategy is illegal, but many companies use it in subtle and not so subtle ways in international markets to gain market share. The final key is to *always* seek legal counsel if there is *any* doubt that a business practice is predatory, illegal, or both.

Conclusion

The primary reason for engaging in product differentiation is to avoid some of the ruinous effects of price competition.[8] Producers are involved in a never-ending process of introducing new products and services and then observing economic behavior. By having several products, producers can experiment and watch economic behavior as consumers will focus on the features and products that are most desirable. The benefits of being a monopolist via differentiation are short-lived, however. Just as cattle are attracted to water, producers are attracted to excess profits.[9] As long as profit potential makes it feasible, competitors *will* enter the market and begin to drive profits to zero.[10]

In this chapter, we have illustrated that there are three approaches to price discrimination and product differentiation. Each pricing strategy is employed under various contexts in practice. The key takeaways include the following:

- First-degree price discrimination, also called personalized pricing, involves charging different prices to different customers for the same product.
- It is difficult to implement first-degree price discrimination because of the difficulty in measuring each consumer's willingness-to-pay, because some consumers may be irritated when they find out they paid more for the same good, because of arbitrage issues and finally because of the potential legal issues.
- Second-degree price discrimination is referred to as product versioning and bundling.
- Versioning involves offering a high-end product for nonprice-sensitive consumers, and a low-end product for price-sensitive consumers.
- Bundling is a special form of versioning in which two or more products are offered as a package at a single price.

- According to Goldilocks pricing, three versions may be just right. The key is to make the versions different enough so that consumer groups can be segmented.
- Third-degree price discrimination involves setting different prices for different groups of consumers such as seniors and students and other groups. It is often based on the price sensitivities of the groups.
- In some instances, price discrimination can be illegal. If there is any doubt that a business practice is in violation of laws, legal counsel should be sought.

CHAPTER 3

Differentiation in Action

Joan's Handcrafted Jewelry Boxes

Joan started out as a tinkerer in her garage. She had a band saw and a table saw and started making wooden toys for her kids. She then decided to make a jewelry box for her daughter. Her daughter and husband were so impressed that she showed the box to all of her family and friends. Word started to get around and soon Joan was getting calls to make the jewelry boxes for numerous customers. She sold the jewelry box for a flat price of $40. It costs Joan about $20 for the wood, the fasteners, and decorations. Joan made a tidy little profit of $20 per box. She enjoyed being a craftsperson and enjoyed the extra income.

Joan worked as an economist for the city government and decided she would like to start a side business making jewelry boxes. She named her business Joan's Handcrafted Jewelry Boxes. Joan subsequently started applying her economic training to launching her jewelry box business.

She knew that understanding how much consumers are *willing-to-pay* for different products and services was critical to running any business. Over the course of several years, Joan had offered the jewelry box at several different prices and, as a result, she had a good feel for the demand for her jewelry boxes at different price levels. She also had many discussions with her customers and potential customers on the amount they would be willing to pay for a jewelry box. She would actually ask her friends and customers how much they would be willing to pay for pearl inlays, exotic woods, and gold-plated hinges. Joan would sometimes send out questionnaires to customers who bought her jewelry boxes asking them what they liked and did not like about their jewelry box.

Joan took the task of understanding consumer preferences and the demand for jewelry boxes very seriously. Joan went so far as to sell her jewelry boxes with different woods and features on a local Internet auction. The Internet auction gave her very precise information on how much customers would be willing to pay for the jewelry box features. Joan had a friend who was in the jewelry business and she also asked her about market demand.

Joan took all the information, integrated it with local demographic and economic information, and developed a forecast and demand curve for her jewelry boxes in the surrounding county. There were approximately 720,000 families in the region and Joan estimated that she could, at most, sell to 0.5% of these families over the course of a year in the current economic environment. She was confident that income levels would not change dramatically over the next year. Joan then used all these information to develop a monthly demand curve for jewelry boxes.

Figure 3.1 presents a 1-month demand curve for Joan's jewelry boxes in her county. The curve was derived after Joan determined that if she charged $60 she could sell 100 units, at $40 she could sell 200 units, and at $20 she could sell 300 units. Joan also spent time examining all the costs that she would incur building the jewelry boxes in her newly remodeled garage. Her garage was now a small factory. She found that the variable and fixed costs are different for each type of jewelry box. After spending considerable time examining the costs and the revenues, Joan decided to sell only one type of jewelry box at a price of $40.

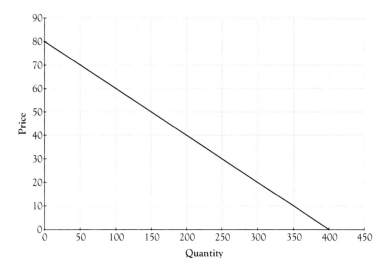

Figure 3.1. Demand curve for jewelry box.

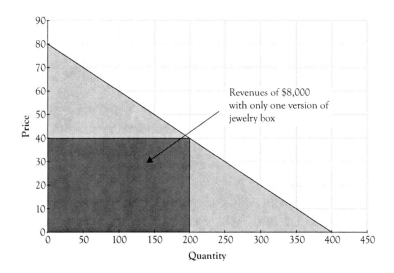

Revenues of $8,000
with only one version of
jewelry box

Figure 3.2. Revenue with one type of jewelry box selling for $40.

Joan determined that she could make a small profit by selling the box for $40. The revenue generated by selling only one model of her jewelry box is illustrated in Figure 3.2. Her fixed costs, consisting of rent, utilities, and tool maintenance, would run about $2,000. The variable costs for the wood, fasteners, and decorations would be about $15 when bought in bulk quantities. The monthly revenue from the business would be $8,000 ($40 × 200) and the profit from the business would be $3,000. The contribution margin is the difference between the selling price and the variable cost to produce each jewelry box. The contribution margin for each jewelry box is $25. The calculations for profit, using q as the quantity and p as the price, are as follows:

Total revenue = $p \times q$
Total revenue = $40 × 200
Total revenue = $8,000
Profit = Total revenue − Total variable costs − Total fixed costs
Profit = $p \times q - V_c \times q - F_c$
Profit = $40 × 200 − $15 × 200 − $2,000
Profit = $8,000 − $3,000 − $2,000
Profit = $3,000

Price and Product Differentiation and Enlightenment

Joan really enjoyed owning a business and being an entrepreneur, but she wanted more. After rereading an interesting article on price discrimination by Hal Varian,[1] Joan decided to expand her product line. Expansion was easy because she had plenty of floor space and could hire one of her talented nephews to assist in producing the boxes. Joan understood the relationship between price discrimination and profitability and this led her to design an additional high-end version and a low-end version of her jewelry box.

The fixed costs for the two new products were about the same. In addition, the variable cost for the high-end jewelry box was $30 and the low-end jewelry box was $10. As illustrated in Figure 3.3, this resulted in additional revenue of $2,000 for the high-end jewelry box and $2,000 for the low-end jewelry box. Now that there is a high-end jewelry box, 100 customers will purchase the high-end box instead of the middle-level box. There are also 100 new customers who will now be willing to pay for a $20 jewelry box. The total revenue for the three boxes is $12,000. The

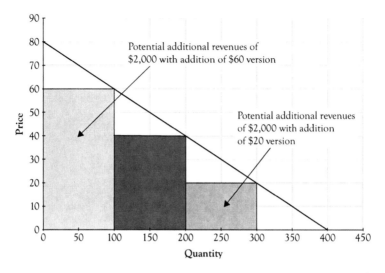

Figure 3.3. Potential revenue when adding versions.

net profit with only one type of jewelry box was $3,000. The net profit with three versions was $4,500 as illustrated in the following calculations:

Profit = ($60 − $30) × **100** + ($40 − $15) × **100** + ($20 − $10)
       × **100** − $2,000 ← {*fixed costs*}
Profit = $3,000 + $2,500 + $1,000 − $2,000
Profit = $6,500 − $2,000
Profit = $4,500

Notice that there are only 100 additional people purchasing the $40 box because 100 customers are now purchasing the high-end jewelry box for $60. There are also only 100 people who will purchase the low-end box. If Joan just adds the high-end box, her profit will increase from $3,000 to $3,500. If she just adds the low-end box, then her profit will increase from $3,000 to $4,000. If she adds both a low-end and high-end box, her net profit will increase from $3,000 to $4,500. The decision to expand and offer additional product versions is complex and will have a profound effect on her business model. She will of course examine her current operations and cost structure and make decisions on what versions, if any, that she will produce.

After considerable soul searching and analysis, Joan decides to introduce three different jewelry box versions. Figure 3.4 illustrates the financial profile for the three jewelry versions designated as the Athena, the Stryker, and the Natural. Figure 3.5 provides an overview of how the features of each version of the jewelry box are used to differentiate each version.

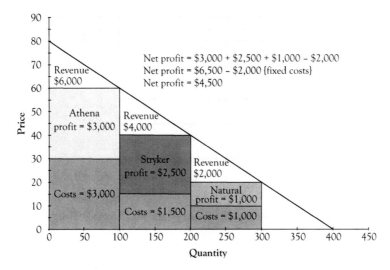

Figure 3.4. Financial structure for three versions of Joan's jewelry boxes.

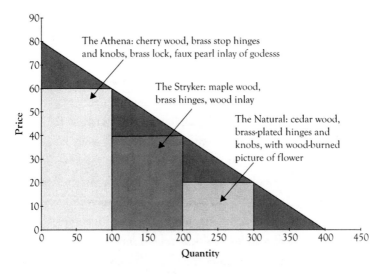

Figure 3.5. Differentiating features for three versions of Joan's jewelry boxes.

The Athena jewelry box is a high-end product targeted toward non-price-sensitive consumers. It is part of what we refer to as a Midas product that was extravagantly engineered and designed. The Natural jewelry box is a Hermes product and is targeted toward price-sensitive consumers, and it was frugally engineered and contains basic features. The Stryker jewelry box is an Atlas product designed for the middle ground. The Stryker has several attractive features; yet it is still priced between Midas and Hermes versions. The Stryker is a mainstream version that appeals to the widest audience. Additional motivation behind the three versions will be presented in chapter 5.

Generating Additional Revenues: Willingness-to-Pay

It might appear obvious that the goal is to extricate as much as possible from the universe of consumers. But many large and small businesses, for reasons of simplicity, turn to the one-product, one-price solution in order to have a simplified management agenda. Adding additional product versions introduces complexity and requires additional investment in the supply chain as well as having an impact on the cost structure for each version. The one-version, one-price approach is a natural solution for the harried entrepreneur who has gazillion things to worry about. However, offering just one version is not a good strategy for several reasons.

If Joan offers only the high-end version, then the profit accrued will be $1,000 [($60 − $30) × 100 − $2,000]. If Joan offers only the low-end version, then the profit accrued would be $1,000. If Joan decides to offer only one product, then it makes sense to go with the middle-level product and the middle-level price, where the profit is $3,000. However, such a strategy leaves a lot of money on the table. First, the high-end consumers would be willing to pay more for the product. Economists call this additional amount they are willing-to-pay as consumer surplus. The consumer surplus is the difference between the amount the nonprice-sensitive or affluent person would be willing to pay for the high-end product and how much they actually paid for the product. Second, price-sensitive consumers can be drawn into the market if an affordable option is made available.

By adding two additional versions, Joan has dramatically increased the present value of her business. A very simple way to calculate the value of a business is to use the perpetual annuity formula of *cash-flow/cost-of-capital*. If we assume a cost-of-capital number of 10%, then having one product leads to a firm value of $360,000 (12 × $3000/0.10). The present value of the business with three products is higher at $540,000 (12 × $4,500/0.10). The business is worth $540,000 rather than $360,000. There is a $180,000 difference. (Additional discussion on the time value of money and how it affects the value of the firm will be presented in a later chapter.)

From the above discussion, we can infer that offering two or more versions of a product is a better strategy than offering only one version. We believe that the best strategy is to always offer at least three different versions of a product; that is, a high-end version, a middle range version, and a low-end version. Varian refers to this type of price discrimination as Goldilocks pricing. However, the value of price and product differentiation goes above the short-term profit considerations. Versioning is critical for long-term survival of the firm because price and product differentiation puts the firm closer to consumers. Versioning helps the seller to understand what product and features are desired by consumers. Versioning is a form of experimentation that affords the seller the opportunity to conduct experiments by introducing versions of products with different features and observing how consumers react.

Price and product differentiation permits consumers to acquire goods that they want at their price point. Consumers come in a variety of sizes with different wants and satisfaction levels and different levels of discretionary income. They have different degrees of their willingness-to-pay for products and services. Price and product differentiation can not only facilitate the extraction of money from the affluent, but it can also benefit the four billion people who live on less than $1,500 per year.[2] This is the so-called bottom-of-the-pyramid. Indeed, price and product differentiation is the basic strategy for selling to the bottom of the pyramid and for providing pharmaceuticals, health care, and many other products to the poor.

We are sometimes asked whether the low-end product will cannibalize the demand for the higher-priced products. That is, will affluent consumers with more money who are less price-sensitive buy the low-end product and ignore more expensive products? This can, of course, occur if the products are not perceived as being adequately differentiated with higher-end features and additional functionality. The key activity for the producer is to conduct experiments by offering differentiated products and watching economic buying behavior unfold.[3] The information garnered from these experiments can then be used to continually refine product offerings and understand the willingness-to-pay functions of your consumers. In essence, if the buyers flock to the low-end product, then this information can be used in future product design decisions.

Demand and Differentiation Dashboards

We have developed a spreadsheet tool that can be used to assist in product differentiation. You are encouraged to visit http://glsanders.wordpress.com/ and obtain the newest version of the spreadsheet. You are also encouraged to read the Appendix of this chapter because it contains an overview of the math for identifying the optimal price and quantity for a demand equation.

Figure 3.6 illustrates the demand spreadsheet for Joan's jewelry. The demand dashboard spreadsheet is used to calculate the slope and the maximum amount consumers would be willing to pay for a product. Figure 3.7 presents a differentiation dashboard spreadsheet. The differentiation dashboard is used to determine the profitability due to product differentiation. The differentiation dashboard also computes an optimal solution for the demand curve when only one version is offered. The optimal price would be $47.50 and, at that price, Joan would sell 162.5 jewelry boxes. As you can see from the solution in Figure 3.7, the monthly cash flow using the optimal solution yields a monthly profit of $3,281.25, which is still not very close to the monthly net profit of $4,500 with three versions. The value of the business would be $393,750 if we assume a cost-of-capital value of 10% (12 × $3,281.25/0.10). The optimal solution is very helpful for identifying a starting point for selecting a price point for one product and for identifying price points for additional versions. The differentiation dashboard is very useful for conducting sensitivity analysis and what-if analysis for differentiating up to three products and services.

Demand dashboard version 4.1 MAC and PC compatible

Only change input values in orange

Enter product name here:	Joan's Jewelry
Demand slope:	-0.2000
Price where there is zero demand	$80.00
Maximum revenue	$8,000
Optimal price	$40.00
Optimal quantity	200

This solution is optimal. →
It will change when variable cost are added
in the demand dashboard

Estimated demand from points

Demand slope (estimated from points):	-0.2000
The slope of the demand curve is between → and between at the 95% confidence level →	-0.2000
Price where there is zero demand:	$80
Maximum revenue from statistical estimate:	$8,000
Optimal price for demand estimate:	$40.00
Optimal quantity for demand estimate:	200
Correlation coefficient price & quantity:	-1.0000

← There will be no confidence
interval if only 2 points are entered

Number of points	4

Point	Price	Quantity
1	$60.00	100.00
2	$40.00	200.00
3	$20.00	300.00
4	$10.00	350.00
5		
6		
7		
8		
9		
10		
11		
12		
13		
14		
15		
16		
17		
18		
19		
20		
21		

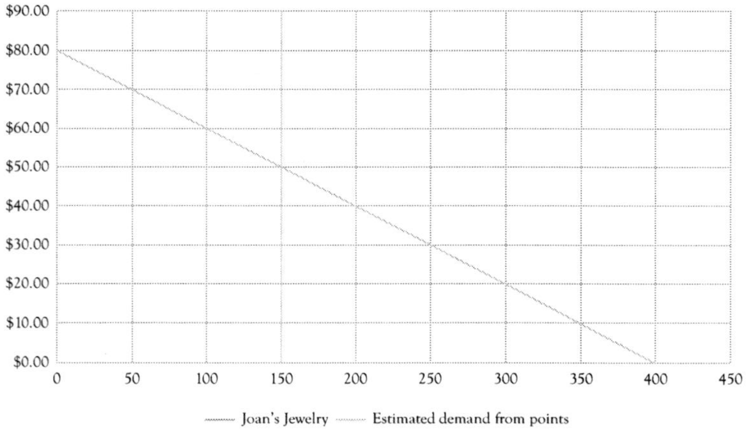

Joan's Jewelry ——— Estimated demand from points

Figure 3.6. Demand analysis dashboard.

Differentiation dashboard version 4.1 MAC and PC compatible

Only change input values in orange

	Joan's jewelry
Enter product name here:	
Demand slope:	-0.2000
Price where demand is zero	$80.00

Midas product	
Price	$60.00
Quantity sold	100
Variable costs	$30.00
Profit (before subtracting fixed costs)	$3,000

Atlas product	
Price	$40.00
Quantity sold	100
Variable costs	$15.00
Profit (before subtracting fixed costs)	$2,500

Hermes product	
Price	$20.00
Quantity sold	100
Variable costs	$10.00
Profit (before subtracting fixed costs)	$1,000

Differentiation strategy	
Fixed costs:	$2,000
Net profit with 3 versions	$4,500

Optimal solution with only Atlas product	
Optimal price	47.50
Optimal quantity	162.50
Total revenue	7718.75
Total variable costs	2437.50
Fixed costs	2000.00
Optimal net profit with 1 version	3281.25

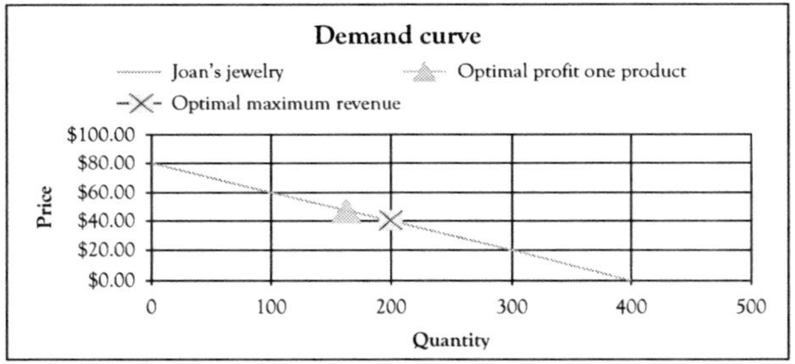

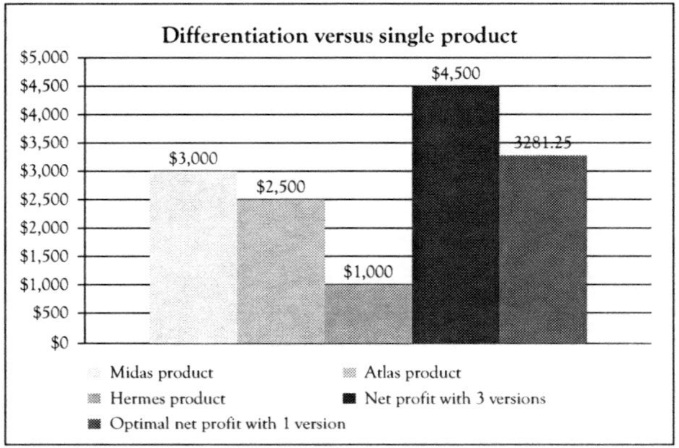

Figure 3.7. Differentiation dashboard using demand analysis dashboard input and financial data from Joan.

Monopolistic Competition at Work

Monopolistic competition involves many buyers, many sellers, and easy entry and exit with one difference. The sellers in these markets sell products that are closely related, but not identical. Joan sells jewelry boxes that are similar to other jewelry boxes in function and form, but they are nevertheless different. They are differentiated from the competition. Joan's products are unique and differentiated because of their features (handcrafted, unique words, styling, etc.) and her unique brand.

As noted earlier, a purely competitive market has many buyers and sellers and each individual firm is a price taker. In this market, the price for a product or service is determined via market interactions (buying and selling) between consumers and producers. In perfectly competitive markets, there are many sellers, many buyers, and entry into and out of the market is easy. In a perfectly competitive market, Joan would price her jewelry boxes at prevailing market prices where marginal revenue equals marginal cost. In actuality, Joan can function as a quasi-monopolist or as a near-monopolist in the short term until the competition recognizes that they can make money selling unique jewelry boxes.

Independent, Complement, and Substitute Goods and Services

Most of the action in business involves not just the product line, but also the markets for related products and services. There are three key concepts related to product and service differentiation and the type of related goods being offered; they are *independent*, *substitute*, and *complementary* goods and services.

Two goods are *independent* if their consumption or use is not related. The use of toothbrushes, for example, is not related to the consumption or use of motorcycles. Independent goods are goods that are not dependent in any way on how the other good is used. Since demand for one does not affect the demand for the other, product differentiation has little impact on these types of product trade-offs.

Much of the interesting economic activity in terms of strategy and differentiation comes from *complementary* and *substitute* products and services. *Complementary* goods are typically used together. When the demand for one rises, for example, burgers, it leads to a rise in demand for the other product, for example, fries. Examples of complementary products and services include toothbrushes and toothpaste, PCs and monitors, travel services and global positioning systems, console game systems and broadband demand, and operating systems and business applications suites. In the case of Joan's jewelry boxes, a complementary good would be an expensive wood polish to maintain the wood or perhaps a limited line of earrings that could be placed in the jewelry box as part of a gift.

Substitute goods are goods that are alike. In other words, substitute goods have an equivalent function and one substitute good can be consumed or used in place of another. They are largely interchangeable and when the demand for one substitute increases, the demand for the other good decreases. Examples of substitute services include cable systems and satellite systems. Although they work very differently, they can be effectively substituted for one another. Other examples include margarine and butter, satellite phones and cell phones, powdered and liquid laundry detergent, and CDs and MP3 files. None of these products are actually perfect substitutes because they all have slightly different features and have different performance characteristics. A *perfect substitute* works essentially the same way and has the same features and qualities as another technology. In practice, many competing technologies are imperfect substitutes. MP3 files are imperfect substitutes for CDs because CDs produce better sound than MP3 files. However, MP3 files are smaller and more easily copied than CDs. Butter and margarine are slightly differentiated in terms of taste and the way our bodies assimilate these two fats. In the case of Joan's jewelry boxes, product substitutes would be any jewelry box or container that could be used to house jewelry. This would include a plastic food storage container, a vase, or even a glass.

Price Discrimination and Price Differentiation

It is a fundamental economic principle that the way to maximize profits is to charge a price that equates to the value of the product to each consumer, instead of selling at a uniform price to all consumers. This is the idea behind price discrimination.[4] Pure price discrimination involves selling the same good at different prices to different consumers. Flat pricing can have perverse consequences, because it encourages the producer to sell to the high end of the market.[5] The producer simply starts at the top price of the demand curve and then ratchets the price down. The flat price selected is a function of how the fixed costs and variable costs lead to the highest profit. Producers who understand differential pricing have a strong incentive to supply several versions of a product because they will usually make more money. Rather than sell the same exact good at different prices, the goal should be to modify a product and sell a differentiated product at different prices. This could be accomplished using the following strategies:

- Adding and subtracting product features
- Adding and subtracting convenience
- Adding and subtracting durability
- Adding and subtracting design appeal
- Adding and subtracting speed of delivery and processing
- Changing the level of customer service
- Advertising and branding and perhaps generating a cool factor and snob appeal

There are two situations that lead to very high demand for products. The first involves scarcity. When a product is scarce, it is usually in demand. Price discrimination is easy for scarce products, even though such situations are sometimes transitory (e.g., snow blowers during extended winter storms, games consoles at launch, and oil consumption in the winter). The other approach to generating high levels of demand is to design products that make people and their kids look smarter or more attractive. Products that give kids an academic edge are always in demand. Parents will flock to such products because they may be able to differentiate their children from the competition.

Irritating Consumers

There are several lessons that can be learned from monopolistic behavior (and misbehavior) for those interested in engaging in monopolistic competition. The first lesson that can be gleaned relates to the behavior of the cable TV companies. Monopolies tend to take their customers for granted, as was the case with cable TV subscribers in previous decades. As soon as alternate products became available with better features, such as those provided by satellite and optical fiber carriers, consumers started to abandon the cable TV ship. They felt little allegiance to cable providers because of the years of neglect. The cable provider's strategy was to make a profit by providing few existing and new features, keep raising subscription rates, and providing poor service. There was enduring ill will toward cable providers because they did not constantly differentiate and improve their services and they were unwilling to streamline costs. Service has improved dramatically and, in some instance, surpasses the competition, but the remnants of ill will survive.[6]

Companies have to be very cautious how they use price differentiation to personalize prices lest they incur the wrath of customers. Amazon found this out in 2001 when they started to sell their DVDs at different prices.

> The price test, which ran early last week, affected dozens of Amazon's top-selling titles. Because of the test, which assigned prices at random to customers as they shopped, some customers found DVDs at prices up to $15 greater than other customers. Amazon spokesman Bill Curry said that Amazon would reimburse customers who ordered DVDs affected by the test for the difference between the price they paid and the lowest test price. Although Amazon has no plans to do any more pricing tests, the company guarantees that should it run another one, customers will pay the lowest test price even if they order goods at a higher price during the test.[7]

Personalized pricing can tick-off consumers when consumers find out that they are paying a premium for the same product or service. Some of the current ill will directed toward the airline companies is related to the wide range of prices charged for identical seats and, of course, to their very proficient use of versioning in the form of baggage surcharges, meals, early boarding, and fast tracking through security. In 1995, the average

U.S. domestic price for an airplane ticket was $292.[8] In 2009, the average airplane ticket price was $309. This is equivalent to $220 in 1995. The airlines turned to product differentiation in order to achieve profitability.

It is sometimes necessary for producers to use approaches that disguise personalized pricing approaches. Here are a few of the strategies used by businesses to engage in product and service differentiation; some of them are more acceptable to consumers than others:

- Charging higher prices where you have bundled other products with low variable costs with the original product.
- Charging lower prices if the customer buys a product or service that will be consumed 6 months or a year into the future.
- Permit customers to purchase products at a reduced price because they are part of a price-sensitive customer segment such as the student or senior citizen populations.
- Make a customer submit a rebate coupon in order to get a lower price.
- Offer the product at a lower price if they wait a couple of days before they receive the product. Offer the customer a lower price the next day.
- Give customers the opportunity to play a game that lets them win the product at a lower price.
- De-bundle services and charge for each service (airlines are a good example).

It should be noted that some consumers will figure out how to game these systems. They will then pass this information on and it will eventually reach a substantial number of consumers as the specter of efficient markets looms its ugly head.

Waves of Innovation Fueled by Substitutes and Complements

Innovation comes in waves. It is driven by consumers in the form of demand for better products and services: "I need a smaller product with more features and capabilities at a lower price."

Substitute and complementary products are part of the engine that drives innovation. For example, transportation has spurred the development of substitute energy sources such as steam, electric, fuel cells, and solar energy. The emergence of the automobile was the driving force behind the development of better roads, fueling stations, and diners. Demand for clearer and faster communication has been the key driver for many modern-day substitute products as illustrated in Figure 3.8. This has in turn driven the development of a wide range of products to support the communication process.

Arbitrage: Producer's Paradise and Consumer's Dread

When I was a youngster in Helena Montana, I wanted to learn how to play the bongo drums like Desi Arnaz.[9] I went to a local store and inquired

Figure 3.8. Innovation driven by substitute and complements.

about the cost for a set of bongo drums. I believe that they wanted $40; this was too much money and I decided to forgo the purchase and take up the tuba because it was available through the school.[10] I found out a year later that the same bongos were available in a mass-market catalog for a lot less money. I possessed inferior information on the value of the bongos. Information asymmetry occurs when the seller has better information about the value of a product than the buyer. In many situations, it is the seller who knows more about the value of a product than the buyer; however, it is possible that the buyer knows more about the value of the product than the seller. Selling a product at a higher price in a market where consumers are not knowledgeable or privy to the true market price is called arbitrage. Arbitrage can lead to excess profits and inefficiencies in the supply chain because the consumer cannot turn to other suppliers and because the consumer does not know the competitive price for the product and/or cannot get access to competitively priced products. Arbitrage presents the opportunity for suppliers and producers to exploit the consumer's lack of product knowledge and earn higher profits.

Arbitrage is very important to commodity traders. Arbitrage enables the seller to buy a product, such as a commodity, in one market and sell the product in another market for a higher price. The arbitrageur makes money by taking advantage of the price disparity by selling in one market while simultaneously buying in the other. Excess profits are symptomatic of asymmetric information and inefficient markets. When someone knows more than someone else about a product, they will often use that information to achieve above-average profits or to secure resources at a steep discount. The benefactor of the windfall rarely views good deals as gluttonous. The number of suppliers and consumers for bongos in Helena Montana during the 1960s was very small, and there were very few opportunities to locate musical instrument catalogs that contained bongo drums. This is asymmetric information at work. A market is *efficient* when price discovery is easy and information is transparent and readily available to all market participants.

Arbitrage can also hurt the producer of a low-cost item. Someone could buy all of Joan's low-cost jewelry boxes, repackage the jewelry box, add a little do-dad, and then sell them at a higher price in the same market. This could effectively reduce her high-end revenues. Continuous product differentiation along with marketing and searching for the most up-to-date information can reduce the impact of arbitrage. This can be summed up in the following relationship:

Information Asymmetries → Arbitrage → Bad Deals.

Conclusion

As we have seen in this chapter, product differentiation leads to additional revenues and is the basis for conducting experiments for determining what products and product versions to introduce in the future. We have also discussed how substitute and complementary products and services further drive innovation. Subsequent chapters will explore how product differentiation forms the basis for experimentation, innovation, and product development.

In this chapter, we have illustrated how price discrimination could be applied to Joan's jewelry box case and optimum prices for product versioning could be derived. The key takeaways include the following:

- By adding additional versions, Joan has dramatically increased the present value of her business.
- Many large and small businesses, for reasons of simplicity, offer products using a one-price solution in order to have a simplified management agenda.
- By adopting a one-price solution, companies overlook the high-end consumers and the premium prices that they will pay for a product.
- A one-price solution also ignores the price-sensitive consumers who could be drawn into the market if an affordable option is made available.
- If a high-end product is not perceived as being adequately differentiated with higher-end features and additional functionality, the low-end product could cannibalize the demand for the higher-priced product.
- Two goods are independent if their consumption or use is not related. For example, cell phones and lawn mowers are independent goods.

- Complementary goods are typically used together like toothbrushes and toothpaste.
- Substitute goods have an equivalent function and one substitute good can be consumed or used in place of another. Examples are CD players and MP3 players and cable TV carriers versus satellite TV carriers.
- Companies have to be very cautious how they use price differentiation to personalize prices lest they incur the wrath of customers.
- Information asymmetry occurs when the seller has better information about the value of a product than the buyer and vice versa.
- Selling a product at a higher price in a market where consumers are not knowledgeable or privy to the true market price is called arbitrage.

Determining the Optimal Selling Price Using Demand, Revenue, and Cost Equations

Even though Joan is an economist, her knowledge of the market for jewelry boxes was based on experience and insight. She understands the market because she has bought and sold jewelry boxes and their raw materials and she has built them from scratch. Joan decided she should put some of her economics training to work and determine the ideal price and quantity to sell that would generate the most profit.

The typical demand curve has the price on the y-axis and the quantity demanded on the x-axis and is downward-sloping.[11] A demand curve can be represented as a linear mathematical formula with quantity as the dependent variable ($q = -5p + 400$) or with price as the dependent variable ($p = -5q + 80$). A demand curve is a very useful diagram for describing the relationship between the price level and the quantity demanded at each price level. In general, as the price of a product increases, the demand for the good decreases. Similarly, as the price of a product decreases, the demand for the good increases. This section discusses how the demand curve can be used to identify the optimal price and quantity for selling just one version of a product.

Since Joan is a near-monopoly working in a market characterized by monopolistic competition, she can set her variable costs and fixed costs within certain limits related to the features she has established for her Jewelry boxes. Joan used algebra to come up with the optimal selling price for her standard jewelry box. This is the price that generates the greatest profit given the $15 variable costs and the $2,000 fixed costs.

Her first task was to develop a demand equation. The demand equation relates the quantity of the good demanded by consumers to the price of the good. Demand equations are in the form: Price = constant + slope*Quantity. This can be calculated by finding the slope of the curve using any two points (see Figure 3.9). We will use the points $(q1, p1)$ or $(100, \$60)$ and $(q2, p2)$ or $(200, \$40)$. The slope is the rise over the run or:

Slope = $(60 - 40)/(100 - 200)$
Slope = $20/-100$
Slope = -0.2

The constant is calculated by determining where the demand line crosses the y-axis or, in this situation, the price or P-axis. This is accomplished by using the point slope form of the demand equation and any point such as $(100, \$60)$. The resulting constant is 80.

$p - p1 = \text{slope}(q - q1)$
$p - 60 = -0.2(q - 100)$
$p = 60 + 0.2q + 20$
$p = 80 - 0.2q$

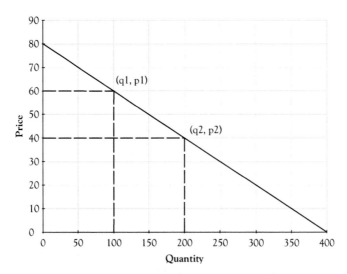

Figure 3.9. Two points are used to derive the demand curve.

In many instances, the demand curve is expressed in terms of p because the price determines the amount demanded. You can just substitute a price into the following formula and find out how many units will be sold.

$q = -5p + 400$

So if Joan decides to price each box at $50, then she will be able to sell 150 units.

Now that the demand equation has been found ($p = -0.2q + 80$ or $q = -5p + 400$), Joan's next step was to determine the quantity where profits are maximized. This is accomplished by identifying where marginal revenue equals marginal cost. This is completed in two steps. The first step is to substitute the demand curve equation into the total revenue equation in order to get the total revenue calculation in terms of the quantity sold or q.

$p = 80 - 0.2q$
Total revenue = $p \times q$
Total revenue = $(80 - 0.2q) \times q$
Total revenue = $80q - 0.2q^2$

The above equation can be used to express the total revenue as a function of the quantity produced. We can check this answer by substituting 200 into the total revenue equation. For example, the total revenue when production is 200 units would be $80 \times 200 - 0.2 \times 200^2$ or $8,000. This is the same value for total revenue using the $p \times q$ equation for total revenue ($40 \times 200 = $8,000).

The second step is to find the quantity where marginal cost equals marginal revenue. This is accomplished by taking the first derivative of the total revenue equation with respect to q. This is then set to the marginal cost and then solved for q. The marginal cost is actually the variable cost in this example. The marginal cost to produce one additional jewelry box is $15.

Total revenue= $80q - 0.2q^2$
Marginal revenue = $dtr/dq = 80 - 0.4q$
Marginal revenue = Marginal cost
$\quad 80 - 0.4q = 15$
$\quad -0.4q = -65$
$\quad q = 162.5$

The 162.5 quantity is rounded up to 163 and then substituted into the $p = 80 - 0.2q$ equation.

$$p = 80 - 0.2(163)$$
$$p = 47.4$$

The 47.4 price was rounded down to $47. This is the short-term optimal revenue solution.

Profit = $47 × 163 − $15 × 163 − $2,000
Profit = $3,216

Joan decided after her analysis to produce fewer jewelry boxes since she could make more money selling fewer boxes at a higher price. She could have done a similar analysis using spreadsheet software and come up with a similar solution. She would, however, still need the original demand function along with an understanding of her variable and fixed costs to produce the jewelry boxes.

Optimal Solution for Three Versions of Jewelry Box

The demand dashboard can also be used to determine the optimum solution when there are three jewelry boxes. The optimum solution is calculated using a mathematical programming algorithm that is usually referred to as a solver add-on in spreadsheet programs (see Figure 3.10). The solver essentially identifies the price for the Athena, the Stryker, and the Natural that would maximize profit with all the other variables such as the variable costs remaining the same.

As you can see from Figure 3.10, the optimal Athena price would be $76.25 and about 19 units would be sold. The optimal price for the Stryker would be $57.50 and about 94 units would be sold. The Natural would be priced at $33.75 and would sell 119 units. The net profit for all three versions would be $5,672. This is in contrast to the non-optimized solution of $4,500. Joan just picked prices for each version using her intuition and insight into what consumers would be willing to pay.

Differentiation dashboard version 4.1 MAC and PC compatible

Only change input values in orange

	Joan's jewelry
Enter product name here:	
Demand slope:	-0.2000
Price where demand is zero	$80.00

Midas product

Price	$76.25
Quantity sold	19
Variable costs	$30.00
Profit (before subtracting fixed costs)	$867

Atlas product

Price	$57.50
Quantity sold	94
Variable costs	$15.00
Profit (before subtracting fixed costs)	$3,984

Hermes product

Price	$33.75
Quantity sold	119
Variable costs	$10.00
Profit (before subtracting fixed costs)	$2,820

Differentiation strategy

Fixed costs:	$2,000
Net profit with 3 versions	$5,672

Optimal solution with only Atlas product

Optimal price	47.50
Optimal quantity	162.50
Total revenue	7718.75
Total variable costs	2437.50
Fixed costs	2000.00
Optimal net profit with 1 version	3281.25

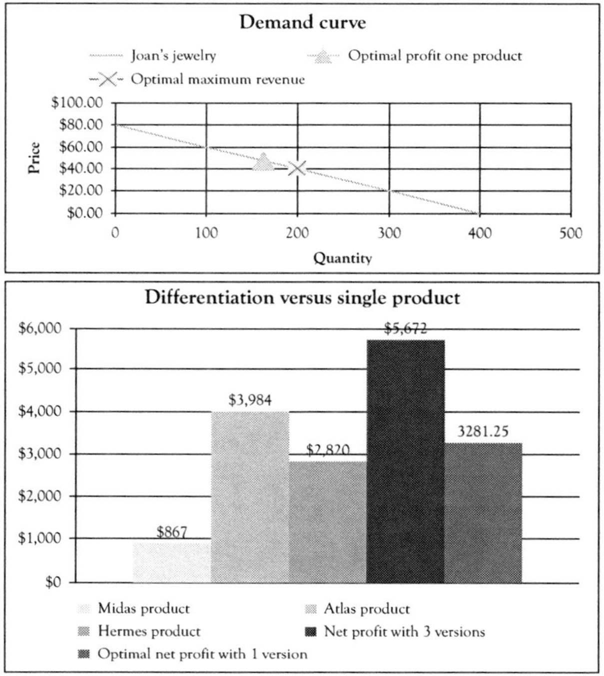

Demand curve

Legend: Joan's jewelry — Optimal profit one product — Optimal maximum revenue

Price axis: $100.00, $80.00, $60.00, $40.00, $20.00, $0.00
Quantity axis: 0, 100, 200, 300, 400, 500

Differentiation versus single product

$6,000
$5,000
$4,000
$3,000
$2,000
$1,000
$0

$5,672
$3,984
3281.25
$2,820
$867

Legend: Midas product, Hermes product, Optimal net profit with 1 version, Atlas product, Net profit with 3 versions

Figure 3.10. Optimal profit with three versions of jewelry boxes.

You should note that the optimal solution for only having the Atlas product is $3,281. This is little different than the $3,216 solution obtained using the algebraic solution detailed in the last section because we rounded the price and quantity in the algebraic solution.

The optimal solution provides insight into the demand curve and the product mix, but it is not a magic potion for setting prices and developing versions. There are a number of factors that go into identifying the price and the characteristics for each version. There might be significant setup costs for constructing the Athena or, perhaps, it would be difficult to find artistically talented employees to work on the fake pearl inlays for just a couple of hours. Perhaps Joan does not want to focus on the Natural because she wants to eventually focus on upscale jewelry boxes and she is concerned that her product would not be considered a high-end offering because of the proliferation of inexpensive jewelry boxes. And, of course, it is very difficult to actually know if the demand curve is valid for all levels of prices.

Linear and Nonlinear Demand Curves

The demand curve for a good does not have to be linear or straight. As illustrated in Figure 3.11, the demand curve could be curvilinear. It appears that the price at which there is no demand is $80 and that there is essentially unlimited demand for jewelry boxes that cost <$15. Let us examine how a different and, in particular, a nonlinear curve could influence the amount of revenues generated. Using Figure 3.11, if Joan charges $60 for the Athena unit, she would sell 50 units. If she charged $40 for the Stryker model, she would sell 50 units (100 − 50). If she charged $20 for the Natural, she would sell 150 units (250 − 100). If Joan still had the same variable cost structure as before, she would generate the following revenues and profit:

$$\text{Profit} = (\$60 - \$30) \times \mathbf{50} + (\$40 - \$15) \times \mathbf{50} + (\$20 - \$10)$$
$$\times \mathbf{150} - \$2,000 \leftarrow \{\textit{fixed costs}\}$$
$$\text{Profit} = \$1,500 + \$1,500 + \$1,500 - \$2,000$$
$$\text{Profit} = \$4,500 - \$2,000$$
$$\text{Profit} = \$2,500$$

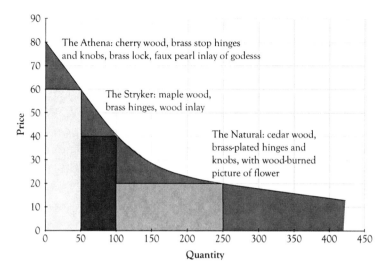

Figure 3.11. Nonlinear demand curve for Joan's jewelry boxes.

This amount is noticeably less than the $3,216 algebraic solution ($47 × 163 − $15 × 163 − $2,000) for the single version where it was assumed that demand was linear. This example illustrates that a slight miss in identifying the appropriate demand function can have a dramatic impact on profitability. Even though the demand and differentiation dashboards can only deal with linear relationships, we can estimate a linear function using only a portion of the demand curve. It appears that there is a linear relationship within the price range of $20–$80. The price where demand is zero (the *Y* intercept) and the slope of the demand curve were both estimated using the demand analysis dashboard as illustrated in Figure 3.12. Figure 3.13 shows the solution for the nonlinear demand curve using the differentiation dashboard. The key difference for this solution versus the solution that was presented earlier in the chapter is that the demand curve was estimated using points that were not linear with a linear regression algorithm. This leads to several interesting results.

The profit for one product using the optimal solution for the nonlinear curve is $1,415.69. Using Figure 3.13, again you can see that when the

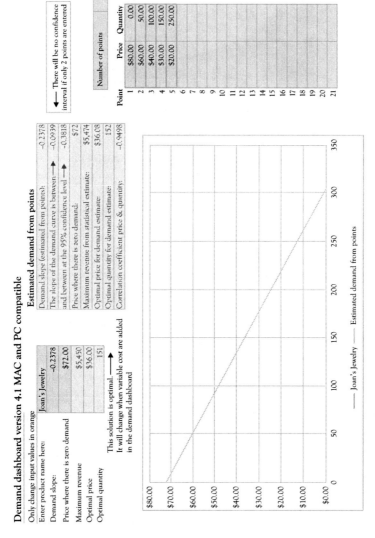

Figure 3.12. Demand curve for nonlinear estimation.

Differentiation dashboard version 4.1 MAC and PC compatible

Only change input values in orange

	Joan's jewelry
Enter product name here:	Joan's jewelry
Demand slope:	-0.2378
Price where demand is zero	$72.00

Midas product

Price	$60.00
Quantity sold	50
Variable costs	$30.00
Profit (before subtracting fixed costs)	$1,514

Atlas product

Price	$40.00
Quantity sold	84
Variable costs	$15.00
Profit (before subtracting fixed costs)	$2,103

Hermes product

Price	$20.00
Quantity sold	84
Variable costs	$10.00
Profit (before subtracting fixed costs)	$841

Differentiation strategy

Fixed costs:	$2,000
Net profit with 3 versions	$2,458

Optimal solution with only Atlas product

Optimal price	43.50
Optimal quantity	119.85
Total revenue	5213.41
Total variable costs	1797.73
Fixed costs	2000.00
Optimal net profit with 1 version	1415.69

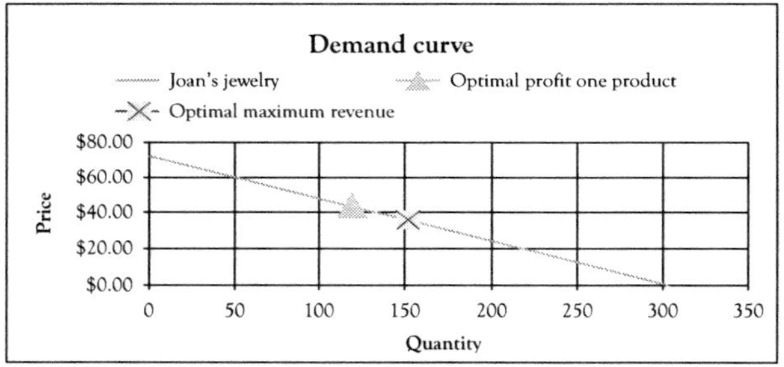

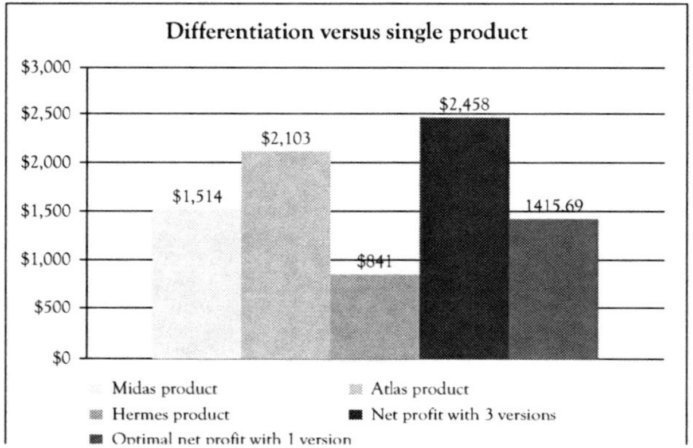

Demand curve

— Joan's jewelry   —✶— Optimal profit one product
— Optimal maximum revenue   ✕ Optimal profit with 1 version

Price: $80.00, $60.00, $40.00, $20.00, $0.00
Quantity: 0, 50, 100, 150, 200, 250, 300, 350

Differentiation versus single product

$3,000 · $2,500 · $2,000 · $1,500 · $1,000 · $500 · $0

1415.69
$2,458
$841
$2,103
$1,514

Midas product · Hermes product · Optimal net profit with 1 version · Atlas product · Net profit with 3 versions

Figure 3.13. Joan's profit using estimates of nonlinear demand.

original variable and fixed costs are entered in the differentiation dash-board, three versions produce a net profit of $2,458. This is in contrast to the $4,500 profit for the three versions using the original linear demand curve.

When the demand is nonlinear, economists use "tricks" to transform a nonlinear demand data into a linear formula.[12] For example, they take the natural log of the price and quantity data and then perform the regression analysis in order to develop an estimate of the function. The trick I used was to estimate the demand function by only using prices between $20 and $80.

If a new product is being introduced, then there may not be any data available for estimating a demand curve. Historical data are often scarce or nonexistent for new products and significantly revised versions of products. Sometimes, the entrepreneur has only two points for esti-mating demand. The first point is where the price crosses the Y-axis. This is essentially the maximum amount that most consumers would be willing-to-pay for a product. The second point is also a guestimate using a hypothetical question. What demand would result if we were to introduce a product at the prevailing market price using typical product features?

The key takeaway is that it is difficult to model consumer demand when products are new and untested, and even where there is a pro-liferation of historical data, it is still a difficult task. Another takeaway is that *versioning* will almost always generate more revenues and also greater profits in the long run. The crucial activity is to constantly experiment and continuously introduce product versions in order to understand the constantly changing nature of consumer behavior. Quantitative tools can provide insight, but they should be used to pro-vide insight and not used as a sole solution for pricing and versioning products.

From an economist point of view, the primary goal of versioning is to capture consumer surplus. As one of my economist colleagues (Bill Hamlen) noted, it is very difficult to develop a reasonable math-ematically grand optimal solution for capturing consumer surplus with even two versions. Economists have not attempted to tackle the problem of versioning because of the mathematical complexity. I have taken the liberty of using the same demand curve for all the versions. In reality, there is a separate demand curve for each version. Bill Hamlen suggested that since it is so difficult to find a grand optimal solution, that I should continue the approach used in the book because it still provides an insight into the important issue of capturing consumer surplus from a strategy perspective.

CHAPTER 4

The Role of Dynamic Tension in Constructing Versioning and Product Differentiation Curves

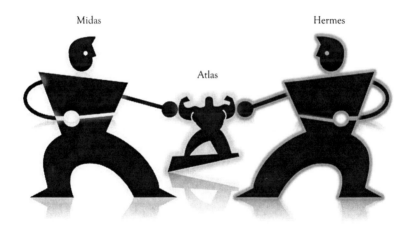

The demand for a product is influenced by a number of factors including product availability, the utility or usefulness of a product, consumer income levels, product features, marketing efforts, product awareness, the quality and performance of substitute products, fashion and the cost of complementary products. This chapter illustrates how product differentiation curves (PD curves) can be used to increase revenues and continually deliver updated products and services. We will sometimes refer to PD curves as versioning curves. The focus will not be on the math or even on the actual form of the demand curve. Our focus will be on using product differentiation or versioning curves as a conceptual tool for developing different product versions.

A PD curve is very useful in illustrating the relationship between price and the quantity demanded. But there is one major difference between the PD curve and the typical demand curve. The PD curve can include different versions of a product on the curve and also segments each product version according to willingness-to-pay characteristics of the buyer groups as illustrated in the case of Joan's jewelry (see Figure 4.1). These major groups are Midas, Atlas, and Hermes consumers. The primary purpose of the PD curve is to assist in identifying product versions and prices levels for discriminating each product version. The process for matching products to the willingness-to-pay segments is rooted in experimentation and the continuous introduction of new versions of products and services.

The PD curve is very useful for product positioning. Product positioning is the process where sellers and producers try to create an image, an identity, or an emotion toward a product or a service in the minds of consumers. This is the essence of the brand concept. A brand is simply something that lives in the head of consumers.[1] The brand is a composite of the mental associations that are generated when you see or think about a certain product. Our focus will be on positioning products and services according to the different customer segments' willingness-to-pay and price sensitivities. The PD curve can of course be used to illustrate

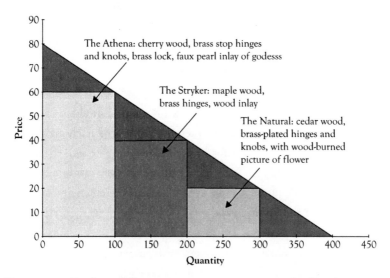

Figure 4.1. Product differentiation or versions curve for Joan's jewelry.

how a single standardized product can be differentiated by geography, by market segment, and through branding efforts.

One promising application of the PD curve is that it can be used to identify the so-called Blue Ocean markets. A Blue Ocean market is a market that does not in exist. The goal is to create a new product that is radically differentiated from existing products that are being offered and to create the Blue Ocean market.[2]

Versioning and Goldilocks Pricing

The idea behind versioning is to engage in differential pricing by offering different types or editions of a product.[3] Ideally, the different versions should be perceived as having different levels of quality. The number of versions can also be related to the number of distinct market segments. In many instances, it is difficult to identify the optimum number of market segments, and it is also difficult to develop products for each market segment. Goldilocks pricing, and therefore versioning, is a rule of thumb that suggests that you should start out with three price levels.[4] The idea behind Goldilocks pricing is that offering 1 product is too few, 10 products is too many, and offering 3 differentiated products is just the right amount. A case was made in the chapter discussing Joan's jewelry boxes for having more than one product because of the increased potential for generating revenue for Joan.

If a company does not introduce multiple versions of a product, they will be leaving money on the table. If a company does not have a high-end product for consumers who are affluent or price-insensitive, then they will not have extracted the consumer's surplus from affluent customers or customers who simply do not care how much the product costs, they just want it. On the other hand, a business will also leave money on the table if they do not have a lower-end product for price-sensitive individuals because price-sensitive individuals will not purchase products that are above their willingness-to-pay. Price-sensitive customers, such as students, also present another opportunity; they can be the foundation for establishing a long-lasting relationship when they have more discretionary income.

There is one additional reason for offering more than one product to consumers. Introducing multiple versions of a product permits a company to experiment and observe consumer's economic behavior in action. The company can monitor purchase behavior and determine which features and products consumers deem most desirable. Such experimentation is actually the most effective activity for conducting research and engaging in new product development.

Using Dynamic Tension Differentiation to Develop Products and Services for the Entire Demand Curve

In their book on developing creative approaches for solving problems, Barry Nalebuff and Ian Ayres describe the "What Would Croesus Do?" approach.[5] The gist of the approach is to consider how a consumer would solve a problem when he or she has unlimited resources. Need tech support, have the tech sit outside your office, and enter when called. Bored, become a cosmonaut. This approach can help to identify high-end products and services for the consumer who is not price-sensitive and is interested in many different features (see Figure 4.2). We have renamed *Croesus* to *Midas* products because it is easier to remember and because it imparts a very colorful and explicit image of high-end features. *Midas* products and services are designed for consumers who are not price-sensitive and demand high-end features. Products that are designed with

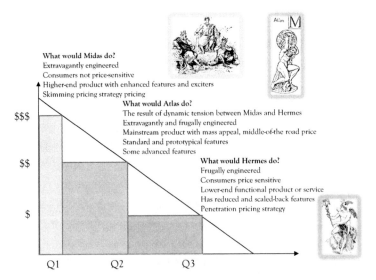

Figure 4.2. Dynamic tension between Midas and Hermes leads to Atlas products.

high-end features for individuals who are affluent or individuals who are simply interested in high-end products are designed using extravagant engineering. Extravagant engineering is less concerned with costs and more concerned with using new technology and concepts to develop innovative and perhaps even radical products and services. In general, products and services that are extravagantly engineered contain advanced features and attributes.

Pricing high-end *Midas* products and services is tricky and very important. The goal is not only to cover variable costs but also to make a profit. There is more at stake with Midas products. Another objective is to get consumers to focus on the attributes of a Midas product that distinguish it from other products. The point is to determine what product features customers value the most. This is accomplished partly by marketing research but also through economic experiments in the form of introducing products with different features and observing buying behavior. Bertini and Wathieu have identified several strategies that can stop consumers from fixating on price and focus on product features.[6] One noteworthy approach is to willfully overprice the product in order to stimulate curiosity. It appears that some consumers are more inclined to analyze product features and even buy a product when there is a high price premium in the 30–80% range.

There is a part of the demand curve where the consumers are price-sensitive. This segment could include students, seniors, and, in general, individuals with low levels of discretionary income or individuals who are truly value-conscious. In designing products and services for this group, you can use the "What would Hermes Do?" approach. Hermes was the god of the traveler, the shepherd, the athlete, the merchants, the cunning, and was linked to invention and commerce. We are now designating Hermes as the patron for the part of the demand curve that does not have a patron.[7] *Hermes* products and services are designed for consumers who are price-sensitive and demand features that are functional for the task at hand. Hermes products and services are still functional, but they have reduced and scaled-back features. There are a variety of very interesting products and services that have been developed for *Hermes* customers occupying the price-sensitive end of the demand curve. An important reason for offering Hermes products and services is to acquire customers who might eventually become Midas consumers. For example, students become less price-sensitive as they enter the work force and generate more discretionary income. Consumers' tastes can also change as they become more familiar with a product line or because they get caught up in the hype around fashionable product. Designing Hermes products requires skills in frugal engineering.

Frugal engineering is the ability to design useful low-cost products and services for price-sensitive consumers.[8] Frugal engineering is the clean slate approach for engineering and designing products and services. The first step is to identify the fundamental or essential functions of a product or service. The next step is to concurrently design or redesign the existing product or service and the manufacturing process so that the process is very efficient and the components and materials used are inexpensive. The individuals using Hermes products can be price-sensitive because they are thrifty, but they can also be Hermes customers because they are part of the approximately 4 billion people in the world with a purchasing power of <$1,500 per year or consumers who are looking for a bargain.

Midas and Hermes products have an important role in developing new ideas for products and services for the middle of the demand curve. Midas gives product developers the license to create ideas that are unique and perhaps superfluous. Hermes products and services establish a minimal baseline for a product or service with the additional prompting of being inexpensive to produce. Hermes products should be less expensive to produce because they are meant to attract price-sensitive customers.

Dynamic Tension Between Midas and Hermes Spawns Atlas

From the producer's perspective, the idea is to get the creative juices flowing and use the top and bottom of the demand curve to generate new ideas for products and services by drawing on both extravagant and frugal engineering approaches to develop *Atlas* products. The mass-appeal or mainstream products in the middle are called *Atlas* products. *Atlas* was a Greek mythological figure that supported the weight of the heavens on his shoulders. Atlas products support the broad-based customer segment in the middle that requires products that have standard features and also have slightly differentiated features to meet the demand of monopolistic competition. The point is to create dynamic tension between the two ends of the demand curve, anchored by extravagantly engineered and designed Midas products and frugally engineered and designed Hermes products. The result of this dynamic tension is an Atlas product.[9] This is a product with attractive features and with an attractive contribution margin. The result is also a robust process for continually inventing and reinventing the products and services to stave off the competition and establish a strong foundation for survival.

Midas, Atlas, and Hermes Versions

The three categories for product versioning and experimentation are the high-end or Midas product, the mass-appeal or Atlas product, and the low-end or Hermes product (see Figure 4.3). We will often use the terms version and product interchangeably; however, a version is usually related to a particular product. The Midas product is targeted toward the consumer who is not price-sensitive and is interested in many different features. Midas products might have an extended warranty or may be bundled with other products and services. Examples of Midas products include Cadillac, Acura, Lexus, TurboTax Premier, and specialized

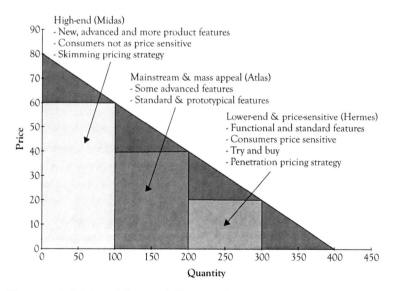

Figure 4.3. Midas, Atlas, and Hermes characteristics.

boutique stores. Sometimes, a Midas version is not even different than the Atlas version of a product or even the Hermes version of a product. Marketing efforts via branding may have infused the notion that the product is better than another product with the same features. This happens in the commodities markets, the car-rental business, and in electronics markets where standardized products such as CDs and DVDs are being sold.

Mass-appeal or Atlas products and services are developed to appeal to a large percentage of consumers. Mass-appeal products and services will contain elements of what is essentially a prototypical product. A prototypical product is the archetype product that other products are patterned after. In order for this product to appeal to the masses, it usually has a minimal set of standard features. In order to distinguish a prototypical product from the competition, there will also be a few features that are differentiators or there will be standard features that have been enhanced or amped up a bit to discern the product from other mass-appeal products. Examples of mass-appeal products include the Camry, the Accord, the Malibu, and TurboTax Deluxe. Examples of mass-appeal retail outlets include Sears, Safeway, and Amazon.

Low-end or Hermes products and services are designed for markets where the consumers are price-sensitive. These products have the essence of the prototypical product, but they are scaled back in order to meet the price sensitivities of this segment. These groups could include students,

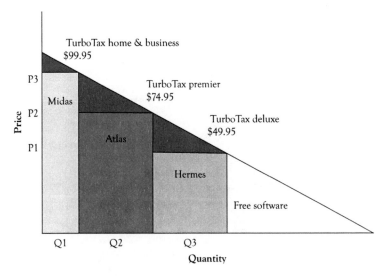

Figure 4.4. TurboTax versioning.

seniors, and, in general, individuals with low levels of discretionary income or even individuals who are value-conscious. Examples of products and services designed for the Hermes customers include TurboTax Free Edition, the Honda Fit and Tata Nano, and many of the large lot stores such as Sam's Club, BJ's, and Costco. Figure 4.4 presents the all-to-familiar price and product versioning that is used by Intuit for TurboTax.

Bottom of the Pyramid

Low-end, low-cost products and services are of emerging importance because of the huge market at the so-called bottom of or base of the pyramid (BoP).[10] Price and product differentiation can benefit the 4 billion people who need pharmaceuticals, health care, personal grooming, and low-priced durable goods and electronics. In the past, many businesses have ignored this substantial collection of individuals. But there is money to be made at the BoP because there is demand for inexpensive products by these consumers. Price-sensitive consumers have many of the same wants and desires as the affluent consumers.[11] They just have to spend more money on the basic necessities of life and have little discretionary income. Products can actually be designed at the high end and the mass appeal levels, and then scaled back so that they can be sold to individuals at the BoP. As noted above, price-sensitive customers can be the foundation for establishing a long-lasting monetary relationship when those customers attain more discretionary income. Here are a few additional examples of versioning approaches. The next chapter will provide many more examples of how versioning has been used by various businesses.

Versioning Restaurants, Hotels, and Motels

Competition in the restaurant, hotel, bars, and motel businesses is fiercely monopolistically competitive. Typically, these businesses compete on atmosphere, the level of service, and the uniqueness of their offerings. A Midas high-end hotel can have boutique rooms, spas and fitness rooms, and a vast array of food choices from room service to expensive high-end dining. In contrast, the Hermes hotel can be clean, Spartan, and in close proximity to fast food and casual dining outlets. The drama is in the

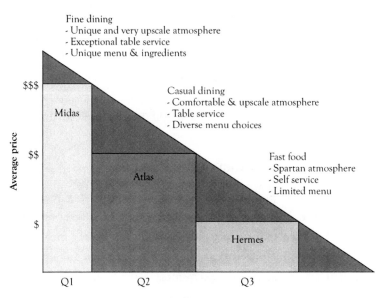

Figure 4.5. PD curve for restaurants.

details. Fresh flowers in the room, a free breakfast, and free cookies can attract customers. In most instances, the benefits of a given differentiation strategy are transitory, and new features have to be added or existing features need to be refreshed in order to compete effectively. Figure 4.5 illustrates a PD curve for fast food, casual dining, and fine dining restaurants.

Versioning Commodity and Standardized Products

Standardized and commodity products can also be versioned. Sometimes, the high-end product is not even that different from the mass-appeal product or even the low-end product. Marketing efforts via branding may have instilled the notion that the product is better than another product with the same features. As illustrated in Figure 4.6, the way to sell a standardized product to the high end is to have a distinct brand, offer extended warranties, deliver products and services faster, or all three. This happens in the auto business, commodities markets, and the entertainment industries. There are also ways to sell a standardized product to the low end without upsetting individuals who purchased a product at a higher price. This can be accomplished by offering customer rewards programs, having customers use coupons, and delaying the shipment of a product. If you buy months ahead from the airlines, you can sometimes get a better price than an individual

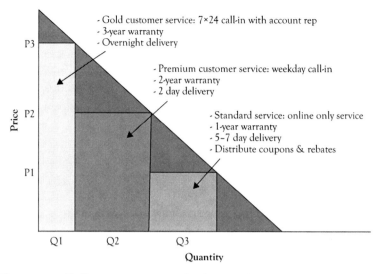

Figure 4.6. Differentiating a standard or similar product.

who buys ticket days before departure. Rebates are also a way to sell at a lower price for standardized product. The product is not the same because of the hassle of filling out the documentation and the uncertainty that comes from not knowing whether the rebate or coupon will be honored.

Versioning Strategies

There is no superset of features that can be used for product and service differentiation because demand is subject to the development of new technologies, changing wants, the social context, culture mores, and the fickleness of fashion. Here is a subset of the attributes of products and services that can be modified:

- Focus on the uniqueness of the product or service.
- Have a version that is simpler and easier to use than other products or services.
- Introduce a product or service that uses new emerging technology.
- Design a more attractive product and frequently refresh the product.
- Use creative and attractive packaging and labeling and continuously refresh the packing.

- Increase or decrease the size and weight of the product.
- Differentiate the product by performance, including speed and capacity.
- Offer different levels of convenience. Offer convenience that is not available in the marketplace.
- Product or service is available quickly and price-differentiated by availability.
- Use packaging and labeling that are unique and up-to-date.
- Offer products and services that are more reliable and durable than competitors.
- Have better customer support and warranties than the competition. Differentiate your products by the length of the warranty and the level of customer support.
- Increasing the cool factor, prestige, and elitism related to the product or service.
- Focus on how the product improves health and personal attractiveness.
- Focus on how the product or service improves some form of intelligence such as reasoning, verbal abilities, analytical skills, social adaptation, and emotional adaptation.
- Focus on how the product improves physical abilities and the ability to compete in sports.
- Illustrate how the product improves the children and family in some way so as to differentiate them from the masses.
- Focus on how the product or service facilitates connectivity and communication and social networking.
- Improve the brand through marketing and promotion efforts.
- Modify the price.

As you can see from the above list, and from the chapter, there are numerous strategies for versioning. Some of them require significant product and development and research and development (R&D), and others require modest investments and change in a product or service. Some of them require repositioning of the product through marketing and promotion efforts. The FAD (features, attributes, and design) template, which is introduced in chapter 7, is very useful for identifying features and attributes that can be used to version products and services for Midas, Atlas, and Hermes customers.

Version Rollout Strategies

Many companies start by introducing and designing the mass-appeal or Atlas product first. The objective is to get the product out the door and generate as much revenue as possible by setting the price and developing the features in such a way that profit and cash flows are near the optimum level. That was the strategy used by Joan's jewelry. She then introduced a high-end Midas version to attract affluent consumers. This is sometimes followed by introducing a scaled-back Hermes version with easy-to-produce features after the production process has been fine-tuned. Some businesses introduce a low-end Hermes product at the same time that the Atlas and Midas versions are introduced. Their objective is to use the low-end version to attract buyers to the mass-appeal and high-end products. Sometimes, a version is given away or is offered on a try-and-buy basis. This is referred to as a *freemium* version.

The key consideration is to design products and services so that features can be easily added and subtracted and new versions can be quickly introduced. This of course implies that the producer will use modular design approaches and agile production processes in product development.

Customer Segments and Midas, Atlas, and Hermes Versions

A customer segment is a group of prospective consumers with similar products and services. Potential segments can be based on age, gender, income, family structure, affluence, city size, location within a country and around the world, interests, life style, behavior, psychological characteristics, culture, and product function. Segmentation is also found in business-to-business relationships. Businesses can be segmented by product and service needs, business function, and industry, location within a country and around the world, culture, and by the size of business.

The goal of segmentation is to target and sell to consumer groups that have similar characteristics and demand habits. Segmentation can be useful in describing the target market, but it should be used sparingly. Potential customers can be a member of many segments. There is a tendency toward oversegmentation. There are three key criteria available for developing and using a customer segment. The first question relates to whether the customer segment is easily identified and whether the customer segment make sense? The second question is related to the first and asks if the individuals in the customer segment are relatively homogeneous? The third question relates to being able to target and reach those customers in the segment. Can the organization effectively use advertising and promotion to target those customers in the customer segment?

Segmentation and grouping are typically based on age, gender, income, family structure, affluence, city size, interests, life style, behavior, psychological characteristics, culture, and product function. However, many businesses and marketers use more detailed and descriptive words to describe their customer segments. Here are a few of the many words that can be used to describe customers segments:

> Traditionalists, Conventionalist, Survivalist, Easterners, Westerners, Northerners, Yankees, Southerners, Pioneers, Enthusiasts, Gamers, Minimalists, Organics, Granolas, Back-to-Naturists, Adventure Seekers, Risk takers, Romanticists, Aficionados, Connoisseurs, Fast trackers, Soccer Moms, Techies, Umbrella/Helicopter parents, Seniors, Oldsters, Middle Agers, Middle age crises and cruisers, Teens, Goths, Hip, Impulsive, Tweeners, Generation X, Millennials, Baby Boomers, Hippies, Yuppies ...

It is interesting to note that many of the customer segments are related to the meaning that consumers attach to products and services. Additional discussion of the importance of the meaning underlying a product or service will be presented in chapter 7. The best use of segmentation is to provide additional insight and to describe in greater detail the consumers who will be buying the Midas, Atlas, and Hermes versions.

Usually, a product or service is targeted toward a particular customer segment. For example, suppose a company wanted to develop a global positioning system for Adventure Seekers and Risk Takers. After they identified the customer segment, they would then develop two or three versions (Midas, Atlas, or Hermes) of the product that were linked to price sensitivities. Here is another example. Suppose a company wanted to develop high-end head phones for listening to MP3 songs using a new speaker technology. They could target both the Tweeners and the Baby Boomers with different versions and marketing campaigns. They could also develop three versions (Midas, Atlas, or Hermes) of the product for Baby Boomers according to their price sensitivities as well as three versions of the product for Tweeners. Usually, but not always, businesses identify the customer segment or segments first. They then engage in versioning to obtain more revenues and to assist in identifying the product features that are attractive and in demand. The bottom line is that versioning complements and assists in the customer segmentation. Here is a summary of how customer segments fit into product development:

1. Conceptualize product or service
2. Identify appropriate customer segments for product or service
3. Design and develop two or three versions for each customer segment
4. Obtain feedback from potential customers, employees, vendors, and interested parties
5. Revisit step 1

This is of course not a linear process. For example, step 1 and step 2 often occur at the same time. It is similar to the creative problem-solving process discussed in chapter 6. There are periods where product developers are engaged in leaning-about customers, emerging technologies, and other products offered in the marketplace. There are also periods of learning-by-doing, where prototypes are built and scrutinized, and where the feedback is obtained from relevant parties. It is, however, a never-ending process of refinement and experimentation.

Pricing and Product Differentiation Strategies

Pricing plays a key role in developing and formulating a market strategy. The use of PD curves in developing products and services incorporates several important pricing and product strategies.[12] Modern businesses often turn to product-line pricing strategy to offer a number of products with differences in quality, design, size, and style in order to maximize profits. The product portfolio can include products that are complementary and even products that compete with each other.

The use of PD curves is also in line with the two major pricing strategies for marketing new products: skimming pricing and penetration pricing. Skimming pricing is used to tap into the so-called "cream of the market." It is an attempt to attract the high end of the demand curve where price elasticity is low. That is, the customers are not price-sensitive. The objective of using this strategy is to facilitate profitability with a slowly maturing innovative product, covering the high cost of R&D. In many instances, marketers introduce the high end first and then go for the mass market by lowering prices. Penetration pricing is a strategy of entering the market with a low initial price in order to capture a large share of the marketplace. One objective of this strategy is to tap into the demand curve where the price elasticity is high and customers are price-sensitive. It is used to lure customers, get at a large mass Atlas market, discourage competition, and build economies of scale.[13]

Dynamic Tension in Action at Singapore Airlines

Singapore Airlines (SIA) is a prime example of a business that uses dynamic tension to deliver high-end, innovative, differentiated services and still be efficient and cost-effective. SIA has garnered numerous awards for their world-class service in their coach, business, and first class offerings.[14] The rest of the story is that they have one of the lowest cost structures compared with any other airline at just under 5 cent per kilometer per seat. Here is an overview of how Heracleous and Wirtz describe SIA's strategy for delivering world-class services and still being a cost leader.

They keep their fleet young and up-to-date. Their planes are much younger than most of the competition. This translates to fewer mechanical failures, more air time, lower fuel costs, reduced maintenance costs, and happy customers. Salaries are linked to SIA's profitability. SIA provides twice as much training to their 14,500 employees than the industry average. They also recruit top-notch university graduates. SIA realizes that their employees are the critical touch point with their customers. SIA also realizes that their employees can be the first line of defense in cutting costs.

SIA holds town hall meetings where senior executives stress the importance of reducing costs in order to remain competitive. SIA also staffs most of their flights with more cabin crew members than the industry standard. SIA encourages their employees to find ways to reduce costs. For example, cabin crew recommended carrying less food for late night flights and they stopped putting jam jars on every breakfast tray because some passengers did not use them. SIA's back-office costs lag behind that of their competitors and its sales and administration costs are low and lean.

The secret sauce of SIA's success includes harnessing the power of its employees, using technology effectively and appropriately, and pursuing the dual strategies of creative differentiation and reducing costs. SIA understands that long-term success is a function of balancing the dynamic tension between delivering high-end Midas services with the Hermes cost reductions.

Conclusion

In this chapter, we have illustrated a model for constructing PD curves that draws on the dynamic tension that exists between developing Midas and Hermes products. The key points are the following:

- PD curves are used to increase revenue and foster experimentation and R&D.
- A versioning curve is the same thing as a PD curve.
- Midas products and services are feature-rich versions of a product that are developed using extravagant engineering and design. Midas versions are high-end products for nonprice-sensitive consumers.
- Hermes versions of products and services are developed using frugal engineering and design. Hermes versions are for price-sensitive consumers.
- Atlas products and services are the result of the dynamic tension created between Midas versioning and Hermes versioning.
- Atlas products and services are designed for mainstream consumers. Atlas products and services incorporate the product design features that will attract the broadest customer base and will also be profitable.

- Even standardized products can be versioned.
- There are a variety of version strategies available and some of them require R&D and some of them can be developed through packaging and marketing.
- A customer segment is a group of prospective consumers with similar products and services. Versioning complements and amplifies customer segmentation.
- Versioning assists in developing and executing pricing strategies.

As noted earlier, we believe that using a combination of pricing and product-versioning strategies facilitates product experimentation and the ability to observe economic behavior in action and perform research and product development. It allows the company to monitor purchase behavior and determine which features and products consumers deem most desirable. The next chapter will introduce a variety of product differentiation versioning strategies that are being used by businesses to compete.

Addendum on Pareto Economics, Welfare, and Efficiency

Price discrimination and product differentiation leads to more efficient markets. Many contemporary discussions of economics begin by addressing the issue of the so-called Pareto efficiency or optimality. Vilfredo Federicao Damaso Pareto was an Italian intellectual during the later part of the 19th century and early part of the 20th century. A Pareto optimal distribution of a bundle of goods is one where all parties agree that the allocation cannot be improved upon without hurting at least one other party. It does not mean that everyone is happy with the distribution; it just means you cannot improve on the distribution without creating a disadvantage for one of the groups or parties. I like to use the word Pareto OK rather than Pareto optimal. A Pareto OK distribution of goods takes into account the idea the distribution of goods is equitable and the welfare of all is optimal given a distribution of incomes and consumer wants. A Pareto OK distribution is also more in tune with Pareto's original conceptualization of optimality and welfare economics. The so-called Paretian welfare economics is built on three principles:[15]

- Each individual is to be treated as the final judge of his or her welfare.
- The welfare of society depends on the welfare of the individuals who make up the society.
- If one person's welfare increases, other things being equal, then societal welfare increases.

These three principles can be distilled into a single maxim: "as far as social choice is concerned, all that matters is the satisfaction of wants" (Robert Sugden, p. 507).

One goal of developing multiple products and using a product and price differentiation strategy is to deliver products that satisfy wants. Economists are always worried about economic efficiency and societal welfare. The natural questions related to price differentiation is whether this leads to efficient markets and whether society is better off. I propose the following definition of market efficiency:

A market tends to be efficient when the market participants have complete knowledge about the prices and features of products and services offered in the market.

This definition is somewhat different than the traditional definition because it incorporates the idea that market participants are knowledgeable about prices and that they are also knowledgeable about the features of a product. Efficient markets emerge when information is freely available. Dynamic and adaptive markets emerge when there are a variety of products and services available and market participants have the tools available to gather information on the products and services. Search engines and auctions are extremely effective tools for gathering information and developing knowledge about pricing and features and that is why the Internet has been such a powerful force for facilitating efficient markets.

CHAPTER 5

Examples of Product Differentiation and Versioning Curves

In this chapter, more examples of product differentiation and versioning curves are presented. As noted earlier, the purpose of the product differentiation curves (PD curves) or versioning curves is primarily conceptual. However, the underlining rationale behind the curves is to generate more revenue and to provide a foundation for conducting economic experiments on what features attracts consumers. In essence, introducing multiple versions of a product permits a company to experiment and observe economic behavior in action. The company can monitor purchase behavior and determine which features and products consumers deem most desirable. Such experimentation is actually the most effective activity for conducting research and engaging in new product development. This chapter presents several examples of how versioning is being used for a variety of products and services.

Versioning Automobiles

Figure 5.1 illustrates a PD curve for Toyota cars that uses sales estimates from 1 month projected to a year. This PD curve also illustrates that demand curves are rarely linear and this is particularly true at the high end and low end of the demand curve for Midas and Hermes versions. It is difficult to obtain precise sales data and the graph should be used to understand how Toyota differentiates their cars and not to illustrate actual sales figures for the company. This is true in many of the graphs used in the book. There are other products in the company's lineup, but these are their primary products for the Midas, Atlas, and Hermes customers. Within each line, there is also product differentiation. Figure 5.2 illustrates the product price and product differentiation for the Camry line. Toyota actually has another high-end product, the Lexus line. This line is actually more luxurious than the Toyota Avalon model and appeals to individuals at the highest income levels. The PD curve in Figure 5.3 illustrates

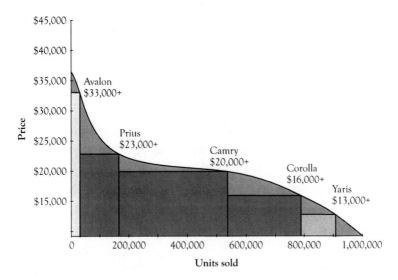

Figure 5.1. PD curves for Toyota passenger cars.

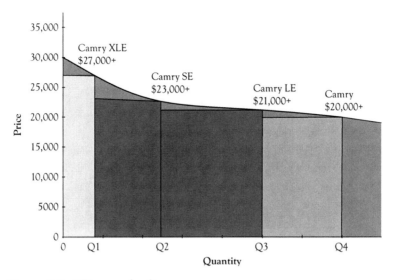

Figure 5.2. PD curve for Camry.

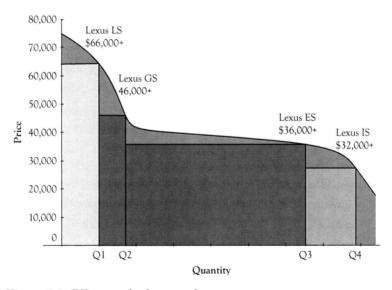

Figure 5.3. PD curve for Lexus sedan.

that there is also Midas, Atlas, and Hermes versions for the Lexus sedans. The width of the Lexus ES quantity reflects the fact that the ES sedan dominates Lexus sedan sales. The top of the line for the Lexus sedans can be found in the hybrid cars. The Lexus hybrids start around $45,000 and scale all the way up to around $120,000 for a fully loaded LS hybrid.

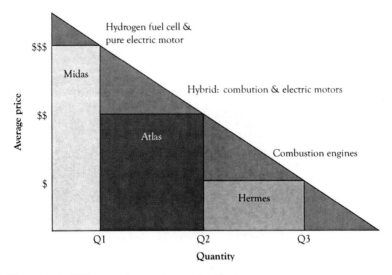

Figure 5.4. PD curve for engine technologies.

Motor technologies can also be placed on PD curves. Figure 5.4 illustrates that combustion engines are at this time occupying the lower end of a PD curve. However, the hybrid cars that involve both internal combustion and electrical components are emerging as mass-appeal technologies. The hydrogen fuel cell autos and pure electric cars occupy the high end of the PD curve.

Versioning at Dell

Dynamic differentiation is the ability to sell personalized closely related, but not identical products to consumers. In a perfectly competitive market, there are a large number of knowledgeable sellers selling a standardized product to a large number of knowledgeable consumers. In such a market, product and price differentiation is difficult, if not impossible. In such a market, it is also impossible to extract any additional money from such consumers even if you can identify how much each consumer is willing-to-pay. That is why businesses turn toward product differentiation and the monopolistic competition model. As noted before, over 99% of the approximately 23+ million businesses are involved in monopolistic competition.[1] The king of monopolistic competition is certainly L'Enfant terrible Michael Dell and his creation, Dell.com.

Michael Dell started out with three guiding principles:

1. Always listen to the customer.
2. Never sell indirectly.
3. Disdain inventory.

It appears that *always listen to the customer* is the driving force behind his model, but in reality, *never selling indirectly* is the engine behind the Dell model. Dell believes that the best way to listen to his customers is watch the customer select from a menu of system features and let the customer tell them what they value. This is the epitome of dynamic differentiation. By selling directly, Dell is very close to the customer and Dell can constantly adapt to subtle shifts and changes in customer preferences. Because they know what features are in greatest demand, they can move them to the high-end products. It is indeed manipulation, and a way to extract consumer surplus. And as an added benefit, Dell can carry very little inventory because they are listening to their customers and building the systems as the orders arrive.

Dell has of course adapted its model and has put more emphasis on listeneing to their customers. They are now selling products indirectly in the USA, in China, and all over the world. This is, in part, because PCs and laptops are becoming commodity products and less differentiable, but also because Dell has been listening to their current and potential customers. Some of them want the instant gratification of buying and taking it home today and some of them want to touch and feel before they buy.

Dell's Migration and Evolution

At one time, Dell was more-or-less a pure pull company, just like Amazon. com. Much of their entire production system was driven by actual orders from customers. Part of their production process has also pushed products to consumers, but they are on balance a pull process company. They have been drawn toward the dark side and push production because of the demands of the marketplace. In a push production process, orders are forecasted and some products are scheduled for production based on forecasts and retailer demand rather than end-consumer. This change in

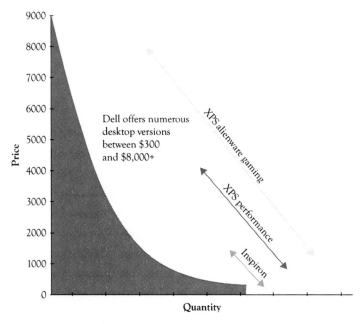

Figure 5.5. Differentiation at Dell.

attitude toward selling directly also coincides with Dell's move to sell off their manufacturing units. They are attempting to alleviate the risk inherent in manufacturing products before customers order them. The risk is of course excess inventory and Dell disdains inventory. After Dell sells their manufacturing facilities, their systems suppliers will then absorb some of the risk of carrying excess and outdated inventory.

Dell, because of its direct selling and the ability to install numerous features, is a prime example of dynamic differentiation. They offer literally thousands of different product configurations or versions. As illustrated in Figure 5.5, Dell has feature points over a broad range of prices (these statistics approximate Dell's line in 2011).

Versioning at Microsoft[2]

Microsoft over the past couple of years has jumped on the price discrimination bandwagon. It was difficult for them to engage in product and price differentiation because they were generating piles of cash as a monopoly. Microsoft is a monopolist in the operating systems arena and with their office suite of applications. The marginal cost to produce incremental levels of software and other information goods, such as DVDs and music, is essentially zero. But as usual, the fixed costs are substantial, and because Microsoft is a price setter, they chose to sell at a price that covers their fixed costs but still permits them to make a large profit without irritating too many consumers.

For many years, Microsoft was not interested in price discrimination based on geography, market segment, or per capita GDP. But Microsoft had to move toward price discrimination because the willingness-to-pay for software was related to software piracy. Students and individuals with low incomes are price-sensitive and will simply turn to piracy when the price exceeds their willingness-to-pay. They also had to offer certain market segments lower prices because piracy was essentially rampant. Microsoft began to realize that they were leaving money on the table because they did not take dramatic steps to price discriminate through product differentiation. They have, in general, avoided unwanted attention by the FTC by attempting to follow the three guidelines outlined in chapter 2.

Sometimes product differentiation does not work.[3] Microsoft tried to differentiate the Vista operating system (see the snap shot of Windows 7 and Vista Versioning in Figure 5.6). But Vista never gained legs for a variety of technical, customer support and marketing reasons. The product was not ready for prime time. They continued to product differentiate and price discriminate with the release of Windows 7. Home Premium was priced at $199.99, Professional at $299.99, and Ultimate at $319.99. They definitely used the Goldilocks versioning. It appears that Windows 7 was a success because it was a stable, fast, and friendly operating system.

Of late, Microsoft has also had to contend with Google's foray into the online office application suite called Google Docs and IBM's offering of open-sourced Linux-based applications. The competition is heating up and the Microsoft monopoly is under attack on many fronts. Monopolies are often transitory as the competition looks for a crack in the armor and a chance to drink from the fountain of plenty. The growth of cloud computing (where data storage and CPU cycles move toward the utility model) and the availability of net-centric applications could continue to erode Microsoft's market share. They have, however, started

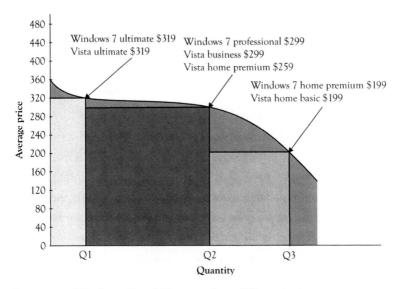

Figure 5.6. Windows 7 and Vista product differentiation.

to address the attack by introducing a cloud-based Office 365 and the Azure development platform.

Versioning Wireless Communications

The most important activity in the history of humankind has been in the area of communications. As illustrated in Figure 5.7, the desire to communicate has been the driving force behind most of the advances in modern technology. The wireless phone is the current battle ground for the universal communication device that will be used for talking, texting and tagging friends and colleagues, scheduling, listening to music, reading eBooks, and in location assistance. Apple and Nokia's strategies are distinctly different. Apple has gone after the cream and focused on the high end, competes primarily in the smartphone arena, and is also beginning to compete with the net-book laptops. Smart-phones have applications such as scheduling, location assistance, email, and Internet access.

Nokia is not only interested in the high-end smartphone market, but they are also selling to the price-sensitive demographic and have an even bigger target in their sight. They want to become the biggest entertainment

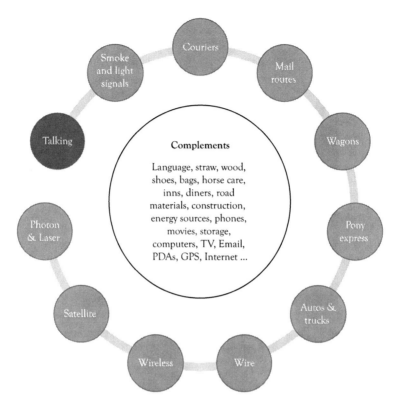

Figure 5.7. Communication drives innovation.

media network in the world.[4] They are trying to reach the entire market by using research and development (they have numerous research laboratories throughout the world) and by pursuing a comprehensive differentiation strategy. Nokia offers devices to satisfy every budget and they are trying to make their products and services indispensable. They have, however, been under an intense attack by Apple and Android-based phones. Android-based phones are very versatile and there are numerous models available at many price points.

Figure 5.8 illustrates a PD curve for several cell phone devices. Apple and Android-based phones have been making steady gains in the smartphone business. Apple has been willing to offer a downscaled version of the iPod to the price-sensitive masses with the Nano and Shuffle. We suspect that iPhone technology will be adapted to the price-sensitive tail of the demand curve because of the competitive pressure of Android-based phones.

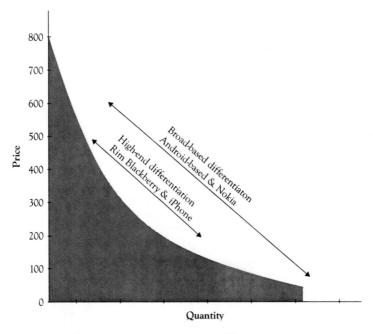

Figure 5.8. Broad-based versus high-end differentiation strategies for cell phone devices.

How Wireless Companies Compete on Price: Hide the True Price

One way to compete on price is to make it difficult for the consumer to know the true price of the product. Companies sometimes use differentiation to hide the true cost of purchasing products and services. Many companies accomplish this task by offering very complex pricing and bundling plans (numerous versions). Wireless service and long-distance providers have become very good at this strategy. These providers rarely offer simple plans such as 5 cents per minute for a certain level of usage or 3 cents per minute for a certain level of usage. Instead, they offer customer's very complex pricing schemes and service bundles that are difficult to disentangle. This helps these providers as well as providers of cable and Internet services to reduce the damage of price competition. Consumers have to engage in a large amount of price and feature comparisons in order to understand the features provided in the tableau of products and services. This is essentially a form of product differentiation but it is more precisely service differentiation.

Versioning at Apple

Because Apple had such a strong brand and was very successful, they were able to secure part of the ongoing revenue stream that AT&T received as a wireless carrier. The success of the iPhone resulted in extreme demands on the AT&T network and this led to the introduction of a pay-for-level-of-use program in the middle of 2010 when the Apple iPhone 4 was introduced. One objective of the service differentiation plans was to reduce network traffic, but it also gave Apple and AT&T the ability to extract more revenue from their existing customer base and to attract new more price-sensitive customers. The original data plan was $30 with no restrictions on the amount of data streamed. Under the new pricing structure, customers with deep pockets and less sensitive willingness-to-pay functions would readily pay $25 for 2 gigabytes of streaming and $10 for each additional gigabyte. Apple has recently introduced new iPhones at substantially reduced prices than their earlier launches. The iPhone models entered in at what we view as Atlas levels of $199 and $299. Apple also revamped their data plan to capture some Hermes-level customers by introducing a revamped data plan. The new low-end plan was $15 and this included 200 megabytes of

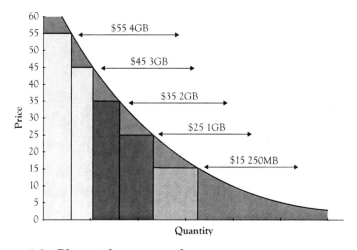

Figure 5.9. iPhone 4 data stream plans.

streamed data for more price-sensitive customers. These plans will of course evolve as Apple and AT&T conduct further competitive experiments on the right combination of phones and data plans. Figure 5.9 illustrates the service differentiation curve for the data plans.

Versioning e-Books

One particularly interesting area of competition is in the e-book arena. The Amazon Kindle started out very strong and looked like a strong contender to capture the market for electronic books. Apple founder Steve Jobs was not impressed and stated, "It doesn't matter how good or bad the product is, the fact is that people don't read anymore."[5] Well he did release an e-book reader, the iPad, that also had additional functionality. Amazon responded by releasing three Kindle versions and by developing an iPad app for downloading and buying books from Amazon. Figures 5.10 and 5.11 illustrate PD curves for the iPad and Kindle, respectively. It is apparent that the Apple has taken great pains to develop versions for a wide range of individuals with differing price sensitivities at the high end.

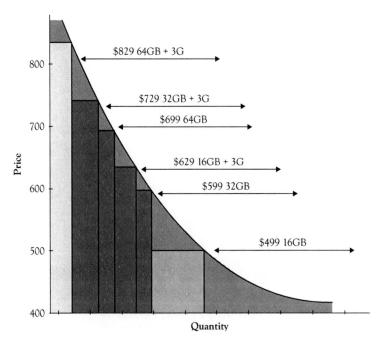

Figure 5.10. iPad differentiation.

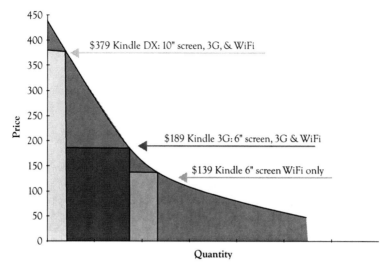

Figure 5.11. Differentiating the Kindle.

Versioning Digital Content

AOL Time Warner lost over $98 billion in 2002. This happened after AOL had purchased Time Warner for $106 billion in 2001.[6] The Time Warner content was supposed to propel AOL, the king of distribution, to the next level. Differentiating content and getting people to pay for the content is one of the most difficult problems facing many companies including newspaper and magazines publishers. As illustrated in Figure 5.12, it is possible to differentiate content, but it is still difficult to get the consumer to pay for digital content. Many consumers simply do not want to pay for the content because much of the content on the Web was free in the past and even when it was not free, it could be read indirectly by creative searching and by pirating.

One way to make all contents desirable is to deliver the content faster and more conveniently than any other business. This can, in some instances, change the demand curve and increase the amount consumers are willing-to-pay for a content version. One way this is being tested is through the use of tablet computers such as the iPad or the Kindle. Delivering content faster and more conveniently than the competition amplifies the value of the content, even aggregated and repackaged content.

One of the challenges of providing content is to develop versions for mobile devices, for traditional Web browsing, and for print media.

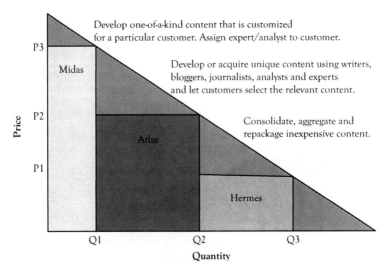

Figure 5.12. Digital content differentiation strategies.

Content has to be written so that it can be used simultaneously for perusal on a mobile device, on the Web, and in traditional print media.[7] The key is to have different versions of content available that do not cannibalize each other. Headlines can effectively make-or-break a business model. For example, a headline received from a mobile phone should not only be interesting enough so that it is passed on to others, but also tweak the interest of the reader so that they will turn to more in-depth content on the Web or in print. If it provides too much information, then the reader will be satisfied and will not look toward other media outlets. Versioning via the type of media outlet is critical to the survival of content providers. Content needs to be carefully crafted in terms of its length and the information provided so that it conveys some information, but not too much; yet it has to be compelling so that it entices the consumer to delve into other outlets. This is the essence of the versioning process.

Versioning Digital Entertainment

The primary characteristic of entertainment and media content is that the fixed costs for development are very high and the variable costs for reproducing digital movies, video game software, television programs, electronic books, and music are very low. The key is to find ways to sell at low price levels for those individuals who are price-sensitive and to capture some of the consumers' surplus from customers who are price-insensitive. Movies are typically consumed only once and it is important to try to meet demand when there is a lot of hype around the release. In the case of movie releases, this is accomplished by charging more for movies attended in the first 3 or 4 weeks of introduction at theaters, charging less when they are released on pay-per-view, and even less when they are rented on DVD. Consumers who want the movie for a repeat view will pay a price that is usually above the price of attending the movie at a theater.

Video game publishers have found a unique way of differentiating their product on launch day by offering unique packaging and complementary items that are useful to game play and other items that are collectibles. These bundles amplify the consumer's feelings of game uniqueness, but in reality the game is essentially the same. Microsoft used this strategy when they released Halo Reach. The standard game was sold for $59.99 and essentially just came with a disc and brief manual. The limited edition cost consumers $79.99 and the Legendary edition cost $139.99. They were packaged differently and they also contained supplementary materials, such as journals, unique armor that could be downloaded and worn during battles, and statues of the virtual team members who support the game players during battles. The game was a resounding success, and sales on the first day were estimated to be in excess of $200 million. Soon after the launch, the $139.99 legendary version was discounted to

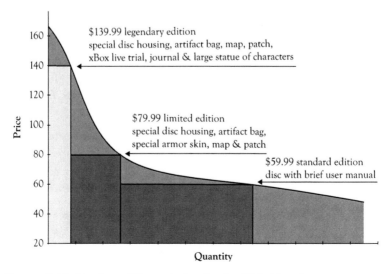

Figure 5.13. Product differentiation for the Halo Reach game.

$99.99. This illustrates that even a successful product can be overoversioned and overpriced. Consumer behavior on the upper (Midas area) and lower (Hermes area) parts of the demand curve is difficult to predict. There is a large measure of demand uncertainty at the extremes of the demand curve. Consumers expect prices to be in a certain range and when they are not, it is difficult to predict the demand. Figure 5.13 presents a product differentiation graph for Halo Reach on launch day.

Versioning Disease Treatments

According to the American Cancer Society, the estimated number of new cancer cases in 2010 was over 1.5 million.[8] One of my classes recently analyzed a case involving NovaCure, a company that developed a promising approach for treating cancer.[9] NovaCure developed a technique to disrupt cancer cell division using electromagnetic waves, called Tumor Treating Fields. Early clinical trials suggest that when the Tumor Treating Fields are used in conjunction with chemotherapy, the survival time of glioblastoma patients improves significantly. NovaCure estimates that the therapy might be suitable for treating 200,000 different types of cancers including brain tumors, head and neck tumors, presurgical breast treatment, nonsmall lung cancer, and pancreatic cancer. Since the NovaCure approach is not a drug, but a medical device, the approval process is abbreviated, but it is still extensive and expensive. The question raised during the case analyses was whether versioning could be applied to treating diseases?[10] The total expenditures for life sciences' R&D in the USA in 2010 were over $59 billion and over $133 billion globally.[11] Life sciences include pharmaceuticals, medical devices and equipment, and biotechnology. The approval of pharmaceuticals and medical treatments and the accompanying R&D can exceed hundreds of millions of dollars. Versioning can even help solve the difficult problem of covering costs of developing expensive treatments for diseases and treating a substantial number of patients.

Figure 5.14 illustrates a hypothetical demand curve for a hypothetical treatment for a hypothetical cancer that affects 200,000 individuals a year. The made-up variable costs for treating the cancer were set at $4,000. This is the base or minimum variable cost. As illustrated in Figure 5.14, if the company only sold one version at $35,000 per month, they would

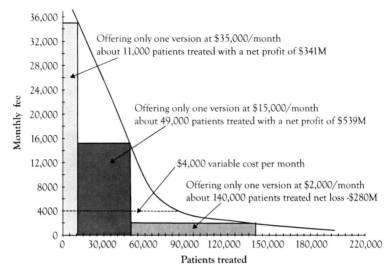

Figure 5.14. Net profits when only one version of the treatment is offered.

net $341 million per month. If they sell only the Atlas version at $15,000 per month, they would net $539 million per month. If they sell the Hermes version at $2,000 per month, they would lose $280 million per month.

The first thing that has to be dealt with is that there are two conflicting goals. The drug and medical devices community want to cover the cost of development and eventually makes a profit. The goal of patients, doctors and some policy makers is to cure as many people as possible. This situation also illustrates that there is a difference in the willingness-to-pay and the ability-to-pay. In most situations, consumers are engaged in a never-ending calculus involving how much money they have to spend and how they want to allocate their money. These calculations are hidden, yet ongoing, and always involve trade-offs related to wants and desires and the consumers' willingness-to-pay for a product or service. When there are decisions related to sustaining life, the life-sustaining trade-off dominates. There is a mismatch between the willingness-to-pay and the ability-to-pay. Versioning can help.

Figure 5.15 illustrates how a hypothetical drug or medical device company could make a nice profit by versioning the cancer treatment and also treat 70% of the patients having the disease. The company could just offer one version of the product and net $539 million and treat 49,000 patients,

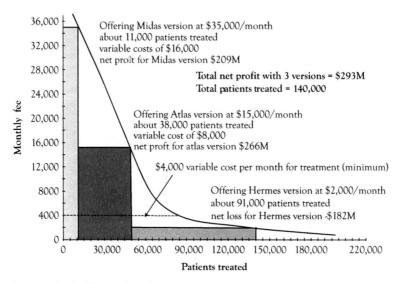

Figure 5.15. Net profit when three treatment versions are offered.

or offer three versions and net $239 million and treat 140,000 patients. This should cover the fixed costs of product development. The actual implementation of versioning would of course be subject to a variety of inputs and serious dialog involving the public, the drug and medical device companies, insurance companies, the health care community, economists, policy makers, and politicians. And of course arbitrage would have to be dealt with. Some sort of mechanism would have to be in place to prevent the purchase of a Hermes treatment and selling it in the Midas market. As we have demonstrated throughout this book, versioning is a keystone foundation of the current competitive marketplace. Versioning has the potential to bring beneficial medical products and services to a broader base of individuals suffering from serious diseases. It will just take a concerted effort on the part of the various constituencies to develop a versioning solution.

Conclusion

In this chapter, we have illustrated a variety of product differentiation and versioning strategies that have been used by businesses. The key points are the following:

- Versioning concepts can be applied to products and services, including new product development, enhancements, digital content, and medical services and devices, and to emerging technologies.

- Some companies focus on versioning at the high end where consumers are less price-sensitive. Some businesses try to offer products across the entire demand curve from price-sensitive Hermes consumers through less price-sensitive Midas consumers.
- Versioning can be applied in a variety of ways including new product development, adding and subtracting features, offering complementary products, and packaging and marketing.
- Versioning also has the potential to be used in delivering medical treatments to a greater number of individuals suffering from serious diseases.

This chapter has illustrated the various ways firms have used to differentiate their products and services in order to compete effectively in contemporary markets. There are three general categories for differentiation. They are the high-end Midas products and services, the mass-appeal Atlas products and services, and the low-end Hermes products and services. There are identifiable revenue benefits for using a product differentiation strategy, but there are also R&D implications. As noted earlier, offering several products permits a company to conduct economic experiments that will help delineate trends in the marketplace and to actually create new markets.

CHAPTER 6

Facilitating Creativity and Innovation

The engines behind research and development are creativity and innovation. Creativity is typically defined as the ability to generate ideas. Creativity is actually a subset of innovation and refers primarily to the process of idea generation. Innovations are defined more narrowly as the ideas, the products, the services, and processes that (a) are perceived as being new and different and (b) have been designed, built, and commercialized. Innovation thus includes both creative idea generation and the actual implementation of the idea.[1] An invention is an innovation that is not ready for prime time. Inventions are ideas that have been built or conceptualized, but not widely used and available and usually not commercialized.

Creativity is the force behind innovation and invention. Creativity has been studied for many years and a variety of models and insights have been developed in order to understand and facilitate the creative process. Figure 6.1 illustrates an updated five-phase model of the creative process that incorporates problem solving, leaning-about, and the learning-by-doing concepts.[2] Here are the details of the model:

Trigger. This is the problem or opportunity that initiates the creative process. The trigger could occur at home, work, play, or while traveling.
Learn-about activity. This involves searching for information and synthesizing that information. It also involves struggling to understand the information and the creation of new knowledge by analyzing the problem or opportunity. The learning-about activities include reading books and magazines; one-on-one dialog with colleagues and knowledgeable individuals; looking at competitor offerings; interaction with suppliers,

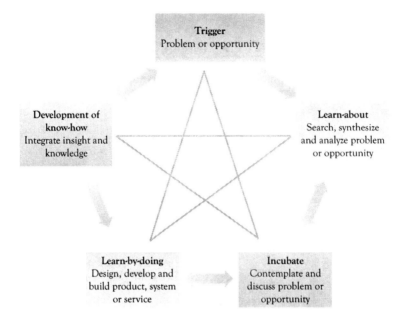

Figure 6.1. Creative problem solving and the creative star model.

customers, universities and research institutes; and attending courses, trade shows, symposia, and conferences.

Incubate. Incubation gives the mind time to work on the problem in the background. This not only involves contemplation, but also involves engaging in one-to-one dialog with family, friends, and colleagues on the problem or opportunity.

Learn-by-doing. This involves designing and constructing a solution to the problem or opportunity. It also involves designing and building a proto-type, modeling with diagrams, drawing pictures, developing flowcharts, drawing digital or CAD diagrams in 2D or 3D CAD, conducting simulation, identifying system specifications, developing system mock-ups, developing business plans, and even the use of narratives. Designing and constructing might include very rough diagrams or developing mock-up pictures of the product or service by using sketching, drawing software, photo software, or presentation software. If the product is a software, then a mock-up screen can be designed by using a word processor, presentation software, or mock-up software. If the idea behind the product or service involves a complex process or business process, then flow diagrams can be constructed or a business process diagram can be developed with presentation software or specialized flowchart and business process diagramming software.

Development of know-how. This is the expertise, skill, and knowledge that can be used to produce a product or service.[3] It is the outcome of the creative process that can be used to provide insight and to build and construct products, services, and business processes. It is the applied and practical knowledge that can be used to make the product or service. In start-ups and small organizations, this knowledge is in the minds of the owner, management and staff, and developers. The knowledge may be codified in lists or in what we refer to as Knowledge Books. These Knowledge Books can be maintained on tablets and spiral notebooks and in computer files. They can contain the following information:

- Descriptions of procedures for providing services and products
- Descriptions of what organization is good at and what it is not so good at
- Job descriptions and links to individuals with certain expertise
- Descriptions of how business processes and tasks are completed.

The Creative Process is Inherently Nonlinear

As illustrated in Figure 6.1, the process is iterative and not always linear. It is indeed a rare instance that creativity emerges through a simple linear process. For example, leaning-by-doing can spur additional learning-about activity and vice versa. This, in turn, can lead to a series of little *ahas* that eventually translates into the big *aha*. The big *aha* is sometimes referred to as illumination where a solution is found to the initial problem or opportunity identified in the beginning of the creative process. This is similar to what Peter Sims refers to as investing in little bets.[4] Investing in little bets leads to little *ahas*, which eventually lead to the big *aha*.

Search is very important as we have seen in an earlier chapter, but in the early stages of developing a solution for a problem or taking advantage of an opportunity, searching should be limited to a couple of sources. Hal Varian, chief economist at Google and one of the most insightful economists in this generation, details the following approach for generating economic models.[5]

> I think that you should look for your ideas outside the academic journals ... in newspapers, in magazines, in conversations, and in TV and radio programs. When you read the newspaper, look for the articles about economics ... and then look at the ones that aren't about economics, because lots of the time they end up being about economics too. Magazines are usually better than newspapers because they go into issues in more depth.... Conversations, especially with people in business, are often very fruitful.... In many cases your ideas can come from your own life and experiences.... However, my advice is to wait a bit before you look at the literature. Eventually you should do a thorough literature review, of course, but I think that you will do much better if you work on your idea for a few weeks before doing a systematic literature search. There are several reasons for delay.

> First, you need the practice of developing a model. Even if you end up reproducing exactly something that is in the literature already you will have learned a lot by doing it ... and you can feel awfully good about yourself for developing a publishable idea! (Even if you didn't get to publish it yourself ...)

> Second, you might come up with a different approach than is found in the literature. If you look at what someone else did your thoughts will be shaped too much by their views ... you are much more likely to be original if you plunge right in and try to develop your own insights.

> Third, your ideas need time to incubate, so you want to start modeling as early as possible. When you read what others have done their ideas can interact with yours and, hopefully, produce something new and interesting.[6]

The takeaway from this discussion is that the creative process is recursive and iterative. For example, you can spend a little time on learning-about by examining just a few magazines or talking to a few people and then go to learning-by-doing after you let the idea season in the incubation phase. Then, you might go back to the learn-about stage or even the trigger stage as you begin to converge on a solution to the problem. The initial search process should be limited to a few sources and then expanded in order to take advantage of ideas that might have been missed in the early stages of the creative process.

The Lonely Genius

A common theme that pervades the creativity literature is that creativity demands discourse, tension, dialog, and debate among the interested parties.[7] Creativity endeavors are driven by interaction, search, and solitude. One of the most pervasive myths is the notion of the lone genius. The lone genius is the individual who toils away in the confined small room developing a grand theory and innovative ideas with little or no interaction. In reality, many inventions and innovative ideas are derived not in a vacuum of isolation, but rather in a sea of collaboration that is countered with periods of solitude and incubation. The prototypical lone genius is Albert Einstein. Einstein worked as a patent examiner during the time that he developed his ideas on relativity and theoretical physics. Einstein did not develop his ideas in solitude. His knowledge was based on intellectual foundations including his university studies, contemporary research papers of his time, and patent applications he viewed at the patent office. There is also evidence that he drew extensively on his academic contemporaries including Marcell Grossman (a classmate), Michele Besso (a friend at the patent office), and Mileva Einstein (his first wife) as sounding boards for his ideas.[8] The point is that anyone can become a wizard of *ahas* if they engage in serious learning-about and learning-by-doing with a pinch of collaboration and dialog. Curiosity and questioning are central to the success of creativity.[9] We are assuming that curiosity and questioning have not been completely driven out of the creative DNA that is hardwired in all humans.

The Habits of Successful Entrepreneurs

Creativity, as we have suggested earlier, can be learned. Dyer, Gregersen, and Christensen investigated the habits of 25 successful innovative entrepreneurs (e.g., Steve Jobs, Jeff Bezos, etc.) over the course of a 6-year study.[10] Here is an overview of their findings related to entrepreneurs:

- They make unusual and unique associations and combinations of processes, products, and technologies.
- They are good at asking questions related to the why, why not, and what-ifs processes, products, and technologies.
- They like to observe and scrutinize processes, products, and technologies.
- They are experimenters with processes, products, and technologies.
- They are good at networking.

The authors of the study also note that these skills can be developed through practice and by creating an environment conducive to their development. The following section presents a series of steps that we have identified to create an environment that fosters creativity.

Environmental Factors Affecting Creativity and Innovation

Creativity, invention, and innovation are driven by a series of little *ahas*.[11] When the little *ahas* are stitched together, they lead to innovative products, services, and business processes. Creative ideas are built on a tapestry of other ideas and the little *ahas* are the basis for both incremental and radical innovation.

Although innovation and creativity can emerge in a variety of settings and situations, some environments are more conducive to the creative process. In one large study, it was found that having a vision, being task-oriented, and engaging in external communication had a strong relationship to creativity and innovation.[12] The following section presents the environmental factors that encourage the creative process.

They are drawn from a variety of sources including Sawyer,[13] Amabile, Hadley, and Kramer,[14] Goldenberg and Mazursky,[15] and Nalebuff and Ayres,[16] and Michalko.[17] The following environmental factors can facilitate the creativity and innovation in individuals, departments, and organizations:

Need a shared mission that is focused on a single goal. Creative and intellectual energy is not unlimited. If an individual or a group is working on too many projects, then it is difficult to focus on one particular problem. If the group has a shared mission, this will also lead to group cohesion and further contribution to solving a problem.

Create an atmosphere that facilitates one-on-one collaboration. Group meetings can sometimes provide focus and insight, and assist in bringing focus to the team. It, however, is the one-on-one collaboration that is most effective in fostering the little *ahas* and individual creativity. It is like reciprocal tutoring. Through discussion and dialog, both individuals, the tutor and student, are better able to understand and grasp their particular problem. This is true even when one individual has more knowledge than the other. The teacher often learns more than the student during discussions.

Promote risk-taking and permit failure. There are many paths in life that can lead one astray. Sometimes we can avoid them by gathering additional information, but many times we cannot know that a path is a dead end or is too roundabout until we travel the path. Risk-taking should be encouraged even when the risks are daunting. The road less traveled may be the right path. The idea of learning by making mistakes is the essential part of the learn-by-doing approach. Consider Steve Jobs. He is the prototypical example of failure leading to success. The path to success was fraught with disappointments including the Apple Lisa, the Power Mac G4 Cube, NeXT computers, and perhaps Apple TV. Counter these failures with the iPad one of the most successful technologies ever released.

Experimentation not only invariably involves some level of failure, but also leads to understanding and insight into what works. As illustrated in a later chapter, investing in a variety of projects diversifies risk and provides opportunities for the future. Making the right investment decision on the right projects and the right products is a combination of having the right information, intuition, and luck by learning-by-doing. Steve Jobs (Apple) and Jeff Bezos (Amazon) intuitively or explicitly invested in real options by exploring the applicability of emerging technologies to create unique products and services.

Allocate quiet time and solitude in order to help individuals think inside the box. There are some creative people who have a special place to go when they want to solve a problem. Quiet time and solitude are essential for the creative process and generating the little *ahas*. Quiet time can be in an office, in a special room, inside a refrigerator box, during an evening run, on the treadmill, in bed, or in the shower. Isolation and quiet time facilitate the creative process. The first thing solitude does is to help us focus on the problem. Even if you are not focused on the problem during quiet time, the mind works in the background reorganizing knowledge and ideas to help solve a problem. For many people, the best time for solitude and creative work is during the first 2 or 3 hours in the morning. I call these hours the Golden Hours. The mind has spent the previous 8 hours organizing knowledge and is primed for problem solving and insight. There is some evidence that artists have their Golden Hours after 10 pm.[18] These so-called Night Owl Learners seek the cover of night and solitude to produce their creative endeavors.

Make things by developing prototypes and experimenting. A prototype is a real, workable, and quasi-usable system built economically and quickly with the intention of being modified. As noted earlier, a key strategy for sparking creative activity is the learn-by-doing process. Learning by doing means that you make and build things, try experiments, and construct prototypes. Prototypes can be built for products and services, including software. A prototype is essential for learning about what you are trying to invent and also for illustrating proof of concept. The prototype is part of a continuous ongoing process of experimentation and review. If you need to write something or develop something that is artistically creative, then the same advice applies. The initial writing, photograph, painting, or sculpture is the prototype. The mantra of those involved in creative pursuits should be *Prototype or Perish* or *Build or Bust.*

Anyone can be creative. Half of the battle of being creative is convincing yourself and others that anyone can be creative. I sometimes hear friends and students say that they are not creative. Anyone can be creative; it just involves applying all of the following strategies:

- Have a mission and focusing on a single goal
- Need one-on-one collaboration
- Take risks and permit failure
- Need quiet time and solitude
- Need to prototype and experiment
- Work hard

In an ideal world, management would be responsible for creating an environment that is conducive to creativity. In reality, it is the individual's responsibility to create such an environment by balancing time at work, at play, and at home that will match the desired level of creative activity. Everyone needs a bit of *aha* in his or her life.

How to Hinder Creativity

The first way to hinder creativity is to reduce thinking time and try to eliminate solitude. Management can accomplish this in six easy steps:

1. Schedule many meetings. In addition to weekly project meetings, schedule daily meetings to solve all kinds of problems and to show off what has been accomplished.
2. Have each team member account for all of his or her time in detail.
3. Tell people not to talk to each other about their tasks.
4. Interrupt individuals whenever possible. Give team members new tasks to accomplish. If problems arise on other projects, then send them over to help out.
5. Change the product specifications and put in new features at the last minute.
6. Have the team members stay at work 12 hours per day and have them work on weekends.

Lack of time and interruptions are enemies of the creative process. Creativity is diminished when individuals are under-the-gun and the workdays are fragmented with many meetings, with busy work and interruptions.[19] Creativity is not very efficient. It takes time to understand a problem and to develop ideas.

Embrace Some Adversity and Avoid Chronic Stress

There is some indirect evidence that some adversity can make you stronger. Researchers such as Mark Seery, Alison Holman, and Roxanne Cohan Silver found that a certain level of exposure to adverse life events resulted in better mental health and well-being outcomes.[20] They found that a history of lifetime adversity, in contrast to low and high levels of adversity, was related to lower global distress, lower levels of functional impairment, less post-traumatic stress, and high levels of satisfaction. Yes, some levels of adversity can make us feel better.

Chronic stress, however, can have a negative influence on health, the immune system, cognitive performance, learning, memory, and brain development in general.[21] When the brain detects some sort of threat, it releases hormones that are used to cope with the threat and the body goes into a fight-or-flight response. Extended or chronic exposure to these hormones and the fight-or-flight arousal state can significantly impair health and cognitive functions and, by extension, the creative process. The bottom line is that a little adversity might be ok; but if the adversity leads to chronic stress, then it will damage the individual.

Creativity Techniques

The effectiveness of creativity techniques is unclear. This section presents several techniques that have been used to foster the creative process. They are essentially problem-solving strategies for generating new ideas for product and services. This section is a compendium of ideas from a variety of places. You are encouraged to look at the various books that are available for additional insight into the approaches.[22]

Challenge Assumptions by Recombining, Adding, Deleting, or Changing Product Features

Assumptions about how a product should look and perform create intellectual boundaries. As noted by Michalko,[23] they become so ingrained that they are never challenged. Flipping[24] and reversing are techniques for challenging the assumptions. For example, it is assumed that delivered pizzas should be cheap, hot, fast, and have standard toppings. How about cold, slow, and nonstandard toppings? Cold pizza is not a good idea, but perhaps expensive pizza, with slow delivery and gourmet ingredients, could be a winner. The first thing to do in this approach is to list all the features of a product, reverse the features, and then see what features make sense.

Other ideas where assumptions and product features have been challenged include the following:

- Taking your car to the glass shop to have the window repaired
  - New assumption: The glass shop repairs the crack in the car window at your work.
- High-resolution expensive camcorder with many features
  - New assumption: The popular Flip Mino was a low-resolution inexpensive camera with very few features. It was popular at one time because it could easily upload files to the Internet.
- Use global positioning system to get you to a location
  - New assumption: Give other people your location and let them find you or come to you.
- Putting condiments in glass bottles
  - New assumption: Flipping by putting condiments in plastic and turn them upside down (ketchup).
- Have spaghetti tonight, chili tomorrow, and macaroni and cheese the next day
  - New assumption: Have Cincinnati City chili tonight. It includes spaghetti, chili, onions and lots of cheese.

Social networking Web sites have championed the idea of combing services in new ways (often referred to as mashups). For example, Facebook combines blogging, photo sharing, marketing, and instant messaging. Twitter has combined text messaging, mini-blogging, instant news, customer tracking, and paparazzi activities in one simple yet powerful system. All in one printers, multipurpose stadiums and Kansas City Chili are additional examples of how simple ideas can be combined into useful products.

Idea Arbitrage: Steal Ideas and Products From Someone Else

Taking ideas from others is idea arbitrage.[25] If the idea is not patented or copyrighted, it will be copied. And even if it is copyrighted or patented, it will probably still be copied.[26] Legal searching for ideas can come from a variety of sources including basic science journals, the popular press, conferences, and trade associations. As noted earlier, innovation benefits from search. And usually, the more sources you search, the better (this is probably true up to about 11 outside sources). The ideas can also come from other countries and cultures. There is a Web site in China called AliBaba.com where there are literally thousands of products that have never been seen in the West. With idea arbitrage, the goal should be to steal the gem and not the entire crown. Take the best ideas and combine them in order to differentiate your products from the competition.

One interesting application of the idea arbitrage is Etsy.com. Etsy is an online store that provides a market for crafts and handmade items. It has drawn on ideas from both Amazon and eBay and has recently begun to encroach on both eBay's and Amazon's market. It is a superb example of a monopolistic competition marketplace, where product differentiation rules the day.

Midas Approach: Product and Services Developed with Unlimited Resources

The idea behind this approach is that you can generate ideas for solving problems by throwing money at the problem.[27] The problems are the headaches. Even though contemporary life in the USA is pretty much headache free, by 18th-century standards, there are numerous instances where products and services are being developed to relieve irritations.

For example, if you have a problem with technical support, then have a technical guru sit outside the door until you call for his or her expertise. Need help with school and homework? Hire a full-time assistant as a tutor. Having problems with snow on the driveway? Install a heated coil driveway. If you cannot guess when the mail arrives; install a sensor that transmits the status of the mailbox.

Barry Nalebuff and Ian Ayers describe the *"What Would Croesus Do?"* approach in their book entitled *Why Not?*[28] This is essentially a problem-solving approach where you have unlimited resources at your disposal. The goal is to identify products and services for the high end where the consumer is not price-sensitive and is interested in many different features. As noted earlier, we have renamed *Croesus* to *Midas* because it is easier to remember and because it imparts a very colorful and explicit image of high-end features. *Midas* products and services are designed for consumers who are not price-sensitive.

Hermes Approach: Products and Services Developed with Limited Resources

In an earlier chapter, we discussed the Hermes approach to problem solving and developing products and services to relieve headaches. The Hermes part of the demand curve is where the consumers are price-sensitive. This could include students, seniors, and, in general, individuals with low levels of discretionary income or individuals who are value-conscious. In designing products and services for this group you can use the *"What would Hermes Do?"* approach. Hermes was the god of the traveler, the shepherd, the athlete, the merchants, and the cunning, and was linked to invention and commerce. There are a variety of very interesting products and services that have been developed for the price-sensitive end of the demand curve. The idea is to use the top and bottom of the demand curve to generate new ideas for products and services. The point is creating dynamic tension between the two ends of the demand curve and eventually producing the best products for the price-sensitive (Hermes), the high end (Midas), and the middle of the demand curve (Atlas).

Nightmare Features: Think of Ways to Put Your Company Out of Business

An extension of the alleviate headaches approach is to think about ways to put your company out of business or for that matter any company out of business.[29] When using this approach, the individual should marshal all the creativity approaches, including using unlimited resources to generate problem solutions, borrowing ideas using idea arbitrage, flipping ideas, and recombining products and services. Many of the ideas that have led to putting companies, industries, and even countries out of business were the result of disruptive technological innovation (e.g., the printing presses, armaments and tactical innovations, networking, computing, communications innovations, etc.). Disruptive technologies are product or process innovations that eventually eclipse or overturn the existing dominant technology. They are part of a product life cycle described by 19th-century economist Joseph Schumpeter that leads to Creative Destruction.[30] Schumpeter was a strong proponent of the entrepreneurial spirit. It was his position that products and services emerge, die, adapt, and re-combine in a never-ending cycle of birth, growth, and decline.

Fostering Creativity in Meetings and with Your Colleagues

The way we perceive the world is constrained by culture, social mores, institutions, education, and neurobiology. In some cultures and businesses, there is a distinct power distance that separates and modifies social interactions.[31] Power distance is the degree to which powerful individuals in a country, culture, occupation, or an institution accept and indeed demand subordination, obedience, and differential respect. Institutions with high levels of power distance are characterized by bosses pulling rank, requiring subordinates to clear everything with the boss, and having excessive rules for interaction and task completion. In general, when power distance is high between superiors and their subordinates, there is an aura of authoritarianism and class distinction. This is in contrast to work environments where the power distance between superiors and subordinates is low. In this situation, superiors treat individuals as somewhat equal, giving subordinates important tasks, permitting failure, and giving credit where the credit is due.

It should be noted that the appropriate degree of power distance is contextual. There are some jobs where high levels of power distance are needed (e.g., the military, some construction jobs, and police work) and others where low levels of power distance are desirable (e.g., research and development, piloting a plane, and creative endeavors). Malcolm Gladwell described a situation where high levels of power distance between flight crew members contributed to the plane crashes of a Korean Airlines in the late 1990s.[32] Planes produced by Airbus and Boeing are supposed to be flown by two pilots without a significant power distance between them, where one pilot corrects the other when necessary. As a result of the large power distance between the pilots of Korean Airlines, the co-pilot would not correct mistakes made by the other pilot, which in turn led to the fatal mistakes and crashes. There has even been speculation that the Madoff debacle was the result of too much power distance between the Securities and Exchange Commission and Bernard Madoff.[33]

It is important to reduce the power distance relationship within teams and at meetings when the objective is to encourage creativity and innovation. As noted earlier, having a mission, focusing on a single goal, encouraging one-on-one collaboration, encouraging risk taking, embracing failure, and having quiet time can all facilitate creativity. This can, of course, be very difficult to do because the power distance relationship is a somewhat durable, cultural, and institutional variable. Overcoming situations where the power distance relationship is high requires a dramatic approach, such as the *Six Thinking Hats* technique.

Six Hats Approach to Creativity

Edward de Bono has developed a technique for creativity that has been outlined in his book the *Six Thinking Hats*.[34] The objective of his approach is to encourage problem solving and creativity by having team members wear different hats. This approach just might help to reduce relationships where the power distance is high. The following presents a brief overview of how the different hats influence team interactions and information gathering:

- White Hat Thinking: This involves gathering facts and figures related to the problem. It is also used to identify areas where more information is required.
- Red Hat Thinking: This involves emotional thinking. Gut feelings and passionate evangelism are permitted.
- Green Hat Thinking: This is where creativity is encouraged. Creative solutions are in order and you can draw it from the approaches discussed earlier (flipping, idea arbitrage, combining ideas, and unlimited resources).
- Black Hat Thinking: This involves the use of critique and judgment to assess the negative aspects of a solution. Key questions to be asked include whether the solution is viable and whether can it be executed.
- Yellow Hat Thinking: This involves the positive aspects of a solution. It is important to be optimistic about the solution when under the yellow hat.
- Blue Hat Thinking: This involves trying to get a strategic look at the problem. An attempt is made to get at the big picture in terms of where were we, where do we want to go, and how do we get there.

The six hats approach is a useful activity that may help to bring different perspectives into the creative process as well as reduce high levels of power distance. When implemented properly, it encourages participation and helps reduce dysfunctional power relationships among team members.

Conclusion

In this chapter, we have discussed the concept of creativity and innovation, and identified various approaches on how to foster them. There are several all-encompassing lessons that can be derived from the previous discussion:

- Innovation is the result of willful and serendipitous interconnections between the little *ahas*.
- Innovation usually involves intellectual and technological maturity levels so that learning-by-doing is possible.
- Innovation requires dialog, learning-about, encouragement, time, solitude, experimentation, construction, and some pressure, but not too much.
- Learning-about, learning-by-doing using prototyping, and hard work are the keys to creativity and successful innovation.

Innovation is an important driver leading to organizational financial performance.[35] It is after all the catalyst for developing differentiated products and services for competing in monopolistic competition markets. Research and development is driven by the diffusion of science and the translation of basic science into commercially viable products and services. R&D by entrepreneurs may not involve basic scientific research, but it does involve searching for ideas that will lead to differentiated and marketable products and services.

CHAPTER 7

Conceptualizing Products and Services Using the FAD Template

The previous chapters have focused on learning the basic concepts related to product differentiation in the context of monopolistic competition. The focus of this chapter is learning-by-doing. We will use techniques to help transform a nagging idea about a new product to be more explicit and real. The tool for completing this task is called the FAD (features, attributes, and design) template. The FAD template is used to identify the features and attributes that can be used for product and service differentiation. The first part of the chapter will introduce the key concepts necessary to understand and motivate the use of the FAD template. The FAD template will then be introduced and used to demonstrate and structure the development of important attributes and features of a new product or service.

Features, Attributes, Form, Design, Function, and Meaning are Interrelated Concepts

Here are some definitions and concepts that can be used to understand how products and services can be differentiated:

- An attribute is used to describe the characteristics or properties of something.
- A feature is often described as a prominent attribute.
- A function is what something does.
- Form is the external experience or shape.
- Design involves all the above.
- Meaning involves all the above plus the relationship of the product or service to emotional and psychosocial needs.

Figure 7.1. SuperDuper smartphone.

A very simple way to view all the above is that features, function, form, design, and meaning are all attributes, with different levels of information about a product. Consider the SuperDuper smartphone in Figure 7.1. The SuperDuper phone has a keypad (attribute, feature, function, and form), with lighted square keys (attribute, feature, and form), and a high color indestructible screen (attribute, feature, and form) with a black onyx color and coarse texture (attributes, features, and form), which can be used for calling and texting (attributes, features and functions), listening to stereo music (attribute, feature, and function), and locating friends within 1 mile (attribute, feature and function). This smart and futuristic SuperDuper phone (attribute and overall design) creates feelings of connectedness, comfort, and security (attributes and meanings).

Meaning and Product Design

There are three fundamental approaches to design (Figure 7.2). The user-driven design (UDD) school is focused on researching consumer wants and needs. The technology-driven design (TDD) school is not a school per se, but rather an approach that is focused on applying new and emerging technologies to develop products and services. The meaning-driven design (MDD) school focuses on the emotional and psychological relationships that people have with things, objects, and products and

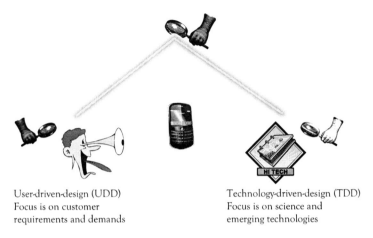

Meaning-driven-design (MDD)
Integrates user-driven design and technology-driven design

User-driven-design (UDD)
Focus is on customer
requirements and demands

Technology-driven-design (TDD)
Focus is on science and
emerging technologies

Figure 7.2. Fundamental design approaches.

attempts to design products that satisfy these meanings. Most products
can be designed using all three approaches, for example, software, custom
houses, furnishings, electronics, clothes, personal care, appliances, and
transportation. Some products such as CPUs' semiconductors and nanotechnology and health equipment are primarily technology driven.

MDD also involves UDD, but it is not the motivation behind the
entire process. In MDD, the company executives and research and development (R&D) personnel design the next-generation product and then
present it to consumers. They still obtain a reaction from potential consumers, but it is not the sole driving force behind the process. The MDD
approach also incorporates technology-push innovation, where innovative emerging technologies are pushed to the market. In essence, MDD
uses elements of both UDD and TDD to deliver innovative products.
The unique part of MDD is the search for meaning. There is a search for
meaning in the way that people relate to objects. This is often accomplished by collaborating with other organizations and with experts in the
product domain on how the product should be designed. The design of
the product is not solely derived from customer pull as is the case of UDD,
but is also driven by the innovator and new and emerging technologies.

In MDD, the innovator synthesizes information from a variety of sources and then uses this knowledge to design innovative products.[1]

The idea behind the MDD School of innovation is to look for meaning in everyday products and to try to determine how they can be changed in a radical way to support the emotional and psychological needs of consumers. The MDD approach to developing a Blue Ocean market involves understanding how customers relate to products and then developing new products that get at the core of what meaning customers attach to products.[2]

Many individuals in the MDD school believe that the user-centered design is a hindrance to developing radical innovations.[3] The focus of the MDDapproach is to find the meaning in the way people relate to objects in their everyday life. The MDD school of innovation not only contemplates beauty and form, but also examines the emotional and psychological relationships that people have with things, objects, and products. Proponents of MDD believe that developing innovative ideas that transcend existing product concepts requires more than just attending to product differentiation. Since the MDD school of innovation uses a push strategy. Product ideas are conceived as a vision and offered to consumers as a proposal. As noted by Verganti: "These proposals are not dreams without a foundation. These proposals eventually emerge as the products users were actually looking for. They end-up being what people were waiting for—and thus are great marketing successes" (p. 116).

We alluded to the fundamental meaning of product in the earlier discussion of the basic functions of products. There are many different types of meanings that can be attached to products, some of them are tangible and some of them are complex and elusive. Key areas of meaning include the following: provide physical and emotional sustenance; facilitate control over the environment; provide entertainment; provide feelings of status, superiority, and elitism; provide a sense of stewardship; provide a sense of altruism; provide feelings of adventure; provide security and comfort; facilitate the completion of some work or home task; provide familial support; support learning and adaptation; help us to change location; provide opportunity for communication and networking; provide for respect and recognition; and, of course, be a source of satisfaction and happiness.

Traditional user-centered design approaches are not focused on understanding the meaning of the relationship that people have with objects. The Wii is not a game machine, it is the campfire surrounded by family and friends. Embedding diamonds in wireless phones contributes little to the calling function. But in some people's minds, diamonds are a symbol of affluence and sophistication and are used to convey that image. The iPhone is not just a phone and the iTouch is not just an MP3 player, they are status symbols that also provide comfort and social networking. A Cirque du Soleil performance is not just a circus or just entertainment, it is a risky adventure in an ethereal world never seen before. The iPad is not a replacement for a netbook or a laptop, it is the adventurer's guide to the galaxy of knowledge and entertainment. It is the present day *Hitch Hikers Guide to the Galaxy*.

Attaching meaning to objects is of course somewhat subjective and strongly influenced by the researcher's background and by social mores. There are numerous types of meaning that can be examined and they are often interdependent.

Designing products that draw on meaning requires creativity and hard work. Creativity can be cultivated and is within the grasp of most people as discussed in chapter 6. The hard work is the never-ending process of determining the proper ingredients that go into the secret sauce to keep people from becoming bored or even worse, ignoring your product.

A key part of the MDD process involves partnering with interpreters. This partnering involves both learning-about and learning-by-doing. The interpreters are the organizations and individuals who are working on products that are similar to the products that you are examining. They can be suppliers and component manufactures, consultants, consumers, competitors, universities, research firms and think tanks, trade association and publications, research conferences, and of course one of the most important interpreters, the search engine.

There are other approaches to design that focus on marketing, project management, product management, portfolio management, product engineering, creativity, and controlling the process. Later chapters will discuss the role of project management, new product development and portfolio management in providing structure to the innovation process.

Many companies use hybrid approaches that draw on UDD, TDD, and MDD. Our focus in this chapter is primarily on MDD. But we also rely on user-centered design for refining products and making them usable. Even Apple, who we believe is the wunderkind of MDD in the USA, listens to their customers. For example, they redesigned Apple TV to become an inexpensive video-streaming device and put buttons on the smallest shuffle because consumers did not like having all the music control buttons on the ear bud cord.[4] UDD is also very important for software development, whether it be in the context of game development, applications development, or social networking applications. A customer-centric agile development process is essential for delivering products that will be used. Ergonomics, ergonomics laboratories, and usability research are the foundation for delivering high-quality software products to the consumers.

There is one more design strategy that can be linked to many product failures. It is a purely functional design strategy that does not incorporate user needs or meaning at all. There is little if any UDD or MDD. This situation occurs where someone thinks that there is a need or demand for a product or service, but the end-users were not listened to or were ignored completely. This often occurs when there is no need or demand for a product or service, but someone thought that it would be a good idea to develop it anyway. I was involved with such a product when I worked as a programmer. Here is the story.

Functional Design and User Ignored

Barlow was the head of our IT group and he was also the head scorekeeper for the plant's golf league. Every Monday morning Barlow would take the golf scores from the past week of play and compute the league standings as well as calculate the handicaps. Barlow had been doing this for years. Someone in human resources thought that he was spending too much time on the league and they also thought it was a burden to Barlow. So HR commissioned a golf handicapping and league scoring system. A complete cost–benefit analysis was actually implemented and the payback was deemed acceptable, so the green light was given to the project. A team of analysts and programmers were assigned to gather requirements and implement the system. Tens of thousands of dollars were spent developing and programming the system. The system was used just a couple of times. It was a pain to use, the results were incorrect, and most importantly, Barlow could finish his calculations faster than it would take to key-in the data and generate the reports. Barlow actually liked his manual system and took pride in his ability to produce weekly updates in a few hours. He said as such, in quiet tones, but he was not listened to.

In the current market context, functionally designed products and services are sometimes at risk, unless the meaning of the design is to convey simplicity and functionality. There are numerous examples of successful products and services that simply do what they are supposed to do, because they are functional. Functionally designed products can be even more successful when they are accompanied by user-centered design and meaning-centered design.

Identifying Key Meanings, Attributes, and Features

One thing is for sure. There are literally thousands of attributes, features, designs, and meanings that can be used to define products and services. This section details the major attributes that should be considered during product and service development.

Functions of the product or service and target customers. What does the product do? What important subfunctions does it perform? What type of customers or customer segment are you trying to attract?

Quality. How well does the product or service conform to specifications? Does the product or service do what it says it is supposed to do in the user manual? Is it effective in performing its function?

Reliability. Does the product or service perform as it is supposed to over the expected life of the product or service. Is it prone to failure? Is it easily maintained? Can parts be obtained at a reasonable cost and are they easy to change? Does the product perform satisfactorily in a variety of environmental conditions?

Ease-of-use. Is the product or service easy to use and can consumers learn how to use it without much trouble? Is the product convenient to use?

A convenient product or service is readily available, performs the task for which it was designed, and reduces the time it takes to complete a task.

Performance. Is the product smaller than the competition? Is it more powerful? Does the product or service complete a task faster? Is the product adaptable to many situations?

Design. Is the external form attractive? Is the product packaged properly? Does the product suggest a certain meaning? Do the materials used in developing a product also contribute to the overall look and feel? Thus, the meaning of a product is derived from the type and color of the material used to construct a product, the texture and feel of the product, the size, the product name, and from the overall form or style of the product or service.[5] Examples of abstract design meanings might include: futuristic, scary, hallow, delicate, intellectual, feminine, masculine, macho, healthy, psychedelic, smart, fashionable, earthy, retro, metal, avant-garde, youthful, personal, worldly, mature, luxurious, elite, western, oriental, simple, sassy, cool, organic, green, and even abstract.

Design attractiveness and innovation also applies to services. Packaging for a service includes the overall look and feel of the service. It is the gestalt or form and configuration of the service as perceived by the consumer. The key success indicator for a service is the customer's perception of the overall experience with the service process.[6]

Technology. Is there an emerging technology or a process that can improve the quality, reliability ease-of-use, performance, value, design, and meaning of the product?

Value creation. Is there any intrinsic value in the product that significantly distinguishes it from other products or services offered by your company or the competition? Does the product or service solve a problem that consumers want to solve and will the solution attract them to the product or service?

Meaning. The meaning of a product or service can be thought of as super-attribute or super-feature that nurtures the inner needs of the individual. Meaning can include the following: provides physical, health, religious, or emotional sustenance; provides feelings of being needed or being listened to; supports artistic and creative needs;

facilitates control over the environment; supports feelings of closeness to the earth and being organic; provides entertainment; supports feelings of status, superiority, and elitism; provides a sense of stewardship or a sense of altruism; supports feelings of adventure; supports gender needs; supports feelings of security and comfort; facilitate and assists in the completion of some work or home task; provides feelings of familial support; helps an individual or a community to learn and adapt; helps us to change location; provides an opportunity for communication and networking; has above-average intrinsic value to some or many people; provide for respect and recognition; and finally, provides a source of satisfaction, happiness, or hope. The meaning of a product or service is very much tied-in to what the product does. For example, communicating is one of the most important and ongoing functions in our lives and we attach significant meaning to products and services that support communication.

Overlap in Meanings, Attributes, and Features

After reading through the list, you can probably notice that there is a significant amount of overlap among the different attribute categories. This is in part related to the imprecision of words in all languages and to the proliferation of synonyms. A Venn diagram illustrating the relationships among words and their meanings would visually depict significant degrees of overlap. This ties in very well with the concept of a brand and MDD. Recall that a brand is simply something that lives in the head of consumers.[7] A brand is simply a composite of the mental associations that are generated when you see or think about a certain product. Another way to think about branding is as a gestalt view of the product. It is more than the sum of its parts (the attributes, features, functions, form, design, and meaning). It is the meaning we attach to the product and all the neural associations that are invoked when the product or service is recalled.

Design Products and Services that Facilitate Control

A fundamental force of adaptation in human beings is our attempt to control the environment.[8] Infants try to get control their environment by crying. Cuteness is a built-in genetic adaptation that augments crying and also facilitates environmental control. As we age, this strategy does not work very well and people control the environment by fitting-in, which is another type of control. Security, freedom, independence, and emancipation are the rewards of obtaining control. Getting wheels and driving, acquiring a secure and comfortable home, obtaining a job, and achieving financial security are milestones in achieving control. One person's gain in control can sometimes lead to a loss of control by another. This is the collateral damage that can occur when someone gains too much control over others. For example, colleagues, family, and friends can facilitate (or hinder) the drive for environmental control. However, that same individual can in turn use the control to dominate those who helped him or her to achieve environmental control. Many individual and group conflicts can be traced to someone seeking excessive control or to someone else seeking emancipation from the excessive control.

The two fundamental strategies used to control the environment are primary control and secondary control. Primary control occurs when an individual tries to directly engage with and change the external environment to fit his or her needs and wishes.[9] Secondary control is a type of control that is directed at changing the self in order to cope with the environment. Secondary control is a goal-directed coping strategy for minimizing losses in primary control and also a mechanism for maintaining and increasing primary control. Individuals that do not engage in primary or secondary control have relinquished control and this is manifested by passivity and helplessness. Individuals engaging in primary control try to fix the environment, and those engaged in secondary control try to adapt to the environment. Both strategies assist in coping with the stress and complexity that are part of the everyday activities in the external environment.

We have found that primary and secondary controls also influence feelings of psychological ownership an individual has towards his or her avatar in an online game.[10] Psychological ownership occurs when people have feelings of ownership towards material things or tangible objects and even immaterial or intangible objects.[11] It occurs when an individual views the object as *mine*. We have found that the key to obtaining lock-in in online gaming environments is to get game players to embrace the system as though they own it. This ownership is the direct result of being able to exercise both primary and secondary controls over their online character by way of the user interface and by successfully interacting with members of the online guilds.

Facebook is a very interesting case of using systems to gain environmental control. It is very difficult for people to actually brag about their day-to-day accomplishments and activities in the *real world* or nononline world. It is much easier, and is indeed acceptable, in Facebook interactions to talk about oneself. There are several mechanisms built into Facebook that encourage bragging. For example, if a picture is added to the photo library or is used to display the image on the Facebook profile, then it is acceptable to brag or tout one's stuff on the accomplishment or the activity. Facebook permits people to control what is known and what is not known about them. It also opens up new lines of communication and it can sometimes alleviate loneliness and even increase recognition and status. LinkedIn is the social networking tool of choice for bragging about professional accomplishments and looking for a job, while Twitter is the outlet of choice for serial braggers and businesses that want to obtain exposure.

The bottom line is that if people can control a product or service or if a product or service helps to actually control the world, people will feel that they own the artifact and thus become locked-in to using that product or service out of loyalty.

There are of course issues of having too much control and having too many options. There is some evidence that having too many choices leads to decision paralysis and some people believe that having too many choices contributes to depression.[12] Novice users of any product or service need directed guidance. A wireless phone or a DVR needs to be easy to use for the first-time user, but also readily customizable as experience grows and new features are sought.

Categorizing the Importance of Product Attributes

Some attributes of products were important 5 years ago, but they are not today. Some product features were not even available last year, but they are mandatory today. Similarly, product designs and their accompanying meanings are constantly in flux. The importance of product attributes changes. The following classification scheme can be used to ascertain whether attributes and features are increasing or declining in importance. The classification scheme was derived from a variety of sources.[13]

Points of Parity and Must-Haves (POPS)

These are attributes that most of the products in a category usually have. They are the basic features found in a product or service. They help to define the prototypical product. A product is something that is tangible and it does something and has a function.[14] For example, it provides sustenance; it provides security and comfort; it helps us to complete some task; it helps us to learn and adapt; and it helps us to change location, communicate, and network. The product should do what it is meant to do, with certain features that are compelling and functional. These features with their accompanying functionality are "must-haves" for a product or service to be minimally acceptable, and preferably strongly desired. If a product does not possess these essential features and functionality, it might be eliminated from consideration. For example, an auto global positioning system (GPS) should have the ability to enter an address and display how long it will take to get to a location; a word processor should have spell-checking capabilities; and a movie theater should sell treats.

Points of Difference and Differentiators (PODs)

These are the attributes of a product or service that assist in distinguishing products from the competition and from similar models in a product line. Product and service features that are differentiators are usually derived from Midas products and are high-end products. They are for nonprice-sensitive consumers. You can think of the demand curve as a steep incline where product features roll down from Midas products to Atlas products. When costs are further driven down, the features become the standard of Hermes products. Hermes products are for price-sensitive consumers. Important differentiators for auto GPSs include Bluetooth capability, voice recognition, and topography maps. A movie theater could have very comfortable seats. A word processor could have voice control. As noted earlier, the features tend to roll down the demand curve and the differentiators become must-haves over time.

Blue Ocean Features and Exciters (BOFs)

These features are typically in the very early stages of R&D and part of a secret plan to develop a new market. BOFs have the potential to deliver a knockout punch by developing a Blue Ocean market, a brand new uncontested marketplace. In general, BOF features are in their infancy—beginning to unfold and emerge. Examples for auto GPS might include location of friends and family in close proximity.

Another way to identify exciters or BOFs is to think about ways you could go about putting your company out of business or for that matter any company out of business. These are nightmare features and technologies. Many of the ideas that have contributed to putting companies, industries, and even countries out of business were derived from radical technological innovation. Examples include the printing press; armaments and tactical innovations; and networking, computing, and communications innovations. These so-called disruptive technologies are product or process innovations that eventually eclipse or overturn the existing dominant technology. Disruptive technologies can lead to sunrise features and to sunrise products. Sunrise features and products are the dawn of new technological and conceptual capabilities.

Extinct and vestigial features (EXTs)

These are attributes that are no longer necessary or on the verge of becoming extinct. They are sunset features. They are features that are on the verge of becoming obsolete and fading into darkness and oblivion. Sometimes EXTs cannot be removed because there may be a small subset of people that demand the feature. In this case, a decision has to be made to abandon the features or keep the feature. Sometimes the decision to abandon is the best way to go because of cost issues and because the company is going down a new technology path. This was the case with recent versions of Microsoft's operating systems that abandoned some of the legacy DOS code. Apple made a similar decision in regards to abandoning DVD drives in the MacBook Air product and the decision not to include a camera in the iTouch. All of Apple's decisions are influenced by product positioning, product costs, and the emergence and decline of technologies.

The next category is actually a subcategory of extinct features. When products or services lead to actual dislike of a product or service, then they should be retired or at a minimum require major redesign.

Dissatifiers (DISs)

There are instances when products and features in existing products can discourage consumers from using your product or your competitor's products. Sometimes features can actually cause consumers to actually avoid using a product. The feature may be a negative attribute of the product. This can occur because the product or service has not been designed correctly and is basically unusable. Numerous products and services have failed because consumers have been dissatified with the design. Consumers can also be dissatified with a product because the consumer does not want the feature in the product or service. DISs are often sunset features. For example, many people did not attend circuses because they were opposed to the use of wild animals in the shows or because they thought that the animals were not interesting. That is one of many reasons why Cirque du Soleil became popular with a larger adult market. Cirque du Soleil simply abandoned the use of animals in their programs.

The FAD Template

The purpose of the FAD template is to try to facilitate and provide a degree of structure for conceptualizing new products and services (see Exhibit 1). The first step in using the FAD template is to provide a description of the product or service that is being considered. The second step in using the FAD template involves describing the meaning of the product. Several product meanings have been listed to provide a starting point. The next step in using the FAD template involves identifying

potential attributes. The attributes can be features, performance characteristics, form, design, and even additional meanings. We have included
a few attributes that are often considered, but you are encouraged to seek
the attributes that are important in the development of your product
or service. One goal of using the FAD template is to facilitate product
differentiation. Focusing on attributes that are exciters and Blue Ocean
features will assist in the differentiation process. It is sometimes helpful
to focus on features that are on the verge of extinction or features that
consumers are not satisfied with or wish they were not there. Considering exciters and disastisfiers helps to expand the way designers view
the meaning behind a product or service, and it allows the designer to
gain deeper insight into how to improve the current performance of the
product.

Prototyping and the FAD Template

The final stage of using the FAD template is to provide a way to visual-
ize the product by: a drawing, a schematic of the product or service,
or a physical model (see several examples in Appendix 1). Learning-
by-doing means that you make and build things. You try experiments
and you construct prototypes. Prototypes need to be constructed for
tangible products, for services, and also for systems applications. If the
product is a tangible product, then a generic mock-up of the product
needs to be constructed as early as possible. The idea is to develop a
very rough prototype of the product or service. There are many different ways to do this. It could be a report developed in a word-processing
program, an interface developed in a presentation program, a sketch
using a vector or raster-based drawing program or even drawn using a
pencil on the back of a napkin, a three-dimensional (3D) model developed in Google's free SketchUp program, or a flow diagram illustrating
a process. If the product is a computer application, then a prototype
can be constructed using a rapid prototyping language or demon-
strated via a presentation package such as PowerPoint. There are also
many excellent applications available for tablet computers that are very
effective for developing mock-ups of applications and for drawing or
sketching preliminary product ideas.

Services should also be prototyped. A uniquely designed service can be used as a way to differentiate a firm from the competition. Service design should always focus on the customer and how the customer interacts with the business in receiving the service. These interactions between the customer and the business are referred to as the touch points or connections. There are many components that go into the design of a service. They include the people, the verbal and nonverbal interactions, the processes, the scripts, the tools, the materials, the infrastructure, and the technologies. Execution of the service is a function of how all the service components work together.

One popular tool for designing services is service blueprinting. It is a visual and descriptive tool for modeling visible customer interactions with employees and processes that also illustrates how the hidden processes support the customer interactions.[15] There are a number of tools that can be used to conceptualize, design, and test the design of the service including drawings, sketches, scenario analysis and task structuring, mock-ups, storyboarding, systems, Lego mock-ups, and many more (see http://www.servicedesigntools.org/repository). Because services often involve queues or lines, simulations can be used to understand how fast or how slow a service will be performed in a particular situation.

The goal of the first-cut prototype is to learn-by-doing, to get other people to understand what you are thinking about, and to help you understand what you are trying to do. Developing a prototype in some form or another is an important part of the learning-about and the learning-by-doing process that *will* facilitate creative insight.[16]

Many prototypes start out with paper and pencil and then become increasingly more sophisticated as they mature. The basic sequence of iterative design with stepwise refinement includes the following:

1. Initial Prototype: In the early stages, develop a pencil and paper picture of the product, the application, or the process. The key is to focus on the key or essential functions of the product or service.
2. Review: Let business stakeholders, family, friends, and eventually potential customers provide feedback on the product or service.

3. Revise and redesign prototype: Use the feedback to refine and improve the design of the product or service. Use more advanced tools as the prototype becomes more refined and detailed. This usually leads to the use of graphics, drawing, and mock-up software. Towards the later stages of development, the prototype might be a functioning product or service or an actual application with some level of functionality.

4. Go back to step 2 after revising and redesigning the prototype.

There are some very exciting prototyping tools for manufactured products. Although currently in their infancy, they have the potential to completely change the way that products are prototyped and eventually how everything will be manufactured.[17] These new tools are part of a new approach for manufacturing called additive manufacturing or desktop manufacturing. Rapid prototyping is becoming a reality because additive manufacturing assists in producing prototypes very quickly. One of the most promising technologies for implementing additive manufacturing is the 3D printer. Very detailed and complex plastic working models of products can be generated using 3D printers.[18] The parts or products are made by using 3D digital descriptions to print successive thin layers of plastic on top of plastic until a 3D solid emerges. Some of these plastic products and parts can be used as final products and not just as prototypes. There are versions of the 3D printers that use titanium powder to construct very complex objects such as jewelry and avionics components. Several aviation companies are investigating the use of very large 3D printers to create entire aircraft wings.

Example of the FAD Template in Wine Aging Cooler

Aged wine has always been attractive to wine enthusiasts and wine connoisseurs, but aged wine is expensive because of the time involved. A merlot can take up to 15 years to age and Shiraz-based wines may require 20 years of aging. Several products have been introduced and patents have been secured and applied for that are purported to speed up the aging process.[19] Suppose an inventor found that it was possible to dramatically speed up the wine aging process by exposing a wine to an electromagnetic field with a very specific magnetic field strength. Suppose that the same inventor found that the taste of all wines could be improved using the special aging process. The net effect is that the technology could reduce the time to produce fine aged wine and also increase the quality of low-priced wines as well as increase the status of the owner of the wine aging product. Appendix 2 illustrates how the FAD template could be used to conceptualize a new wine storage refrigerator that can be used to age wine. This example will be extended in chapter 9 using the Ten–Ten planning process.

Use the FAD Template to Develop the Blue Ocean Strategy Canvas

Chan Kim and Renée Mauborgne developed a technique they call the Strategy Canvas to assist in identifying a Blue Ocean market.[20] A Blue Ocean market is essentially an uncontested new market with high profit and significant growth potential. They use the Strategy Canvas as a tool to assist in identifying Blue Ocean markets. One purpose of the Strategy Canvas is to understand where the competition is playing and investing their time and resources. Another purpose of the Strategy Canvas is to try to identify new customer segments in uncontested market spaces. The idea is simply to create new markets and attract customers.

One area where the Strategy Canvas is deficient is in the identification of attributes and features for competition and differentiation. The FAD template is ideally situated for assisting in that process. The FAD template can be used as an input device for constructing the Strategy Canvas by facilitating the identification of important attributes and features on which to compete.

The following approach can be used to develop a strategic canvas:

- Use the FAD template to identify the key competitive factors in terms of product and process features including price, meaning, technology, performance, design, availability, customer support, technology, size, weight, speed, ease of use, and other product features. These key competitive factors are then placed on the X-axis of the canvas (either at the top or the bottom).

- Then, each competitor and your company are plotted on the *Y*-axis. If a competitor has a high level of a particular factor, then it is plotted above the middle of the *Y*-axis. Similarly, competitors with low levels of a factor are plotted below the middle of the *Y*-axis.

A generic Strategy Canvas with the FAD categories is illustrated in Figure 7.3. It incorporates the essential concepts from the FAD template into the development of a Strategy Canvas. Figure 7.4 illustrates how the Strategy Canvas could be used to position the Nintendo Wii. We identified what we believed is the key meaning of the Wii along with several important attributes and key design issues for the Wii. The feature categories that apply to the attributes are highlighted in bold. For example, the *Appeal to the entire Family* attribute is considered a point of differentiation and a Blue Ocean Feature. The attributes and their values are, of course, contingent on who actually constructs the Strategy Canvas and they will change very quickly according to the whims of the market. Figure 7.5 illustrates a more attractive graphic that was created using the Strategy Canvas data.

| | | Meaning of product or service↓ | BOF POD | BOF POD | BOF POD | BOF POD | BOF POD | BOF POD |
			POP EXTDIS	POP EXTDIS	POP EXTDIS	POP EXTDIS	POP EXTDIS	POP EXTDIS
Attribute name	Price		Quality					
Very High								
High								
Average								
Low								
Very Low								
Not Applicable								

Figure 7.3. Preliminary strategy canvas with FAD categories.

		Meaning of product or service↓	BOF POD POP EXT DIS	BOF POD POP EXT DIS	BOF POD POP EXT DIS	BOF POD POP EXT DIS
Attribute Name	Price	Family campfire	Ease of use	Appeal to entire family	Resolution	Disk space
Very High		Wii		Wii		
High	PS3 Xbox		Wii		PS3 Xbox	PS3
Average		PS3	PS3	PS3		Xbox
Low	Wii	Xbox	Xbox	Xbox		
Very Low					Wii	
Not Applicable						Wii

Figure 7.4. Potential strategy canvas for Nintendo Wii.

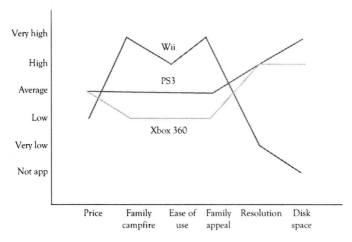

Figure 7.5. Nintendo wii strategy canvas.

Benefits of the FAD Strategy Canvas

The FAD strategic canvas can be used to determine where a company wants to differentiate themselves from the competition. The objective is to determine where you would add, delete, or change the level of a factor in order to identify a Blue Ocean. It can also be used to identify attributes or factors that could be eliminated because the product features are considered low-value, extinct, or dissatisfiers. It could of course be used to assist in identifying unique features that could be added. You can also use the ideas discussed earlier such as combining products, borrowing ideas from other industries and products, and flipping ideas.

It should also be noted that the approach can be used in conjunction with a SWOT (Strengths, Weaknesses, Opportunities, and Threats analysis) diagram to identify the major strengths and weaknesses in the design of existing and new products.

Lateral Marketing, FAD, and the Strategy Canvas

Lateral Marketing, a related concept found in the marketing literature, can also be used to assist in identifying Blue Ocean markets. The goal of lateral marketing[21] is to help create new markets by:

- trying to reach a new set of customers by radically changing the product features either by adding or subtracting features;

- trying to identify substitute products or services that can compete with an existing product or service;
- trying to identify complementary products and services for existing lines;
- trying to reposition a product by having it satisfy different needs for different market segments.

The lateral marketing approach along with the other ideas presented in this chapter complements the Blue Ocean approach as a mechanism for identifying how product features can be added, subtracted, and adapted to create innovative products and services. Not all products and services introduced will be Blue Oceans; nevertheless, the approach using the FAD template and the Strategy Canvas will certainly provide a useful tool for understanding the positioning of your products and your competitors.

Marketing research is a complementary and systematic avenue for identifying key attributes and marketing opportunities for products and services. The literature describes a number of approaches for identifying what features are relevant to consumers:

- Brainstorm to identify a superset of existing and future product and service features
- Use auctions to identify what products and features are relevant to consumers
- Develop consumer surveys and sampling approaches
- Ask consumers what features they think are important
- Ask consumers to evaluate, compare, and rank the features they deem important in a product and service
- Use statistical analysis to disentangle and understand the relationships between customer wants and product features
- Look at consumer and editorial reviews and try to understand what features of a product or service appear to be attracting people.

For additional and more detailed insight into the concepts and approaches for conducting market research, you are encouraged to read

Naresh K. Malhotra and David F. Birk's very thorough book on the topic[22] and the Cavusgil, Knight, Riesenberger, and Yaprak[23] book on conducting international marketing research.

Developing Blue Ocean Markets from Complementary Products and Services

Many innovative products and services are actually complements of the original products. The innovation can be an add-on feature, an after-market service, or a different product or service. Transportation devices have spurred the development of substitute energy sources such as steam, electric, fuel cells, and solar energy. The automobile was the driving force behind the development of better roads, fueling stations, diners, and truck stops. The development of better sailing ships led to the need for complementary devices for navigation tools such as maps, star maps, compasses, sextants, and GPSs. The FAD template and the Strategy Canvas can also be used to identify competitive complementary products and services.

Avoid the Swiss Army Knife Approach to Product Differentiation

One model of the Wenger Swiss Army knife, called the *Giant*, has 87 tools, performs 141 functions, and costs $1,400.[24] If you were sent to a deserted island and were limited to what you could bring, that knife would certainly be on a short list of must-have items. The Giant was probably introduced because Wenger could introduce it and also because it creates a great image in the mind of consumers. Wenger has excellent engineering skills. In general, however, specialized tools perform better than the all-in-one tool. There is a trade-off between having everything in one place that is readily accessible and having superb capabilities and functionality. The cork-screw, the scissors, the magnifier, the golf club cleaner, and the wire cutter in a Swiss Army knife are OK, but they are not the best tools for doing the respective jobs.

Wireless phones have become the Swiss Army knife for communication, networking, and entertainment. Not all the implements (camera, music playing, video, net interface, retail showroom and purchasing, gaming, GPS, social networking, and communications) are stellar; they are, however, always available to the user. Apple has been very successful at integrating features on the iPhone, the iPad, and their other products that are attractive to their customers, but they are very cautious in adding features for feature sake.[25] Some of the hubris exhibited by Apple is attributable to the cache of the superb Apple brand. But there is a secret sauce for Apple's success. There are strong design principles at work at Apple, involving minimalism, attention to quality, and focusing on the design of a high-quality user interface. Apple is also very big on attaching meaning to their entire product portfolio. Their commercials exude the development of meaning. The Flip Mino video camera was once very successful because it was simple and very easy to use. The very young and the old are always looking for easy-to-use products and services.

Feature creep occurs when a new feature is added and many of the old features are retained. Sometimes features are beneficial. Sometimes they become vestigial and forever encoded in the DNA of the product or service. They are like vestigial physical characteristics in human beings that are no longer needed. For example, humans have tailbones or coccyx, but they do not have tails. Once a feature is in place, it is difficult to remove it because some company will use the features to illustrate how they have more features than competition. Automobile GPSs illustrate how feature creep occurs over time. Feature creep has been the boom and the boon of companies that produce automobile GPS applications. Figure 7.6 illustrates the numerous product features that can be found in automobile GPS products. It is unlikely that many people are using the MP3 and photo players on their auto GPSs to play music or view photos, but these features have crept into many of the units sold by GPS manufacturers. The point is that there are instances where it might make sense to scale back on features because the features are either truly vestigial or overkill. This would also reduce the cognitive burden facing consumers because of the numerous choice points. Sometimes the vestigial features hinder design changes and can adversely affect the ability to add new features that are truly valuable to the consumer. One of the greatest impediments facing hardware and software developers in redesigning systems is in maintaining backward compatibility.

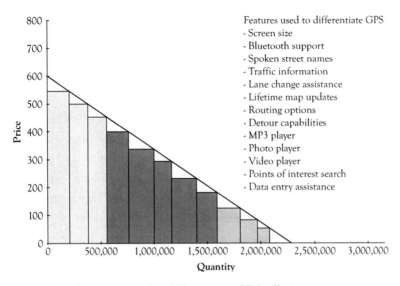

Figure 7.6. Features used to differentiate GPS offerings.

Conclusion

Successful product development should involve both UDD that is focused on consumer wants and needs and MDD that is predicated on understanding the emotional and psychological relationships that people have on products as well as incorporating the importance of new technological developments (TDD). We have also introduced the FAD template. The FAD template is based on the various design approaches and also draws on a classification scheme that can be used to ascertain whether attributes and features are increasing or declining in importance. The FAD template in conjunction with the Strategy Canvas can be used to assist in taking an abstract product concept and preparing a first-cut prototype of the product. The key points are the following:

- The focus of MDD allows the innovators to develop ideas that transcend existing product concepts, conceiving product ideas as a vision rather than only on product differentiation.
- Concentrating on function and ignoring user input is a recipe for failure.
- Identifying key meanings, attributes, and features is an essential step in MDD, including the customer relationship

to the product, quality, reliability, ease-of-use, performance, design, technology, and most importantly, value creation and meaning.

- The meaning of a product or service is very much tied into what the product does.
- Attributes of a product to help users control either their internal or external environments have the power to make a significant impact.
- Psychological ownership of a product promotes user attachment and use, keeping users locked into the product out of loyalty.
- Attending to POPS as well as PODS is necessary to keep your product competitive. POPS ensure that your product meets the minimal essential features. PODS are necessary for distinguishing a product from the competition.
- Disruptive technologies and sunrise features are the dawn of new technological and conceptual capabilities.
- Use the FAD template to facilitate and provide structure when conceptualizing new products and services.
- Create a FAD Strategy Canvas to understand the attributes of your product in the context of your current and potential competitors.
- Seriously consider your feature list in terms of must-haves, points of differentiation, and vestigial features. Try to avoid feature creep, which involves adding features just for the sake of adding new features.

EXHIBIT 1

FAD Template

1. **Product or service description (what will it do or what is its function?). What type of customer or customer segment(s) are you targeting?**

2. **What is the meaning(s) behind the product or service?**

    Potential meanings: The product or service provides physical, health, religious, and emotional sustenance; provides feelings of being needed or being listened to; supports artistic and creative needs; facilitates control over the environment; provides entertainment; supports feelings of status, superiority, and elitism; provides a sense of stewardship; supports feelings of closeness to the earth and being organic; provides a sense of altruism; supports feelings of adventure; supports gender needs; supports feelings of security and comfort; facilitates and assists in the completion of some work or home task; provides feelings of familial support; helps an individual or a community to learn and adapt; helps us to change location; provides an opportunity for communication and networking; has above-average intrinsic value to some or many people; provides for respect and recognition; and finally, the product or service is a source of satisfaction, happiness, and hope.

3. **Identify potential product and service attributes, features, and functions. Here are some ideas for the attributes, features, and functions:**

    Price: How much does it cost?

Quality: How well does the product or service conform to the product specifications? Does the product do what it says it is supposed to do in the user manual? Is it effective in performing its function?

Reliability: Does the product or service perform as it is supposed to over its expected life? Is it prone to failure? Is it easily maintained?

Ease-of-use: Is the product or service easy to use and can consumers learn to use it without much trouble?

Performance: Is the product or service faster, smaller, more convenient, greater capacity, better resolution, compatible, and adaptable? Which features, functions, and processes are unique or distinguishing?

Design: Is the external form attractive? Is it visually, tactilely, audibly, and olfactorily attractive? Is the product packaged properly? Is the service experience attractive and positive from the consumer's perspective? Does the product or service suggest a certain meaning?

Technology: Is there an emerging technology or a process that can improve quality, reliability, ease-of-use, performance, value, design, and meaning?

Value creation: Is there any intrinsic value in the product that distinguishes it from other products or services? Does it solve a problem that consumers want to solve and will attract them to the product or service?

4. **List the key attributes, features, and functions that will be focused on and, in particular, those that reinforce or detract from the meaning. Attribute can be in more than one category. Attributes can refer to the product you are planning to introduce and to existing products,**

Points of parity and must-haves (POPS): List the attributes, features, and functions that most of the products or services in a category usually have.

Points of difference and differentiators (PODs): List the attributes, features, and functions of a product that distinguish it from the competition.

Blue Ocean features and exciters (BOFs): List the sunrise attributes, features, and functions that could be used to develop a new Blue Ocean market.

Extinct and vestigial features (EXTs): List the sunset attributes, features, and functions that are no longer necessary or on the verge of becoming extinct for the product or service.

Dissatisfiers (DISs): List the attributes, features, and functions that can cause some consumers to avoid using your product or your competitor's product.

Design and Prototype Product or Service

Put a mock-up picture of the product or service here (use sketching, drawing software, mock-up software, photo software, or presentation software). If the product is a software, put an example of a critical report or input screen here (use a word processor or presentation software). If the idea behind the product or service involves a complex process or business process, then draw a flow diagram or a business process diagram (use presentation software or specialized flowchart and business process diagramming software).

APPENDIX 1

Examples of Prototypes

Decision support system: location tracking, alerting the chance of disease occurring, micro-climate, web based solution

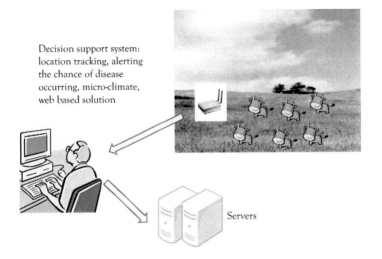

Servers

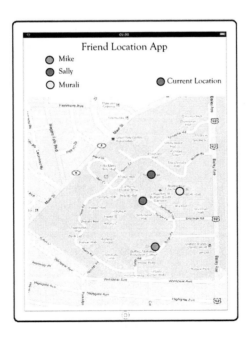

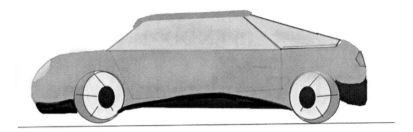

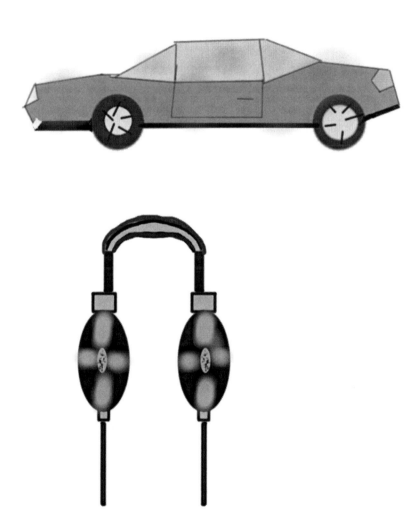

APPENDIX 2

FAD Template for Wine Aging Product

1. **Product or service description (what will it do or what is its function?) What type of customer or customer segment(s) are you targeting?**

   > Uses some type of technology to age inexpensive wines and make them more pleasant. Considering using an electromagnet with a specific magnetic field strength. The potential target customers are wine connoisseurs and individuals interested in fine wine.

2. **What is the meaning(s) behind the product or service?**

   > Appeals to status.

   Potential Meanings: The product or service provides physical, health, religious, and emotional sustenance; provides feelings of being needed or being listened to; supports artistic and creative needs; facilitates control over the environment; provides entertainment; supports feelings of status, superiority, and elitism; provides a sense of stewardship; supports feelings of closeness to the earth and being organic; provides a sense of altruism; supports feelings of adventure; supports gender needs; supports feelings of security and comfort; facilitates and assists in the completion of some work or home task; provides feelings of familial support; helps an individual or a community to learn and adapt; helps us to change location; provides an opportunity for communication and networking; has above-average intrinsic value to some or many people; provides for respect and recognition; and finally, the product or service is a source of satisfaction, happiness and hope.

3. **Identify potential product and service attributes, features, and functions. Here are some ideas for the attributes, features, and functions:**

Price: How much does it cost?

> Unsure but will have two versions priced at $300 and $1,000 price level.

Quality: How well does the product or service conform to the product specifications? Does the product do what it says it is supposed to do in the user manual? Is it effective in performing its function?

> Need to test the effectiveness of the technology in a research setting.

Reliability: Does the product or service perform as it is supposed to over its expected life? Is it prone to failure? Is it easily maintained?

> Unsure. Plan on having a refrigerator function in the high-end version.

Ease-of-use: Is the product or service easy to use and can consumers learn to use it without much trouble?

> Will have either knobs or a digital key pad to program the aging time.

Performance: Is the product or service faster, smaller, more convenient, greater capacity, better resolution, compatible, and adaptable? Which features, functions, and processes are unique or distinguishing?

> We are optimistic that it will be faster than existing wine aging products. Will also have greater capacity than existing products.

Design: Is the external form attractive? Is it visually, tactilely, audibly, and olfactorily attractive? Is the product packaged properly? Is the service experience attractive and positive from the consumer's perspective? Does the product or service suggest a certain meaning?

The high-end model will look like a high-end, high-tech refrigerator.

Technology: Is there an emerging technology or a process that can improve quality, reliability, ease-of–use, performance, value, design, and meaning?

Unsure. However, our approach could be ineffective.

Value Creation: Is there some intrinsic value in the product that distinguishes it from other products or services? Does the product or service solve a problem that consumers want to solve and will the solution attract them to the product or service?

It may attract wine enthusiasts because it has the potential to improve the taste of all wines We also think that it will also appeal to buyers of wine storage devices including refrigerators and coolers.

4. **List the key attributes, features, and functions that will be focused on and, in particular, those that reinforce or detract from the meaning. Attribute can be in more than one category. Attributes can refer to the product you are planning to introduce and to existing products,**

Points of parity and must-haves (POPS): List the attributes, features, and functions that most of the products or services in a category usually have.

Capable of aging			

Points of difference and differentiators (PODs): List the attributes, features, and functions of a product that distinguish it from the competition.

Sophistication aging technology. Aging refrigerator available.	High-tech design		

Blue Ocean features and exciters (BOFs): List the sunrise attributes, features, and functions that could be used to develop a new Blue Ocean market.

Sophistication aging technology	High-tech design		

Extinct and vestigial features (EXTs): List the sunset attributes, features, and functions that are no longer necessary or on the verge of becoming extinct for the product or service.

Traditional wine aging process	

Dissatisfiers (DISs): List the attributes, features, and functions that can cause some consumers to avoid using your product or your competitor's product.

Does not age wine	

Design and Prototype Product or Service

Put a mock-up picture of the product or service here (use sketching, drawing software, mock-up software, photo software, or presentation software). If the product is a software, put an example of a critical report or input screen here (use a word processor or presentation software). If the idea behind the product or service involves a complex process or business process, then draw a flow diagram or a business process diagram (use presentation software or specialized flowchart and business process diagramming software).

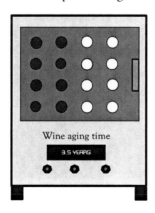

CHAPTER 8

Strategic Planning Approaches for Product Differentiation and Innovation

To be strategic is to have plans of action that provide directions for operating in an uncertain world. In this section, our focus is on developing strategic plans to compete in a world characterized by monopolistic competition. Notice that the emphasis is on plans of action and not on a single plan. There is no single plan or single planning approach that can deal with the complexity of contemporary markets. What is needed is a continuous process for churning out new plans, for differentiated products and services, in order to compete in a dynamic environment. This chapter presents a brief overview of the various approaches to strategic planning and provides an overview of the planning literature. There is a lot of material to slog through, but each approach to planning has something to offer. This overview will set the stage for presenting the Ten–Ten planning process in the next chapter. The next chapter will integrate the various planning approaches and present a simplified, yet robust approach to planning called the Ten–Ten planning process. The key benefit of the Ten–Ten planning process is that it can be used for developing business plans in a very short time span.

Planning Concepts

There are two generic planning strategies that a business can pursue.[1] It can strive to be efficient, it can differentiate, or both. In other words, a firm can focus on delivering Midas versions of products, Hermes versions of products, or both. A firm that employs a strategy of efficiency strives to be the low-cost producer and compete on the basis of charging less than the other competitors. In contrast, a firm that is competing on the basis of product differentiation can charge premium prices. If charging premium prices yields larger-than-average profits, the market will, of course, attract attentions. Competitors will enter the market with a slightly different product, perhaps even a better product, at a lower price and ultimately drive down the premium prices. The firm will then have to embark on further cost-cutting initiatives, improve their product in order to hold on to market share and survive, or do both. The market is relentless and it demands a two-pronged approach of developing differentiated products and services and cutting costs.

The first mantra of the entrepreneur is "differentiate through innovation or perish" or in simpler terms "differentiate or die." The second mantra of the entrepreneur is "strive to reduce costs." The first mantra is accomplished by focusing on Midas versions of products using extravagant engineering and design. Differentiation is the not only engine driving business success under monopolistic competition, but it is also buttressed by attempting to improve costs and product design through frugal engineering. The second mantra is accomplished by focusing on Hermes versions of products using frugal engineering.

As noted earlier, over 99% of the approximately 23 million businesses compete in markets that are characterized by monopolistic competition. That is there are many buyers, many sellers, market entry and exit is easy, and the products are closely related but not identical. There are the two approaches for differentiating products. The first uses marketing and advertising to develop a brand. The second approach is to engage in product development through some sort of research and development (R&D) process and to develop goods and services with updated features. Both approaches are necessary parts of the differentiation process. Marketing and advertising can help illustrate the features and can sometimes delay encroachment by the competition. But in the long run (probably less than a year), successful differentiation depends on product development and R&D.

The Planning Process

Planning can be accomplished in a variety of ways. Figure 8.1 presents a typical model of the strategic planning process.[2] The *mantra* is an often-repeated phrase that provides the basis for the existence of the company. It is a slogan, a watchword, a byword, or a motto that breathes life into the firm's existence. The mantra is not a replacement for the mission statement. The *mission* statement is an overall view of the business at an abstract level. It describes what the company does and why it exists and how it satisfies customer needs. The mission statement can also include a statement reflecting whether the company will focus on product differentiation and niche markets, focus on being price-competitive, or focus on both. The mantra and the mission are rarely static but ever-changing and emerging throughout the life of the firm.

The essence of the planning process consists of looking-inside and looking-outside analysis. *Analysis* involves both introspection and extrospection. The *internal* and *external* organization environments are examined using a number of analytical approaches, several of which are included in Table 8.1. These techniques will be covered in the next section. There is a lot of confusion related to identifying goals and objectives. Many view the terms goals and objectives to be interchangeable. *Goals* are more abstract and broader than objectives. *Objectives* are generally more detailed. The important point that will be discussed in the next chapter is to identify the goals and objectives that will help support the mantra, the mission, and the value proposition over a certain time

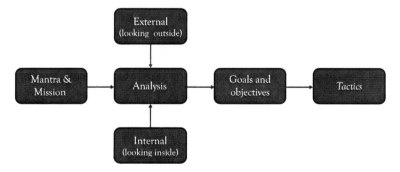

Figure 8.1. The planning process (adapted from May).

Table 8.1. Orientations of Strategic Planning Approaches

	Inter organizational focus	External competitive environments focus	Time to execute
Value and supply chain analysis	High	Low	Moderate
Porter's five force model	Low	High	Long
Resource-based framework	High	Moderate	Long
Strategy maps	High	Moderate	Long
Creating Blue Ocean markets using the strategy canvas	Moderate to high	Moderate to high	Short
SWOT analysis	Moderate to high	Moderate to high	Short

frame. The *tactics* are the activities the organization will use over the next 3 months to a year to reach their goals and objectives. The tactics can include timetables and schedules related to the goals and objectives. The key to the model in Figure 8.1 is that this is not a linear process. Sometimes a new mission emerges after analysis has been completed. Mission statements that change, reflect an organization that can adapt to dynamic environments.

We will revisit the definitions in the next chapter and illustrate how the planning process can be streamlined and made more efficient and facilitate the development of business plans in a very short time span using the Ten–Ten planning process.

Analytical Approaches for Strategic Planning

There are a number of analytical approaches that can be used to develop a process for churning out new plans for differentiation. We will review several of the more popular strategic planning approaches because they all provide insights into the differentiation process. A discussion of planning concepts can be at times boring; however, such discussion is also crucial for developing good plans.

The approaches to be discussed include value chain and supply chain analysis, Porter's five-force model, the resource-based framework, the use of Strategy Maps, creating Blue Ocean markets using the Strategy Canvas, and SWOT (Strengths, Weaknesses, Opportunities, and Threats) analysis. As illustrated in Table 8.1, each of the approaches can be classified as having an internal organizational focus (looking inside) or an external environmental focus (looking outside). Several of the strategic analysis approaches are better for understanding the organization and others are better suited for understanding the competitive environment. This table illustrates that there is no "best" approach for conducting strategic analysis and that a combination of approaches is necessary for completing an examination of the inner workings of an organization as well as the organizational context. Each of the strategic analysis tools will be covered in this chapter.

Value Chain and Supply Chain Analysis

Value chain analysis is a framework developed by Michael Porter that divides the company into primary and secondary activities related to delivering a product or service.[3] The primary activities include inbound logistics, operations, sales and marketing, and outbound logistics. The secondary activities are supporting activities and include the firm infrastructure, human resources, information technology, and procurement. Figure 8.2 illustrates the components of the value chain.

A closely related concept is the supply chain. A supply chain is defined as the connected activities related to the creation of a product or service up through the delivery of the product to the customer. It includes upstream suppliers as well as downstream activities such as wholesalers and distribution warehouses. Figure 8.3 illustrates the supply chain.

In general, the terms value chain and supply chain can be used interchangeably; although the value chain is rooted in the strategic planning literature, the supply chain is linked to the work in the operations management area. The key concept is that products and services have to be created and eventually delivered to consumers and the in-between activities can be referred to as the supply chain or the value chain.

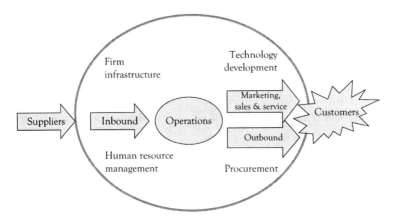

Figure 8.2. The value chain (adapted from Porter).

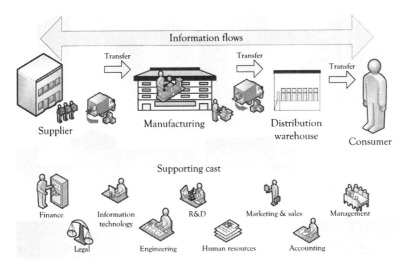

Figure 8.3. Supply chain.

The supply chain is an important visual tool because it can be used to understand where to look for processes that can be reengineered. That is, improvements can be made in connecting, coordinating, and controlling activities across linkages. It can also be used to determine what kind of information should be gathered to improve communications throughout the value chain and where value chain performance could be improved. For example, the firm can investigate where information technology can be marshaled to support the supply chain activity and where technology can be used to automate tasks. The goal, of course, is to reduce transaction costs up and down the supply chain.[4] Transaction costs refer to the effort that goes into choosing, organizing, negotiating, and entering into agreements for products and services.[5] Transaction costs come in a variety of flavors and there is significant overlap among the various costs.

- *Search costs*: In general, these costs are related to gathering information on a product or service, including the costs associated with locating a product and offering a product for sale.
- *Discovery costs*: These costs are involved in locating an acceptable price for a product.
- *Decision costs*: These costs are associated with making a decision on what product to purchase. These include personal cognitive effort and organizational decision processes related to selecting a product or service.
- *Negotiation costs*: These costs are related to agreeing to the terms of a contract including the price, what will be delivered, how much, and when.
- *Acquisition costs*: These costs are involved in transporting, receiving, infrastructure development, and managing the product in inventory.
- *Enforcement costs*: These are the costs that the parties in the contract incur in order to enforce the terms of the contract.
- *Settlement costs*: These are the costs related to paying and getting paid for a product or service.
- *Social costs*: These include costs that are not necessarily picked up by the buyers and the sellers. Examples include pollution costs, health costs, privacy costs, and bankruptcy costs.

Porter's Five-Force Model

Michael Porter has also developed a technique for assessing the desirability of competing in a particular industry and how a firm can compete in that industry.[6] Porter's five-force framework considers the buyers, the sellers, the suppliers, the current competition, and the threat of competition from substitute products. The key idea is that a firm can be more profitable by understanding how the five forces influence the competitive environment, as will be explained next.

Threat of new entrants. This is the degree to which entry into an industry is easy to accomplish. If it is easy to enter an industry and start competing, then there is a threat of new entrants. If an industry has high fixed costs, such as in the case of semiconductor manufacturing, auto manufacturing, or operating systems construction, then there is a low threat of entry. This is in contrast to the situation where entry is easy and relatively inexpensive such as found in online retail stores, home maintenance businesses, and restaurants.

Entry into a market can of course be precluded because of the scarcity of expertise and resources. For example, in the late 1990s, there were very few individuals with expertise in Enterprise Resource Planning systems and in COBOL to handle the Y2K date problem. Numerous firms turned toward India and Singapore to find employees with skills in these areas.[7] Resource scarcity can also limit entry into a market. Examples of industries where resource scarcity is critical include diamond mining, where DeBeers owns a substantial amount of the diamond resources, and oil production where Exxon has access to oil production and installed refining capability.

Threat of substitute products. Substitute products are a constant threat in contemporary commerce. If another product can be substituted for a product in the industry under consideration, then there is a threat of substitute products. It is sometimes impossible to know where your competition will come from. For example, video and audio content can be delivered via satellite, wireless, coax cable, cat 5, and fiber optics. The content can in turn be delivered to a variety of devices including mobile phones, televisions, IPODs/MP3 players, game consoles, DVRs, and computers. A similar situation exists for transportation. You can travel via electric car, bus, and air and, in the future, by way of a personal jet craft or some type of Segway device. Indeed content delivery can be a substitute for transportation. As video and audio becomes more robust and easy to use, it may be possible to be there without actually being there. Families will soon get together by linking-up and interacting with their plasma and LCD screens using a high bandwidth carrier to communicate video and audio feeds of a birthday party or anniversary. This has already occurred in businesses with the emergence of virtual meetings. This brings up another issue. People set aside a certain amount of dollars for entertainment. However, although technology is not a perfect substitute for entertainment outside of the home, it can be a substitute for spending on entertainment. Thus, a console or a game might threaten the launching of a new movie during the holidays or vice versa.

Bargaining power of buyers. If individuals, companies, or groups of companies can influence the price and the features required in a product or service, then the buyers have the bargaining power. This often occurs when there are few buyers or when the buyer is large. The auto companies have bargaining power over the component manufactures. The same goes for Dell's component suppliers and Wal-Mart's suppliers. When a buyer is large and switching costs are small, then the buyer has the bargaining power. Wal-Mart is in such a position with its suppliers. Dell, however, has less buyer power because it cannot simply switch the component suppliers because desktops systems are built around integrated components and the performance of the system can be adversely impacted when components are not integrated.

Bargaining power of suppliers. If a company supplying a product or service can dictate the terms of the transaction, then the supplier has the bargaining power. The bargaining power of suppliers can be derived from many factors including the scarcity of the resource or technology, the number of suppliers, the characteristics and features of the technology, whether the technology is proprietary, and even the brand image. Intel and Microsoft have some bargaining power over Dell, but the hard drive, dram, motherboard, and monitor manufacturers have less bargaining power. The power supply and case manufacturers have even less bargaining power with Dell. The game console and global positioning system (GPS) manufactures have some power over Wal-Mart when they introduce a new model, but a holiday candle manufacturer has much less power. In many ways, the bargaining power is related to the threat of new entrants and the threat of substitute products or services. The key issue surrounding the bargaining power of suppliers is the availability of other sources of the products and services. If alternative or second sourcing is available, then the bargaining power of the supplier is lessened.

Rivalry among existing competitors. This is the degree to which there is competition among the firms. When there are several competitors and the products they are selling are fairly standard or readily obtainable and the competitors cannot easily leave the industry, then the rivalry will be intense. Examples of intense rivalries include breakfast cereals, flash memory, dram and electronics industries, housing construction, online and offline retailing, and the airline industry. Intense rivalries among competitors are again driven by the threat of new entrants and the threat of substitute products and services. In this context, product differentiation is essential in order to reduce the ruinous effect of perfect competition. This is the reason that the producers of GPS systems are constantly refining and adding features to their product line. Airlines, breakfast cereal producers, and the housing industry are constantly looking for ways to differentiate their offerings and at the same time reduce costs.

The Five-Force Model in Practice

The five-force model can be used as the basis for conducting an industry analysis. The goal of an industry analysis is to understand the dynamics of competition and to ascertain how the five forces influence profitability. The following steps are used for conducting an industry analysis:

- Develop a brief description of the target industry
- Identify the competitors, buyers, suppliers, potential entrants, and potential substitutes
- Determine the strength and weaknesses of the forces
- Identify any recent changes in the dynamics of the forces
- Determine the potential for short- and long-term profitability
- Ascertain who in the industry is positioned to be profitable
- Determine where the organization should invest.

Porter's five-force model provides an overarching view of the competitive environment and is extremely helpful for understanding the competitive environment. It does, however, have several deficiencies. First of all, it takes a long time to conduct a full-blown expose of the five forces because many devotees to the approach tend to overanalyze the industry and the competition. This in turn leads to organizational fatigue. Overanalysis is related to the second deficiency. The ideas are very abstract and broad, and the technique requires consulting expertise in order to be applied effectively. Finally, it takes too long to implement for small organizations. For the entrepreneur working under extreme pressure, under the umbrella of monopolistic competition, there is very little time to attend to apply the approach effectively. Even though Porter's ideas are very powerful, they do not resonate with the entrepreneur because they are abstract and difficult to apply.

Resource-based Framework

The resource-based view, also referred to as RBV, is very popular with academics. The intellectual foundations for the RBV approach are many, but the work by Prahalad and Hamel on core competencies[8] and the work by Barney[9] on the link between resources and sustained competitive advantage established a strong foundation. The basic idea of RBV is that some organizations are more competitive because they have access to unique resources or special capabilities and competencies. Resources can be tangible or intangible and include raw materials, land, brand, knowledge and expertise of people, reputation with customers and suppliers, plants, equipments, patents, trademarks, copyrights, and funds. A capability or competence is the ability of a firm to turn its resources into customer value and profits. Capabilities or competencies can be manufacturing prowess, order fulfillment and delivery, customer service, marketing, finance and accounting, management expertise and leadership, and in essence any proficiency or prowess in the supply chain and value chain.

Porter's force model, and the accompanying industry analysis, tends to focus on locating a firm in an attractive industry and then taking steps to achieve competitive advantage over rival firms. In contrast, the RBV approach suggests focusing on competitive arenas where the firm has unique resources and competencies. For example, if you own property with rich productive topsoil, if your workers are diligent, and if your daughter is an excellent agronomist, you will probably be a successful farmer. The key to being successful in the context of RBV is that the resources and competencies are hard to imitate and help to establish a strong basis for competitive advantage. In essence, the status of the internal resources and competencies will assist in pursuing a particular strategic direction. Amazon has a core competency in selling online and it simply kept pursing that competency by selling construction tools, electronics, audio books, eBooks, and developing partnerships with brick and mortar vendors. Most of Google's successful ventures are related to its core competency of *search*. Joan's foray into the jewelry box business discussed earlier was linked to her excellent craftsman skills. Joan had a core competency in jewelry box design and fine woodworking.

Core competencies are the very critical skills that define an organization. For Google, it is their search capability, for Amazon it is their ability to sell online, and for Joan it is her prowess at jewelry box design and her knowledge of the marketplace. In the case of Joan, her knowledge and skills can probably be imitated and replicated in a shorter time frame than the competencies developed by Amazon and Google. But of course, Joan's jewelry box business is more agile and can change direction much faster than Amazon and Google. Eventually, all capabilities and competencies (even Amazon and Google's) can be imitated, replicated, and improved. Even scarce resources and monopolies can succumb to the onslaught of new technology, time, and market forces. There are substitutes for oil, diamonds, and operating systems.

The RBV is a powerful idea for understanding strategic direction, but it has several deficiencies. First of all, it is very broad in scope and hard to implement as part of a concrete business plan. Delineating the unique capabilities, competencies, and resources and then using this information in strategic planning are time-consuming. In addition, there is little guidance on how to build competencies. Indeed, some theorists believe that core competencies cannot be built but simply emerge. For additional discussion on RBV, see Henry[10] and Grant.[11] Later on, we will discuss how this approach can be effectively integrated with SWOT analysis and, in the next chapter, we will discuss how this approach can be integrated with the Ten–Ten planning process.

Strategy Maps

A strategy map is a visual diagram that represents a causal structure of an organizational strategy. The strategy map is an outgrowth of the balanced scorecard approach developed by Robert Kaplan and David Norton.[12] The purpose of the balanced scorecard is to develop a series of measurable performance indicators that are linked and aligned with organizational missions and objectives. Measurement at the operational and tactical levels is a key part of the balanced scorecard approach and essential for developing and benchmarking best practices. Measurement can be used to identify where management should redirect its attention and also to identify whether best practices are already in place.

There are four primary areas where performance indicators can be used. They are the financial performance indicators, customer performance indicators, performance indicators related to internal organizational processes, and performance indicators related to the ability of the organization and employees to innovate and learn. The strategy map is an overview of the causal relationships related to the four perspectives. Figure 8.4 is an example of a strategy map for a railroad. You are encouraged to use Google's image search using the keyword strategy map for additional examples.

In general, the balanced scorecard/strategy maps approach is more suitable for older larger organizations with a lot of time for developing and executing a strategic plan. Kaplan and Norton point out that a strategy map presents an integrated overview of the outcome measures and the performance drivers of outcomes using cause-and-effect relationships. The strategy map can serve as a strategic measurement system and strategic control system that align departmental and personal goals with overall strategy.[13] There are, however, problems in assumptions and the time it takes to implement the approach.[14] The first problem is that the approach is too hierarchical and not particularly suitable for dynamic and complex environments. Some researchers also question the causal relationships among the variables. For example, are there causal links related to enhancing cost control leading to increases in the rate competitiveness, which in turn are leading to improvements in customer satisfaction?[15] In essence, does cost control always lead to customer satisfaction through competitiveness? One hopes that this is the case, but it is not easy to verify from both research and practice perspectives.

The major problem from an entrepreneurial perspective is that the balanced scorecard approach using strategy maps approach is very complex and difficult to implement. In general, strategy maps and the balanced scorecard approach are more applicable to relatively mature

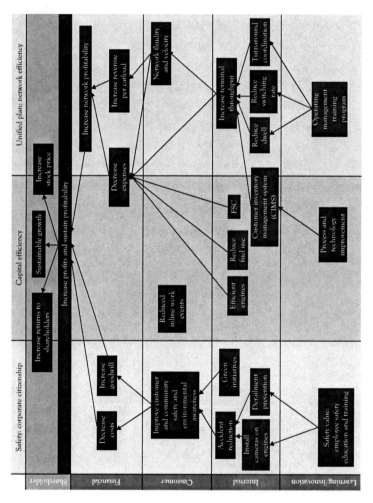

Figure 8.4. Example of a strategy map for a railroad. from the public sector, permission of Wikimedia Commons License Agreement, http://commons.wikimedia.org/wiki/File:Strategy Map.jpg.

companies and are not conducive to new venture development. New ventures, whether they are intrapreneurial or entrepreneurial, need a more adaptive and agile approach. A customer orientation, with an attention to securing and reducing the cash burn rate, a focus on executing the plan by attending to developing internal processes, and focusing on R&D and learning are the most important takeaways from the balanced scorecard/ strategy maps approach.

Creating Blue Ocean Markets Using the Strategy Canvas

As noted throughout the earlier chapters we believe that the Blue Ocean concept is an important contribution to the strategic planning literature.[16] The idea is very similar to the so-called killer-app concept and lateral marketing approach. The goal of the Blue Ocean approach is to identify uncontested market spaces for profit and growth rather than compete in traditional Red Ocean market spaces where there is a tendency to focus on either cost-cutting or differentiation. Table 8.2 illustrates how the concepts developed in the book with Midas, Atlas, and Hermes products relate to the Blue Ocean concepts. This process of developing Blue Ocean market is facilitated by developing the Strategy Canvas and by using the FAD template as an input into the Strategy Canvas.

This is in contrast to the competitive strategy approach where a large and growing already-served market is identified and the entering firm tries to find a way to compete. Several research projects have been conducted on the efficacy of the Blue Ocean approach, and the results suggest that organizations pursuing Blue Ocean markets can in some instances be successful. A Blue Ocean strategy that is focused on intense innovation and on product differentiation and brand creation has been found to be profitable.[17] The Blue Ocean approach apparently helps to insulate a firm from intense competition. In many instances, Blue Oceans are not completely blue, but rather have patches of red. The net effect is that it is sometimes necessary to find a niche in a large market and then use Porter's five-forces model to assess the desirability of competing in a particular industry and how a firm can compete in that industry. The key idea is that a firm can be more profitable by understanding how the

Table 8.2. Red Versus Blue Ocean Strategy

Red Ocean	Blue Ocean
The major goal is to best the competition in an already established market space.	The major goal is to make the competition irrelevant and superfluous by developing a new product or service in a new market space.
Compete on the existing demand curve in the existing market space. Growth is slow.	Compete and capture a new uncontested demand curve in a new market space. Growth is above average.
Develop either Midas, Atlas or Hermes products and services	Develop and introduce Midas, Altas and Hermes products and services
Focused on product differentiation or being a low cost producer	Focused on product differentiation and also being a low cost producer.
Focused on cost cutting, outsourcing, brand management, and advertising.	Focused on research, product design, and learning.

five forces influence the competitive environment. The most important part of the Blue Ocean approach is that is to assist in identifying strategic opportunities for product differentiation using the Strategy Canvas. This was discussed in an earlier chapter where we used the FAD template to develop a Strategic Canvas for the Nintendo Wii.

SWOT Analysis

The genesis of the SWOT approach to strategic planning is usually attributed to Albert S. Humphrey during his tenure with the Stanford Research Institute.[18] Even though the SWOT technique can trace its roots to the 1960s, it is still an important and useful tool that it is constantly evolving and improving to deal with the ever-increasing complexity of contemporary markets.

The objective of a SWOT analysis is to facilitate the development of a strategy for completing a new venture, completing a large-scale project, and diagnosing deficiencies in an existing organization by taking its temperature in a particular environmental context. A SWOT diagram consists of four quadrants (see Figure 8.5). The upper two quadrants relate the internal strengths and weaknesses of the organization. The bottom two

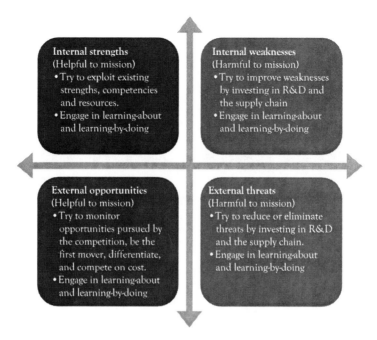

Figure 8.5. SWOT diagram.

quadrants relate to the external organizational environment in terms of the opportunities and threats faced by the organization in the marketplace.

One of the benefits of SWOT is that it can be used to analyze the organization as well as the organizational environment in order to identify areas of competitiveness and areas that need attention. It is a very useful tool for looking inside and looking outside to identify the state of the organization and the competitive environment. In an ideal situation, it draws on organizational constituencies and scans the external environment for opportunities and threats. Several examples of how SWOT can be used to analyze the strategic context are presented below.

Example 1: iPhone 4

Figure 8.6 illustrates a SWOT analysis for Apple's iPhone 4. Substitute products are the greatest threat; however, Apple has been able to counterbalance such encroachment by paying attention to product differentiation through research and product development and, of course, the coolness index.

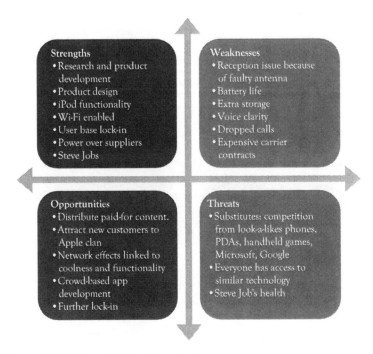

Figure 8.6. iPhone 4 SWOT analysis.

Example 2: Dell's Entrance Into the Chinese Computer Market

Dell decided to enter the Chinese PC market in the 1990s. They faced many impediments to entering such a complex environment. Figure 8.7 illustrates a hypothetical SWOT analysis for Dell as they embark into the Chinese PC market. The Dell supply chain is top-notch as well as their strong commitment to R&D. They have numerous business process patents as well as product patents. One of the earlier knocks on Dell was that the Chinese culture was not conducive to Dell's golden rules of disdaining inventory, always selling directly, and always listening to the customer. They have subsequently begun to listen to the customer and have started to sell through retail outlets.

Integrated SWOT Analysis

Even though a SWOT analysis is fairly easy to understand and apply, it is not necessarily easy to develop a good one. One of the primary criticisms of SWOT is that it leads to a large laundry list of strengths, weaknesses, opportunities, and threat factors. It is also criticized because it lacks

Strengths
• Supply Chain and just-intime manufacturing
• Customer service
• Research and development
• Product customization
• Brand

Weaknesses
• Knowledge of Chinese government
• Knowledge of culture and people
• Adherence to Dell's golden rules

Opportunities
• Market size
• Growing demand

Threats
• Threat of copycat systems
• Intellectual property protection
• Chinese government
• Intense competition
• Wages and payment systems

Figure 8.7. SWOT analysis for Dell entering China.

direction and focus. The net effect is that strategic planners are not sure what variables are important or where to start in the process. This is particularly relevant in a world characterized by strong domestic and global competitions where risk and uncertainty are driven by the winds of technological change, political turmoil, and governmental actions.[19]

The quick SWOT approach alleviates the deficiencies of traditional SWOT analysis by drawing on the other analytical approaches looking at strategy presented earlier. It takes the key variables in value and supply chain analysis, the five-force model, the resource-based framework, and the technology-based strategy approach and uses them to drive the SWOT process. The critical variables or drivers that influence the SWOT are listed below:

- Internal Organizational Drivers
    ◦ Supply and value chain performance
    ◦ Core competencies and organizational resources
    ◦ Emerging technology

- External Organizational Drivers
  - Threat of substitute products
  - Threat of new entrants
  - Bargaining power of buyers
  - Bargaining power of suppliers
  - Local and world economy, culture, and government influence

Some of the variables influence both the internal and external organizational environment. For example, the supply chain boundary affects the internal environment, but it is also part of the external environment and involves logistics and financial institutions. Similarly, the onslaught

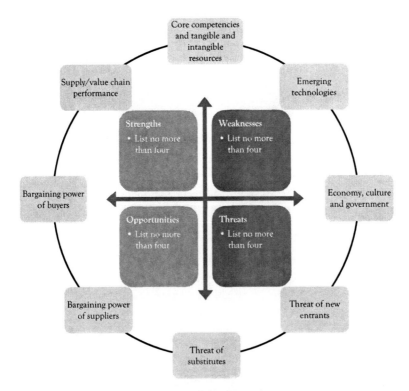

Figure 8.8. Key drivers for quick SWOT analysis.

of new technologies also influences the internal as well as the external environment. Figure 8.8 illustrates the SWOT template along with the key variables that should drive the SWOT analysis.

The Quick SWOT Supported With Strategy Canvas

A SWOT analysis should be conducted very quickly as illustrated below:

1. Conduct a brief external industry analysis.
   - Identify the competitors, buyers, suppliers, potential entrants, and potential substitutes.
   - Understand the industry supply chain and how it works.
2. Conduct a brief internal organizational analysis.
   - Identify organizational capabilities/competencies related to manufacturing prowess, order fulfillment and delivery, customer service, marketing, finance, accounting, R&D, employees, and management. This is essentially the internal supply and value chains.
3. Use a strategy canvas to identify how you can add or subtract features for product differentiation. The idea is to identify new opportunities and perhaps Blue Ocean markets.
4. Develop a 4 × 4 SWOT diagram using the template. Try to limit the number of factors in each quadrant to four factors.
5. Start the process over after 4 months.

The next chapter will provide a simple template as part of the Ten–Ten planning process for conducting an organizational and industry analysis that incorporates the quick SWOT approach.

Monopolistic Competition and SWOT

Monopolistic competition involves many buyers and many sellers offering slightly different competitive products. Producers are always searching for markets with potential. In such an environment, there are several strengths that are critical for survival. Figure 8.9 illustrates the idea that

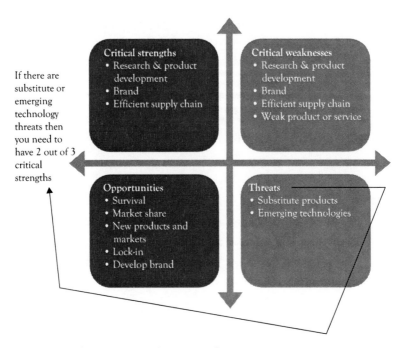

Figure 8.9. Competing under monopolistic competition requires strength in at least two areas.

if there are substitute products or emerging technology threats, then you need to have 2 out of 3 critical strengths. The critical strengths are research and product development, a high performance supply chain, and a strong brand. The optimum situation is to be strong in all three areas, but this is not very common. If any of these three are placed in the critical weakness category, the organization is definitely at risk. It should also be noted that an organization could be strong in all three critical strengths and still fail. Survival is still linked to long-term profitability. Many of the very successful companies are 3 for 3 and have above-average performance in R&D and a strong brand and excellent supply chain.

Conclusion

In this chapter, we have reviewed many popular approaches for strategic planning. The key points are the following:

- The two basic strategies for business planning include product differentiation and striving to be the low-cost producer.

- Product differentiation can be accomplished by focusing on Midas versions of products using extravagant engineering and design. Being the low-cost producer can be accomplished by focusing on Hermes versions of products using frugal engineering and design.
- Planning approaches can be classified as having an internal organizational focus (looking inside) or an external or environmental focus (looking outside).
- The development of an abbreviated SWOT analysis that is supported with a strategy analysis can be used to integrate the key attributes of the various strategic planning approaches.
- The planning process never ends. With continuous pressure from market and competition, firms are suggested to develop new strategy and planning from time to time.

This chapter reviewed the various analytic approaches for strategic planning. There is no single business plan that can be used to deal with the complexity of monopolistic competition nor is there a single planning approach that will take the organization down the right path. A revised analysis tool, called quick SWOT analysis, was introduced that combines the various strategic planning approaches.

This chapter also sets the stage for the Ten–Ten planning process, a simplified yet robust approach to planning. The next chapter will present two templates for developing a business plan. The first template is the Organizational and Industry Analysis template and it incorporates the quick SWOT approach along with concepts from value chain analysis, the resource-based approach, Blue Ocean market analysis, and the other strategic analysis approaches discussed in this chapter. This information is then used to fill in the Business Plan Overview template. The use of the two templates is part of the Ten–Ten planning process. The approach can be used to produce one plan and also to churn out new plans in order to compete in dynamic environments characterized by monopolistic competition.

CHAPTER 9

The Ten–Ten Planning Process: Crafting a Business Story

As noted in the last chapter, the planning process is never-ending because of the ongoing pressure in the marketplace. There is no single plan that can deal with the complexity of monopolistic competition. The first mantra of the entrepreneur is: *differentiate through innovation or perish*, and this is accomplished by focusing on Midas versions of products using extravagant engineering. The second mantra of the entrepreneur is: *strive to reduce costs*, and this is accomplished by focusing on Hermes versions of products using frugal engineering and design. The dynamic tension between delivering Midas and Hermes versions will also lead to mainstream Atlas products. A continuous process for developing business plans is necessary for competing and surviving under monopolistic competition. As discussed in the last chapter, the strategic planning process can be modeled using the diagram in Figure 9.1. The mantra and mission are constantly evaluated and revisited throughout the life of the firm.

The Ten–Ten planning process contains two templates: an Organizational and Industry Analysis template and the Business Plan Overview template that identifies the mantra, mission, money, goals, objectives, and tactics in a very brief format. (These templates can be downloaded from http://glsanders.wordpress.com/) The idea behind the Ten–Ten approach is that once you have gathered some background data related to the industry and the organization, you should be able to complete the two templates in about 20 minutes.[1] This will of course be a very rough first-cut, but it will be the foundation for developing more refined plans. The Ten–Ten process is meant to be quick and to the point, but it can be expanded to 10 hours, 10 days, or in some instances 10 weeks, but rarely more than

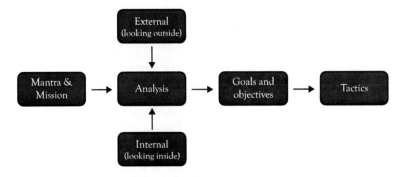

Figure 9.1. Strategic planning process.

that. These templates along with the FAD (features, attributes, and design) template can be used to develop the executive summary. This in turn can be used to develop a full-blown business plan, which is the foundation for building the business. Figure 9.2 illustrates the entire Ten–Ten process from conceptualizing the business idea through building the business.

Organizational and Industry Analysis Template

The first template is the Organizational and Industry Analysis template and it incorporates the quick SWOT analysis using concepts from supply chain analysis, Porter's value chain analysis and five-force model,[2] the resource-based approach,[3] core competencies analysis,[4] and the Blue Ocean Strategy Canvas.[5] The idea is to conduct a brief industry analysis without getting bogged down in the details. This template is contained in Table 9.1. The FAD template is a good source of information related to what products or services are going to be produced and sold. The point of the first planning template is to help you understand the current or proposed organization and the target industry. Questions 1 through 5 assist in detailing the basic question related to what business you are in and what the industry looks like. Question 6 is a simplified SWOT diagram. It is intentionally small so that that it is difficult to enter too many items. Long laundry lists are a recurring critique of SWOT analysis. One area where the simplified SWOT analysis differs from the traditional SWOT approach is that the focus is not on just internal issues, but on any areas where an organization has strengths and weaknesses. For example, the

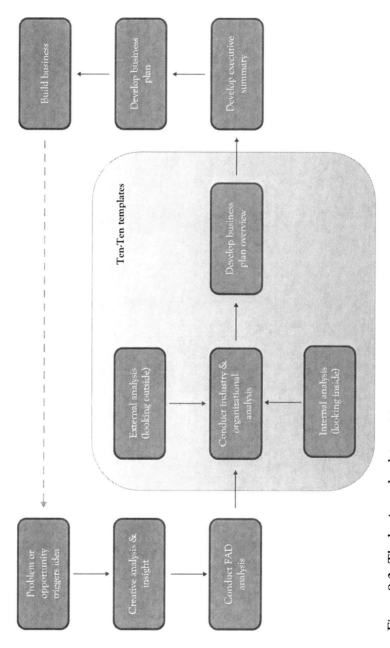

Figure 9.2. The business development process.

Table 9.1. Organizational and Industry Analysis Template (do this first)

1. Give a brief description of your business model including what products or service you are producing or will produce.
2. Describe your target customers and the size of the market?
3. List and describe your current competitors?
4. List and describe your potential competitors?
5. Who will you purchase or acquire materials, components, resources, or other inputs from?
6. SWOT (consider human resources, R&D, marketing, procurement, manufacturing, distribution, engineering, IT, finance, accounting, and legal)
What are your strengths (products, R&D, supply chain, brand, pricing, core competencies, resources, infrastructure, scalability, and interfaces)? — What are your weaknesses (products, R&D, supply chain, brand, pricing, core competencies, resources, infrastructure, scalability, and interfaces)?

What are the opportunities (growth, market share, product lines, Blue Ocean, complementary products, lock-in, brand, and first-mover advantage)?	What are the threats (substitutes, emerging technologies, new entrants, economic climate, government regulations, and social/culture issues)?

7. Strategy Canvas for new product compared with competitor or industry (price and quality are example attributes)

Use the FAD template to add key attributes to the Strategy Canvas (you can continue the table if you need more attributes)

Attribute name	Meaning of product or service↓	BOF POD POP EXT DIS	BOF POD POP EXT DIS	BOF POD POP EXT DIS	BOF POD POP EXT DIS	BOF POD POP EXT DIS	BOF POD POP EXT DIS
Price		Quality					
Very high							
High							
Average							
Low							
Very low							
Not applicable							

BOF, Blue Ocean features and exciters; POD, points of difference and differentiators; POP, points of parity and must-haves; EXT, extinct and vestigial features; DIS, dissatisfiers research and development (R&D) and product development areas are typically considered internal functions, but the supply and value chains along with the brand image are interconnected functions that span the internal and external organizational environment.

Another important feature of the Organizational and Industry Analysis template is the presence of question 7 and the development of a strategy canvas, the Blue Ocean strategy, for identifying the current product features and how they compare with one or more competitors or with a typical product or service found in the industry marketplace. The goal is to assist in illustrating what product features are being used to differentiate the competitors and to identify other areas where you might want to reduce or add features or even increase or decrease performance.

Business Plan Overview Template (Mantra, Mission, Money, Goals, Objectives, and Tactics)

The second template is the Business Plan Overview template (see Table 9.2). This template uses the Organizational and Industry Analysis information and FAD template to identity the organizational mantra, the mission, the money or value proposition, goals and objectives, and tactics. It is essentially a scaled-down business plan that can be used to develop the full-blown business plan that will be discussed in a later chapter.

1. *The mantra*: Guy Kawasaki prefers using a mantra in lieu of a mission statement.[6] He is very critical of mission statements that are crafted by a large committee of 60 at an offsite retreat. We do not see the mantra as a replacement for the mission statement. We see the mantra as an often-repeated phrase that provides the basis for the existence of the company. It is a slogan, a watchword, a byword, and a motto that breathes life into the firm's existence. The meaning of a product as identified in the FAD template is a good place to look for the foundations of a mantra. Examples include the following:

   - Hospital: Service, respect, and excellence in healthcare
   - Software Developer: Quality software through hard work and creativity

Table 9.2. Business Plan Overview Template (do this second)

1. What is your *mantra* considering differentiation through innovation or perish or cost reduction (3–10 words on why your company should exist)?
2. What is the overall *mission* of the business (1–3 sentences on what your company does or will do and your target customers)?
3. How will you make *money* in terms of product differentiation, being the low-cost producer, and what complementary products and services will be offered in order to generate recurring revenues?
4. What are your *goals* and *objectives* over the next 3 months to year (2–6 phrases on precise performance intentions)?
5. What *tactics* will you use over the next 3 months to a year to reach your objectives and mission (2–8 phrases)?

- Manufacturing: Quality is our endgame
- Telecommunications: We hear our customers.

2. *The mission statement:* The mission statement presents a brief overall view of the business. It describes what the company does and why it exists. It should focus on meeting customer needs. It should address at an abstract level what products or services are produced. It can also include a statement reflecting whether the company will focus on product differentiation and niche markets, focus on being price-competitive, or focus on both. The FAD template is also a good

source of information for the mission statement. Examples of a mission statement include the following:

- We use high-quality materials and craftsmanship to develop superior jewelry boxes for the discriminating buyer.
- We develop general purpose and customized charity events planning software for nonprofit organizations.
- We manufacture high-quality measurement instruments for companies involved in oil exploration.
- Our school prepares students to work in highly productive software environments.

3. *The money*: The purpose of this section is to provide an overview for the value proposition. That is how your organization will make money using the two generic business model strategies. The organization can differentiate, be the low-cost producer, or both. As noted earlier, most organizations attempt to differentiate and be the low-cost producer at the same time. Because they are often conflicting strategies, many organizations are slightly better at one or the other. The best performers balance both strategies. One important consideration is the generation of additional sales by offering complementary products and services. For example, a printer company can sell toner, warranties, and maintenance contracts. A phone manufacturer might become a mobile application developer and also sell accessories for the phone. Firms should also discuss the potential size of the market when it is relevant and whether there is potential for a Blue Ocean market. Examples of money statements include the following:

- We will generate profits by constantly introducing jewelry boxes with new features and cutting costs by using building technology to lower costs.
- We generate most of our revenues by developing high-end customizable charity planning software. We will keep development costs down by developing software modules that are conducive to adding and subtracting

features. We will generate additional recurring revenues by offering upgrades and providing customized systems development for nonstandard applications. It is a largely untapped market with excellent revenue potential.

- We will sell a high-end social-networking project management tool for large companies. The companies we will sell our product to are not price-sensitive and we will be able to charge a premium price to cover our high fixed costs. We will generate additional recurring revenues by offering upgrades and providing customized systems development for nonstandard applications.

- We will build an inexpensive house using modular and inexpensive building materials. We will be the low-cost supplier. We will generate additional recurring revenues by offering house maintenance services to our customers.

4. *The goals and objectives*: There is a lot of confusion related to goals and objectives. Goals are thought of as being more abstract and broader than objectives. This is a rather overstated and specious claim that creates more harm than good. This section of the business plan template encourages you to list both goals and objectives. The important point is to identify the goals and objectives that will help support the mantra, the mission, and the value proposition over the next 3 months to a year. Examples include the following:

- Launch new product line in July
- Increase sales by 5% over the next year
- Service 10% more customers than last year
- Reduce waste by 5%.

5. *The tactics*: The tactics are the activities the organization will use over the next 3 months to a year to reach a company's goals and objectives. In the context of the military, the tactics are the techniques used to deploy troops, hardware, aircraft, and ships for combat. In business, this includes the activities related to marshaling human resources, manufacturing resources, acquiring equipment, and related supply

chain activities to attain the goals and objectives. The tactics can include timetables and schedules related to the goals and objectives. Examples of tactics include the following:

- Purchase a high-performance band saw in February
- Hire employees in April to develop new customer interface software
- Develop a radio-marketing plan for introducing new product in November
- Have the sales force contact every customer who has not purchased a product in the last 2 years.

Developing an Executive Summary: Crafting a Business Story

One of the most common reframes we hear from entrepreneurs is that:

They just don't understand our business model.
They just don't understand what we are doing.

Who are *they*? *They* can be friends, family, investors, and even the business founders. In reality, *they* sometimes do not understand because the business concept is faulty, but sometimes they do not understand because you have not communicated the essence of the vision to the relevant parties. The Ten–Ten planning templates can alleviate some of the confusion; furthermore, at some point, the Ten–Ten templates will have to be converted into a well-crafted executive summary that tells an interesting story. This will help further refine the business model, and it will also serve as a platform for communicating with the many *theys* that are encountered.

The executive summary should tell a story in one or two pages or perhaps even three pages. The best way to prepare the business plan is to use Business Plan Overview template information as a starting point and use the Industry and Organizational and the FAD templates for additional input into the development of the executive summary. Here is a general format for the executive summary:

- Paragraph 1: Introduce the idea (four to six sentences).
  - The first line of the executive summary should be a catchy sentence that captures the essence of the *mantra*.
  - The remaining sentences of the paragraph should discuss the *mission* of the company.
- Paragraph 2: Describe your business model and what products or services will be produced (four to eight sentences).
  - Describe your target customers.
  - Describe your product or service and tell what it does.
  - Describe how it will benefit consumers or other businesses.
  - Discuss why your business model will work in terms of product differentiation, being the low-cost producer, or both.
  - If appropriate, describe how your approach and your products are superior to the competition.
  - If appropriate, describe the size of the market and if it is a Blue Ocean opportunity.
  - You can add additional paragraphs if you think that more detail is needed to describe your product or service. Sometimes a technology or a concept is very unique and it needs additional discussion.
- Paragraph 3: Discuss your strengths (three to six sentences).
  - Use the SWOT analysis to discuss the strengths, core competencies, and resources that are keys to the company's success.
- Paragraph 4: Discuss the opportunities and how the goals and objectives relate to achieving the opportunities.
  - Use the opportunities in the SWOT analysis to identify the business opportunities.
  - Discuss how you will make money and generate revenues.
  - Use the goals and objectives in the Business Plan Overview to indicate how the firm will take advantage of the opportunities.

The executive summary can be up to three pages and have additional paragraphs, but you should still aim for brevity, crispness, and clarity.

Remember, the goal of the executive summary is to communicate your business model to the readers by telling a story. One of the best ways to communicate ideas is to keep the readers interested and avoid long meandering discussions. Here are a few ways for increasing attention and interest.

The first thing is to avoid using bullet points in your executive summary. Bullet points create the impression that you have just cut and pasted the presentation into the executive summary. In addition, readers tend to skim bullet points and sometimes even ignore them. You should also vary the length of your sentences. For example, have two short sentences, one long sentence, and one short sentence followed by a long sentence and then a short sentence. The idea is to mix up the sentence structure and create interest. Always try to begin and start your executive summary with a catchy phrase related to the mantra. Finally, editing is important, and having someone else edit your plan is essential. Even if you do not use the edited version, you will obtain insight into where the executive plan is unclear and needs work.[7] One example of an executive summary is exhibited in the Appendix at the end of this chapter.

Extending the Wine Aging Cooler Example Using the Ten–Ten Templates

Chapter 7 introduced the concept of a device that could be used to reduce the time that it takes to age wine. The FAD template was presented in chapter 7 for a storage and refrigerator device that could be used to age wine. This example is extended in the Appendix of this chapter. The Appendix contains a completed template for the Organizational and Industry Analysis and a completed template for the business plan overview. The Appendix also contains an executive summary for the wine aging cooler and the picture of the proposed product. The product was subsequently named the Addvinter Star.

Conclusion

In this chapter, we have illustrated a model for quickly crafting a business plan. The key points are the following:

- The Ten–Ten planning process is very brief yet dynamic and adaptable to a variety of situations.
- It draws on the major strategic planning approaches as well as the FAD template discussed in chapter 7.
- It consists of completing two templates and developing an executive summary.
- The first task consists of collecting internal and external information completing the Organizational and Industry Analysis template. This template also uses information from the FAD template.
- The second task uses the Organizational and Industry Analysis template along with the FAD template to complete a Business Plan Overview template.
- The information gathered using the FAD template, the Organizational and Industry Analysis template, and the Business Plan Overview template are then used to write an executive summary.
- The goal is to communicate with partners, confidants, and funding sources.

Strategic planning is often criticized as taking too long, being too complex, and even being counterproductive. The Ten–Ten approach alleviates many of these criticisms by its conciseness and the way it focuses on learning-by-doing. It is still hard work. However, the author has actually had groups of people complete a Ten–Ten plan in one night. This includes conceptualizing a new business model up through the completion of the business templates. The feedback was generally positive from the experience, although the participants were exhausted.

The business plan serves many purposes. But the primary goal is to foster communication with the business founders, partners, confidants, and funding sources. The Ten–Ten business plan presents a succinct overview of the what, how, when, and why of the business. It provides a concise overview of what the business is about and how money can be made. In many ways, the Ten–Ten documents are a prototype of the business model. This is in essence a scaled-down business model that describes how the business will function and serve as a platform for the business founders to communicate with each other and identify strengths and weaknesses of the emerging firm. In chapter 12, we will present the infrastructure for a full-blown business plan that can be used as a blueprint for operating the business the first year.

Illustrations of Completed Ten–Ten Templates and an Executive Summary for the Addvinter Star

Example of an Organizational and Industry Analysis Template

1. **Give a brief description of your business model including what products or service you are producing or will produce?**

   We will develop high-tech devices that will significantly reduce the wine aging process. Most wines can benefit from aging. The typical Merlot needs 15 years to age and Pinot Noirs and Burgundies sometimes need 5 years to age. Shiraz-based wines sometimes require more than 20 years.

2. **Describe your customers?**

   We will target wine connoisseurs, the wine aficionado, upscale restaurants and clubs, wine enthusiasts, and dabblers in sophistication. The wine connoisseur is one who understands the details, technique, and principles of wine as an art and is competent to act as a critical judge. The aficionado includes individuals who like, know about, and appreciate and fervently pursues fine wines. The enthusiast and dabblers includes individuals who are interested in wine and enhancing prestige at a reduced price.

3. **List and describe your current competitors?**

   Existing wine production companies and distributors.

   Japanese inventor at http://www.timesonline.co.uk/tol/news/world/article576802.ece

Wine aging tester at http://www.vinummaster.com/Eng/InfosClefEn.htm

Wine aging accelerator http://www.amazon.com/Vintage-Express-Accelerator-Bourbon-BEVERAGES/dp/B00I2S308

Wine aging patent: http://www.freepatentsonline.com/7334516.html

4. List and describe your potential competitors?

Any business interested in wine aging technology. Companies currently producing wine refrigerators are also a threat.

5. Who will you purchase or acquire materials, components, resources, or other inputs from?

We will secure local manufacturers to develop the device and will hire local people to assemble the device.

6. SWOT (consider human resources, R&D, marketing, procurement, manufacturing, distribution, engineering, IT, finance, accounting, and legal)

What are your strengths (products, R&D, supply chain, brand, pricing core competencies, resources, infrastructure, scalability, and interfaces)?	What are your weaknesses (products, R&D, supply chain, brand, pricing, core competencies, resources, infrastructure, scalability, and interfaces)?
The idea Creative team of researchers and entrepreneurs	R&D Supply chain Brand Infrastructure
What are the opportunities (growth, market share, product lines, Blue Ocean, complementary products, lock-in, brand, and first-mover advantage)?	What are the threats (substitutes, emerging technologies, new entrants, economic climate, government regulations, and social/culture issues)?
Per capita wine consumption in the USA exceeds 9 liters. http://www.wineinstitute.org/files/PerCapitaWineConsumptionCountries.pdf Gen X and millennial wine drinking high. http://www.winemarketcouncil.com/research_slideview.asp?position=9 Will try to secure wine connoisseurs, aficionados, clubs, enthusiasts, and dabblers.	Market can be easily entered. Our research or our competitors may show that it does not work. Wine companies may go after our product. For example, expensive wine vintners may take out advertisements to attack our product. Wine refrigerator companies: http://www.winerefrigerator.com/

| We also plan on developing a series of complementary products and services. For example, we could engage in wine consulting to producers. We could also introduce a line of wine accessories for consumers. | |

7. Strategy Canvas for existing product compared with competitor or industry

		Meaning	BOF POD POP EXT DIS	BOF POD POP EXT DIS
Attribute name	Price	Sophistication	Wine aging and refrigeration	Design
Very high	Us	Us		Us
High	Us		Us	
Average	Us			
Low		Competition		
Very low			Competition	Competition

Sample Business Plan

Business Plan Overview Template for AddVintner (confidential draft)

1. **What is your *mantra* considering differentiation through innovation or perish or cost reduction (3–10 words on why your company should exist and company name)?**

   AddVintner: Creating fine wine before its time.

2. **What is the overall *mission* of the business (1–3 sentences on what your company does or will do)?**

   We will develop high-tech refrigeration devices that will significantly reduce the time to age wines for a broad range of customers.

3. **How will you make *money* in terms of product differentiation, being the low-cost producer, or both?**

   We plan on offering at least two products. One is targeted at the wine connoisseurs, aficionado, and expensive restaurants/clubs. The other product will be targeted toward wine enthusiasts and dabblers. The high-end products will be prices in the $1,500–$2,500 range. The low-end product will start at $400.

4. **What are your *goals* and *objectives* over the next 3 months to year (2–6 phrases on precise performance intentions)?**

> Sell 5,000 units of $2,000 unit by December.
>
> Sell 10,000 units of $400 unit by December.
>
> Conduct research on the effectiveness of the wine aging process.

5. **What *tactics* will you use over the next 3 months to a year to reach your objectives and mission (2–8 phrases)?**

> Purchase warehouse for manufacturing by March.
>
> Conduct additional research on the viability of the aging process.
>
> Hire additional designers to develop product portfolio.
>
> Develop marketing strategy by March.
>
> Develop production process by May.
>
> Hire 10 employees by June.
>
> Start advertising by July.
>
> Start production by August.

Executive Summary (first draft not for distribution)

It is said that music is the wine of silence. Aged wine is for those seeking silence and comfort in the chaos of everyday life. It is our mission to bring aged wine to the discriminating concern and to give everyone the opportunity to drink aged wine at a reasonable price. A good Merlot can take up to 15 years to age, a Pinot Noir or a Burgundy can take up to 5 years to age, and Shiraz-based wines may require 20 years. We sell the most advanced solutions for improving the aged quality of most wines without having to pay high prices or wait many years for the wine to be ready for the palate.

Our product (see prototype below of the Addvinter Star) can attract variety wine drinkers including wine connoisseurs, the wine aficionado, and expensive restaurants/clubs and wine enthusiasts and dabblers. Our product will help to reduce the time that a consumer has to wait for fine wine, it will also increase the quality of low-priced wines and it will increase the status of the owner of the product. We are strong believers in design-driven innovation and will spend several months experimenting with new ideas and concepts for creating new customer meanings for wine aging. R&D will be the key driver for developing products that are unique, contemporary, and relevant to the wine community. The competition will simply not be able to keep pace with our research-based design-driven products.

We are an idea-driven company and have assimilated a creative team of researchers and entrepreneurs to deliver products to compliment and reflect contemporary tastes. Our marketing and production plans are in place and we have a strong grasp of the critical elements in the supply chain. We are developing an organization that will not just listen to consumers but will also be proactive in developing products that will anticipate and drive demand.

Per capita wine consumption in the USA exceeds 9 liters per year.[8] Wine drinking by the Gen Xers and the Millennial's exceeds the consumption of beer and spirits.[9] We have an opportunity to tap into that huge market and develop products that are relevant to the life style of Gen Xers and the Millennial's. We believe that we can generate nearly $7 million in revenue the first year. It is our goal to enter the market by January with two new products for producing fine wine before its time.

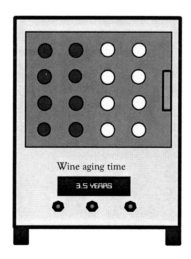

The Addvinter Star

CHAPTER 10

Lock-In and Revenue Growth

Lock-in occurs when there are costs involved in switching from one product or service to another product or service. For example, consider how cable television broadband providers and wireless phone providers have penalties for the customers who terminate a contract within the term of specific agreement period. Switching costs can also involve time and psychological effort. When you switch cable providers, there is a definite learning curve related to using the new station guide and digital video-recording device. Cable providers try to increase monetary and psychological switching costs so that consumers are locked-in to their service. The nature of psychological switching costs can be traced to past use of a product and to the learning effects as consumers become attached to the product and become familiar with the interface and how to control the interface. Economists have identified a related concept that they refer to as the increasing-returns-to-adoption phenomena where the use of a technology leads to greater use and this in turn leads to technological improvements.[1] This "learning by use" approach, which we have also described in an earlier chapter as the *learning-by-doing* phenomena, creates a situation where locking-in customers essentially locks-out the competition.

Lock-In Leads to Network Effects and Increased Product Performance

Lock-in also increases the so-called network effect phenomenon. A network effect occurs when the value of a good is dependent on the number of customers already owning that good. Metcalfe's law states that the value or utility of network is proportional to the number of users of the network.[2] In the economics literature, a network effect typically

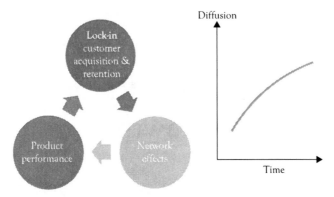

Figure 10.1. Growth and lock-in.

refers to a change in the positive benefit that a consumer receives from a product when the number of consumers of the good increases.[3] Lock-in is also related to Moore's law, whereby the performance of products always increases over time and the cost of the product stays the same or decreases. This increase in performance is a function of technological developments and learning curve effects. When network effects are combined with increased product performance, product diffusion can increase dramatically and result in exponential market growth and sales (see Figure 10.1).

Switching Costs are Everywhere

Switching costs are the costs that result from switching to a new product or a new service. They are often viewed in terms of dollars but they can also be conceptualized in terms of time and psychological effort. Switching costs can include early termination costs, the amount of time and effort to switch, all learning costs required to understand the new product or service, cash outlays for switching, and even the emotional discomfort caused by switching.[4] The goal of buyers is to try and avoid switching costs and not be locked-in to a particular product, service, or technology. Buyers want flexibility and they try to avoid lock-in.

The goal of producers is to essentially lock-in their customers and lock-out the competition. This is accomplished by creating a value proposition for their customers and make it difficult for them to leave the fold because of the high switching costs. Here is a list of situations that result in product and service lock-in:[5]

- High-quality product and service that are in demand. Examples include high-end cars and newly introduced game consoles.
- Products that are sold at a relatively low price while its development costs are recouped through replacement parts, consumables, and maintenance. Examples include printers, razors, and autos.
- Recently purchased products that are relatively expensive will probably be too new to abandon. Examples include new cars, freezers, most durable goods, and houses.
- Products or services that cause customers to continue using the product because it forces them down a particular path. The path can be related to technology and is often proprietary. Examples include operating systems, game consoles, computers, tax software, banking, colleges, social networks, Internet service providers, word-processing, and various other applications software.
- Products, services, and vendors that are usually the lowest cost. Examples include Kohl's, Wal-Mart, Target, Newegg, inexpensive cars, off-brand inks, alternative materials (plastic for metal), discount airlines, and most of the Hermes products and services.
- Brands that customers will turn to because they engender trust, confidence, and quality. Examples include IBM, Audi, Clark's shoes, Expedia, Amazon, Tide, and many of the companies selling Midas products and services.
- Legal contracts for providing products and service. Examples include wireless phone, broadband, cable, and outsourcing agreements between businesses.
- Loyalty programs and frequent use programs. Examples include airlines, retail stores, and in general discounts for repeat purchases.
- Product and services that complement the main product or service. Examples include software applications for operating

systems, mobile phone applications, social networking applications, and maintenance and repairs departments connected with the dealer.

- Customers who are socially and emotionally involved with the product and services. Examples include online and offline social networks, online role-playing games, colleges, and church groups.
- Products that facilitate control of one's environment. If a consumer can control a product or service, then they feel that they own it and thus become locked-in to using that product or service out of loyalty.

Figure 10.2 illustrates the author's view of the degree of lock-in for several business activities. One particular interesting example of lock-in is related to social networking sites such as Facebook, MySpace, and LinkedIn. Social networking sites have an abundance of features that facilitate lock-in. First, they encourage the development of very strong emotional ties among the participants. Secondly, some of them attempt to thwart searching by search engines. And finally, they encourage the customization and control of the home screen. Our research has found that if you can give users the ability to control and customize their environment,

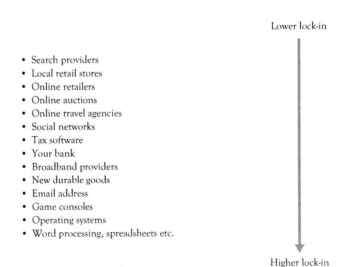

Lower lock-in

- Search providers
- Local retail stores
- Online retailers
- Online auctions
- Online travel agencies
- Social networks
- Tax software
- Your bank
- Broadband providers
- New durable goods
- Email address
- Game consoles
- Operating systems
- Word processing, spreadsheets etc.

Higher lock-in

Figure 10.2. Levels of lock-in for several businesses.

then they will begin to exhibit feelings of ownership toward a virtual place.[6] It appears that in some people, the emotional ties are stronger than the ties exhibited by some individuals toward a house or a car. In addition, there is a positional effect. This can reduce the influence and reduce the network effects:

> Positional goods purchases, consequently, are interdependent: what we buy is partially a function of what others buy. Put another way, the value of a positional good arises in part from social context. The positionality of a particular good is often two-sided: its desirability may rise as some possess it, but then subsequently fall as more possess it.... A particular fast car is most desirable when enough people possess it to signal that it is a desired object, but the value diminishes once every person in the neighborhood possesses one. Nothing about the car itself has changed, except for its ability to place its owner among the elite and to separate her from the crowd. Similarly, part of the appeal of a "fashionable" resort is that only a few people know about it, or are able to afford it. For these goods, the value of relative exclusivity may be a large part of the goods' total appeal."[7]

A Lock-In Index

We have developed a set of questions that can be used to measure lock-in. It can be viewed as a lock-in index. Try to think of a product or service and then answer the following questions:

- The people who use this product are very cool. Add 1 point.
- This product has a strong brand. Add 2 points.
- The product or service is relatively expensive and was recently purchased. Add 1 plus 1 point for each time you use the word *very*.
- The replacement parts for the product are relatively expensive. Add 2 points.
- There is a service contract. Add 1 point for each year.

- There is a significant learning curve for using the product effectively. Add 1 plus 1 point for each time you use the word *very*.
- This product is a social networking application or has social networking features. Add 3 points.

If the score for the product or service is above 9, then this is a product or service with significant switching costs and lock-in. If the score is between 6 and 9, then the lock-in is moderately strong. If the score is between 3 and 6, then the lock-in is average. And if the score is <3, then the lock-in is minimal. If the score is zero, then you are probably buying an off-brand candy bar.

There are some products where the lock-in is transitory. Consider the fashion and clothing industry where the lead designers develop an anchor for next year's fashion.[8] The premier lines typically develop seasonal themes for the fashion community. Everyone copies the anchored themes including the fashion leaders with their slightly scaled-back bridge lines (e.g., Gap Inc. represented by Banana Republic, the Gap and Old Navy and the Armani Group represented by Giorgio Armani, Armani Collezioni, and Emporio Armani). Copying is actually beneficial to the fashion industry. Copying an emerging fashion concept helps to standardize the design for a year or two until the design becomes obsolete. Some level of standardization is essential or chaos would ensue and costs would skyrocket because the supply chain would never stabilize. Nevertheless, the fashion themes are extremely transitory because, in a very short time, a new theme emerges and the old theme is out-of style.

The Downside of Lock-in

A consistent theme of this book is that companies must pursue innovation and differentiation constantly. Locking in your customers does not mean you can abandon innovation and let your products and service languish in mediocrity. Because consumers will eventually abandon your products and services and you will eventually fade from the marketplace. As we have said in an earlier chapter, people want to control their environment and they do not want to be controlled. Google has been very proactive on this front because they realize that lock-in is very transitory and they have attempted to engender trust through innovation.[9] Cable companies were able to lock-in their customers because there was very little competition. The landline cable companies avoided innovation and they treated their customers poorly. It is only recently that they have been able to shirk their earlier image and begin to engender trust and acceptance in the marketplace. All businesses must change, even if it is only in the minds of consumers, or they will eventually be abandoned.

Outsourcing and Lock-in

Outsourcing is a contractual relationship between one business and another. The outsourcee, the company trying to outsource some organizational function, can have the outsourcer company provide manufacturing, product design, product distribution, IT services and infrastructure support, and about everything else including strategic planning support. There are many reasons why companies turn toward outsourcing, including reducing costs, access to expertise, and increased production capacity, as illustrated in Table 10.1.[10] At the same time, there are many reasons

Table 10.1. Benefits of Outsourcing

Simplifies management and can increase flexibility.
Management can focus on core competencies.
Can reengineer and downsize organization.
Helps develop strategic alliances.
Can improve the quality of service to customers and within organization.
Reduces short-term costs and transactions costs.
Possible large influx of cash resulting from transfer of assets to the new provider especially in outsourcing IT.
Access to technical expertise and the ability to free in-house resources. Outsourcer has access to technology and to specialized expertise.
Eliminates a process area that was a headache.
Outsourcer has above-average management skills.
Outsourcer has better cost control because they have benchmarked best of breed processes.
Outsourcer has capacity on demand and bulk purchasing power.

that outsourcing can create problems as illustrated in Table 10.2. There is, however, one major reason that outsourcing creates problems. Outsourcing causes the organization to lose its absorptive capacity in the area that was outsourced. As noted in an earlier chapter, having absorptive capacity means that a company is able to evaluate new technological development because the company or the owner has insight and expertise into a particular area. Organizations with absorptive capacity have developed knowledge structures and insight in a particular domain. Having absorptive capacity gives an organization the ability to understand, assimilate and exploit new knowledge and information, and then to apply it to solving problems and developing commercially viable products. If an organization outsources an ability or capability, which is a core competency, then the organization may not be able to understand and recognize when an emerging technology is important. In the worst case, the organization may not be able to develop products because it does not have the know-how since it has already lost the ability to learn-by-doing and learn-about.

Table 10.2. Risks of Outsourcing

Loss of control.

Costs may be greater than anticipated.

   Transition costs including process reengineering and severance pay.

   Managing the outsourcing agreement.

Vendor may not implement emerging technologies.

Poor customer service.

May lose good staff.

May hurt current employee's morale and performance.

Vendor may not survive.

They know all of your secrets and you might not be able to get away from them.

Very high lock-in and switching costs.

Limits your options and the ability to develop additional core competencies.

Loss of absorptive capacity. They may not be able to recognize a new opportunity or take advantage of a new opportunity.

Because company has lost the ability to do something, they may not be able to do it for a long time.

Customer Acquisition, Customer Retention, and Lock-in

Customer acquisition and customer retention through lock-in are the two primary components of market share. Once customers have been acquired, the next step is to retain them. There has been an ongoing debate on whether to focus on acquisition or retention marketing.[11] Both are important. But there has been significant interest in retention because of the research findings on customer retention. For example, increasing customer retention by just 5% can increase profits by 25–95%.[12]

The point is that customer retention should be a critical goal for all organizations. This is particularly true in the current business climate where substitute products and competitions from unforeseen sources are the norm. Customer acquisition and customer retention are related to the development of a viable business model and having good products, good people, a good brand, successful marketing, a capable R&D process, and an efficient supply chain.

Conclusion

In this chapter, we have discussed the concept of lock-in and identified various issues on the lock-in such as how companies can achieve it, the downside of it, and the lock-in index for practical use. We also have addressed the relationship between the lock-in and companies' absorptive capacity within the framework of outsourcing. The key points are the following:

- Lock-in is pervasive. It is part of the normal day-to-day transactions in business.
- If you are a producer, then you need to take steps to acquire customers so that you can lock them in (see Figure 10.3). This may include giving potential customers money, providing additional complimentary services, and developing attractive incentives for participation.
- Producers will always try to lock-in consumers. It is important that consumers try to get producers to offer incentives in order to offset present and future switching costs.

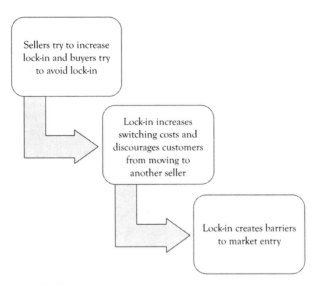

Figure 10.3. Lock-in issues.

- The initial stage of bargaining is important because once the consumer has committed to a seller, then the lock-in has been cast. If you are a business and are considering outsourcing, then you will be locked-in as soon as you sign on the dotted line. In that case, you should look for second sources.
- When a company or an individual outsources, they are essentially merging with another entity that has a competitive advantage in a particular area. Identifying the processes where having a core competency is critical for the firm to survive and to engage in learn-by-doing activity in that area.

CHAPTER 11

Valuing the Business

Everyone is interested in how much a business is worth. The entrepreneur and the entrepreneur's family are interested because they hope to use some of the income from the business to live on or because they are interested in how much they might sell the business for someday. Then, there is a simple curiosity factor: "I wonder what I could get for this?" If the entrepreneur seeks outside funding from friends, banks, angels, and venture capitalists (VCs), they will be very interested in the potential value of the firm. When a public company is being sold, its current trading price establishes a starting point—usually a minimum transaction price—but the acquiring company must still decide on the maximum bid consistent with a profitable acquisition. But when selling a nonpublic company, even that starting point does not exist. The field of *business valuation* has developed techniques designed to estimate the value of a business.[1]

One author gives this thorough definition of business valuation:

A **business valuation** determines the estimated market value of a business entity. A thorough, robust valuation consists of an in-depth analysis by a qualified independent professional who combines (a) proven techniques; (b) analysis and understanding of a specific company and its associated industry; (c) research and analysis of industry, association, and other publications; academic studies; the national and local economy; and online databases with (d) judgment honed by education, training, and experience; and (e) intuition. A valuation estimates the complex economic benefits that arise from combining a group of physical assets with the intangible assets of the business enterprise as a going concern. The resulting valuation, part science and part art, is a well-founded estimate that represents the price that hypothetical informed buyers and sellers would negotiate at arms length for an entire business or for a partial equity interest.[2]

Why are Businesses Bought and Sold?

A major reason why businesses are bought is that parties interested in beginning or expanding business activity often prefer acquiring an existing business rather than starting a new one. Existing businesses are "up and running," and have in place a product or service line, a work force, customers, suppliers, the necessary physical resources, and various intangibles—technology and "know-how," systems and procedures, location, reputation, and the like.

From a seller's perspective, business owners need to have an **exit strategy**, a means of extracting value from their investments of time and resources in the business. A sale may be occasioned by the death or intended retirement of the owner, or by a desire to "cash out" the investment at a time when its value is perceived to be high. Or, an owner may wish to expand the business by taking on new partners, selling a portion of ownership to new parties. Sometimes this is done to reward and retain key personnel by offering them an ownership interest in the business.

Even when no transfer of ownership is involved, a business valuation may be done when seeking major new financing. A valuation provides the prospective lender with an indication of the safety of a loan secured by the business.

Overview of Business Valuation Techniques

The foundations of business valuation techniques and practice lie in the tax law, as it has long been necessary to value businesses for estate and gift taxation. Though over 50 years old,[3] *Revenue Ruling 59–60* is still recognized by professionals and by the courts as an important source of standards for valuation. Section 1 of the Ruling states its purpose:

> The purpose of this Revenue Ruling is to outline and review in general the approach, methods, and factors to be considered in valuing shares of the capital stock of closely held corporations for

estate tax and gift tax purposes. The methods discussed herein will apply likewise to the valuation of corporate stocks on which market quotations are either unavailable or are of such scarcity that they do not reflect the fair market value.

Subsequent rulings enhance and expand these basic standards:

- *Revenue Ruling 65-193* clarifies that the procedures outlined in *RevRul 59-60* apply to intangible as well as tangible assets.
- *Revenue Ruling 68-609* extends the provisions of *RevRul 59-60* beyond estate and gift taxation to any type of business interests and any tax purpose, and provides a "formula approach."

The basis for business valuation is the familiar concept of *fair market value*, which is defined in Section 2.02 of *RevRul 59-60* as follows:

Fair market value [is] the price at which the property would change hands between a willing buyer and a willing seller when the former is not under any compulsion to buy and the latter is not under any compulsion to sell, both parties having reasonable knowledge of relevant facts. Court decisions frequently state in addition that the hypothetical buyer and seller are assumed to be able, as well as willing, to trade and to be well informed about the property and concerning the market for such property.

This definition remains the common definition of fair market value: the price negotiated by well-informed, willing, and able buyers and sellers who are not compelled to act.

Controlling and Noncontrolling Interests

One consideration in determining the value of a business ownership interest is the extent to which that interest can exercise *control* over business activity. **Control** refers to the power to direct the policies and management of the business. Control is most commonly measured by voting power—holding more than 50% of the voting equity of the company. In some cases, when there is no majority stockholder, other circumstances can lead to one owner having effective control.

When there is a controlling interest, other ownership interests are said to be **minority** or **noncontrolling interests**. Such interests represent <50% of the voting power in the company. A voting interest of exactly 50% is neither a controlling nor a minority interest. While a 50% interest cannot cause things to happen, it can prevent things from happening. Having two 50% owners is often considered an inefficient business structure, as a stalemate occurs if the two owners do not agree. However, that structure—*shared control*—appears in many joint ventures.

A controlling interest is generally considered to be worth more, on a per-share basis, than a noncontrolling interest. Among the powers of a controlling interest are the abilities to:[4]

- establish the nature and policies of the business;
- select officers, employees, and directors, and set their compensation and benefits;
- enter into contracts with suppliers, customers, and others;
- determine the existence and amount of dividends;
- decide on acquisition and disposition of assets;
- determine the financing and capital structure of the company.

A controlling owner has different options for disposing of the investment (*exit*) or converting it to cash (*liquidity*) than does a noncontrolling owner. The controlling owner's *exit or liquidity options* include selling the controlling interest, taking the company public, or deciding to liquidate the business. The noncontrolling owner's exit or liquidity options include selling to the controlling owner or selling to another noncontrolling owner. When a buyer does not exist, the noncontrolling owner effectively has no exit option. Continuing to hold the investment is a liquidity option to the extent that the business pays dividends.

Specific Valuation Techniques

A variety of techniques are available for conducting a business valuation. Part of the skill and expertise of a valuation analyst is the ability to select the appropriate technique for the situation at hand. Even when one technique is chosen, valuation under other techniques is often determined for comparative and confirmative purposes. Some analysts present a weighted average of the outcome of several techniques as their final conclusion, while others select a final value from the range of outcomes without resorting to formal weighting.

Factors to be Considered in a Business Valuation

Whatever the technique, the analyst should consider a variety of factors about the business and its industry. Among the factors to be considered are the following:[5]

- What is the stage of the company's development? Is it new, established and growing, mature, or declining?
- What is the current and prospective state of the industry in which the company operates, and of the economy in which it competes? How attractive is the industry to capital suppliers?
- What is the experience and competence of the members of top management and the company's Board of Directors?
- What is the company's position in the marketplace—for example, its market share—and what major competitors does it have?
- Are there barriers to entry in the company's marketplace?
- What are the competitive forces in the company's industry (recall Porter's five competitive forces, discussed in an earlier chapter)?
- Does the company have proprietary technology, products, or services, and what is the nature of the protection, such as patent rights or exclusive licensing?
- What is the nature and quality of the company's work force, including employer–employee relations, pay and benefits, labor supply, and the like?
- What is the nature and quality of the company's suppliers and of the company's customers? Is the company dependent on a small number of customers or vendors, or does it have a broad base? Are the customers and suppliers financially solid?

- Are there strategic relationships with suppliers, customers, and sources of financing? The existence of such relationships may be a positive or a negative factor when valuing the company.
- What is the company's cost structure (operating leverage, fixed-variable mix) and its financial strength indicated by debt capacity, free cash flow, and the like?
- What risk factors does the company face?

The consideration of risk factors is an especially important part of business valuation. Uncertainties or concerns in any of the above areas may signify risks to be considered.

Two simple approaches to business valuation are (a) determining the value of the company's net assets (assets minus liabilities) and (b) identifying the fair market value of a similar business. We discuss them briefly in the following sections, although they often prove unsatisfactory.

Asset-Based Methods

One approach to business valuation involves direct estimation of the value of the net assets to be acquired (=assets to be acquired by the buyer minus any liabilities to be assumed by the buyer). An **asset-based approach** typically begins by examining the firm's balance sheet. However, there are several reasons why *book (recorded) values* are typically unsatisfactory indicators of business value:

- Book values reflect the accumulated effects of applying Generally Accepted Accounting Principles to the past transactions of the firm and have no necessary connection to current economic value.
- Book values may not reflect the impact of changing prices (inflation) or technological change.
- Balance sheets may not include all the relevant assets of the business, especially unrecorded intangible assets.

Given these deficiencies, the analyst attempts to adjust book values to arrive at an overall business valuation. The analyst examines and values each asset and liability to estimate its *fair market value*, using techniques such as the determination of market values for comparable assets, expert appraisals, and price index-based inflation adjustments. It is important to identify and value unrecorded intangible assets, including goodwill, and unrecorded liabilities, such as environmental liabilities, operating leases, and other *off-balance-sheet* and contingent obligations.

Direct Comparison Approach

The logic of a direct comparison approach lies in the idea that similar assets should sell for similar prices, a principle well established in other markets.[6] In real estate, for example, the market value of a house could be estimated by finding recent selling prices for substantially similar houses in comparable neighborhoods. Finding sales of comparable businesses, however, is difficult. Transactions are few, and comprehensive data sources do not exist. Thus, a true direct comparison approach cannot generally be used in business valuation.

However, a form of direct comparison exists when some measure or ratio serves as the link between the business valuation in question and other businesses. For example, professional practices like Certified Public Accountant (CPA) firms often sell for a multiple of billings, perhaps two to three times annual billings. For example, the average price–earnings (P/E) ratio of similar public firms in the industry might be used. If such firms sell for 12 times earnings, we can apply that same measure to a business being valued. The *capitalized earnings* approach discussed later is a version of this technique. As with the *discounted future returns* approach discussed later, one needs to select a particular cash flow or income measure, such as gross revenues. One also needs to select the "other variable"—number of years' billings, P/E ratio, and the like—that will link the business being valued to other businesses.

Direct comparison techniques serve as a quick way of estimating business value, with little need for extensive estimation. However, because the comparison typically reflects an average of other businesses, this technique does not do a good job of incorporating distinctive features of the business being valued.

Payback Method

The payback for an investment is the number of periods management must wait before the accumulated positive cash flows from the investment exceed the initial cost of the investment project plus any negative operating cash flows. Investments are considered acceptable when the payback period is less than some predetermined time period, for example 3 years. Here is the computation:

Beginning investment: $100,000
Cash flow year 1: –$15,000 (with the beginning investment,
                    $115,000 still left to recover)
Cash flow year 2: $50,000 ($65,000 still left to recover)
Cash flow year 3: $60,000 ($5,000 only left to recover)
Cash flow year 4: $60,000
Cash flow year 5: $60,000

In this example, the payback occurs at about 3 years and 1 month. Many people do not consider *payback* to be a discounted cash flow technique because it does not take into account the time value of money. This is not entirely true. A short payback period, say, for example, 2 years, reflects the importance of dollars received in the short term and thus the time value of money.[7] The payback approach does not take into account cash flows that are outside of the payback threshold and they do not take into account the magnitude of the cash flows. Amazon is now a viable business but early investors did not consider the payback to be an important tool for deciding whether to invest in Amazon. This is a normal situation for many start-ups where positive cash flows do not occur until many years in the future. Discounted cash flow approaches incorporate the importance of distant cash flows and the magnitude of the cash flows.

Discounted Future Returns

Perhaps the most common, and conceptually best, technique for business valuation is calculation of the present value of expected future returns from the business. Although present-value computations are easy, determining the relevant inputs is not. Choices need to be made for:

- the type of future return to be measured (income or cash flow);
- estimates of the future amounts;

- an appropriate discount rate;
- the time period for the analysis; and
- the estimation of a terminal value.

We consider each of these areas.

Definition of Future Return

Numerous measures of future return are available to the business valuation analyst. Although *cash flow measures* are the most common, the analyst must still decide on a particular cash flow measure to use. One possibility is **cash flow from operations,** which reflects the cash impact of all *operating* activities during a time period. Others use *free cash flow*, a term for which different definitions exist.

> The most common definition of free cash flow is cash flow from operations minus cash investments in new assets needed to maintain operations. A less common definition is cash from operations minus cash investments in new assets needed to maintain operations minus debt repayments (this measure is designed to approximate cash available to the new owners).

Other analysts use income rather than cash flow measures. There are many variations here as well: net income as conventionally measured by accounting; earnings before taxes (EBT); earnings before interest and taxes (EBIT); earnings before interest, taxes, depreciation, and amortization (EBITDA); and the like. In some cases, especially if a minority investment is being evaluated, **expected dividends** is the relevant measure of future return.

Estimating Future Returns

Estimating future returns is a difficult task. Often the starting point is past returns, perhaps adjusted for unusual and nonrecurring items that have occurred. Knowledge of the business, industry, economic conditions, and other factors must be brought to bear.

One important task is to separate the expected future returns from the business *in its present form* from the expected future returns *under the guidance of the new owner.* Often, the efforts of the new owner will be more influential in determining future success than continuing the same uses of assets already in place. Because the business valuation is usually being conducted to establish a selling price, the buyer should not pay the seller for the buyer's anticipated improvements in the business.

Another consideration is whether to conduct the analysis on a *constant dollar basis* or to estimate revenue and cost increases resulting from inflation. Whichever is chosen, the discount rate should be selected in a consistent manner, as discussed in the next section.

Although discounting expected future returns is a conceptually sound approach to business valuation, it is often not used due to the practical difficulties of implementing it. We need projected returns for several years into the future, and such estimates can be highly speculative.

Choice of Discount Rate

Many considerations enter into the selection of a discount rate. First let us consider the **focus of the analysis**. If the analyst employs **return to all invested capital**, then a discount rate appropriate to the entire capital structure should be chosen. This rate is usually called a **weighted average cost of capital**, because it includes costs for both debt and equity capital. In contrast, a **return to equity capital** focus calls for an equity-based discount rate. Following the well-known **capital asset pricing model** of finance, this rate includes at least two components: a **risk-free rate** and a **risk premium**, reflecting both the risks of general economic conditions and the risks of the specific business and industry. The beta (β) **coefficient** is the typical measure of risk premium used.

Next we consider **adjusting for growth or inflation**. When the estimates of future returns reflect inflation, then a discount rate that includes an inflation component applies. If future returns are estimated on a current (constant) dollar basis, then the inflation component should be subtracted from the discount rate. For example, suppose that an appropriate discount rate, including inflation, is determined to be 25%. The analyst uses this rate to discount estimated future returns that include inflation-based growth in revenues and costs (nominal dollars). On the other hand, if estimated future returns are based on current (constant) dollars, and the inflation assumption is 4% annually, then a discount rate of 21% (=25% minus 4% inflation adjustment) should be used to discount the current-dollar future returns. To express this another way, if the future dollar amounts in the valuation analysis reflect *future prices and costs*, the discount rate should *include* the inflation component. If the future dollar amounts are based on *current prices and costs*, reflecting no growth or inflation, the discount rate should *exclude* the inflation component.

These two discounting approaches do not provide exactly the same answer, but they are close enough. Given the many assumptions that go into a valuation calculation, the slight difference is usually deemed acceptable. For example, assume that the annual cash flow is currently $300,000. An 8-year time horizon is used for the analysis. It is estimated that cash flows will grow by 5% annually. A discount rate of 15%, including growth, is deemed appropriate. The present value of $300,000 annually discounted at 10% (15% minus the 5% growth assumption) and the present value of the growth-adjusted cash flows discounted at 15% are shown in Table 11.1.

Table 11.1. Comparison of Present Values With and Without Growth

Year	Projected annual cash flow without growth ($)	Present value of cash flow without growth at 10% discount rate ($)	Projected annual cash flow with 5% growth ($)	Present value of cash flow with 5% growth at 15% discount rate ($)
1	300,000	272,727	315,000	273,913
2	300,000	247,934	330,750	250,095
3	300,000	225,394	347,288	228,347
4	300,000	204,904	364,652	208,491
5	300,000	186,276	382,884	190,361
6	300,000	169,342	402,029	173,808
7	300,000	153,947	422,130	158,694
8	300,000	139,952	443,237	144,895
Total		$1,600,476		$1,628,604

When multiyear analysis is used, a growth or inflation factor should be considered in some way. If growth is completely ignored in the above example, the present value of a $300,000 annual cash flow discounted at 15% would be approximately $1,350,000. If growth is expected, ignoring it clearly understates the value of the business. Of course, if future *declines* in cash flows are expected, indicating a business with initial appeal but little staying power, ignoring the expected negative growth would overstate the business value.

As seen in the above example, a positive growth assumption can either be built into the cash flow estimates, or incorporated by a reduction of the discount rate. Either approach will increase the business value relative to making no adjustment for growth.

The two present values in Table 11.1 are approximately the same, differing by <2%, which may be more precise than the cash flow estimates themselves or the discount rate selection. Nonetheless, one could easily find the precise discount rate and use that. If one accepts 10% as the correct rate without growth, then the correct rate with 5% growth that would discount the cash flows with growth (fourth column above) to the $1,600,476 present value turns out to be 15.50%. Similarly, if one accepts 15% as the correct rate with growth, then the correct rate without growth that would discount the constant cash flows (second column above) to the $1,628,604 present value turns out to be 9.52%. But for most purposes, the process illustrated above is sufficient.

Most of the literature on the weighted average cost of capital is based on information from public capital markets. Recently, work has been done to try to establish a private cost of capital approach.[8] They identify five different capital markets for private firms: bank lending, asset-based lending, mezzanine financing, private equity, and venture capital. Median rates of returns for these markets (first quarter 2010) were found to range from 6.8% for bank lending to 38.2% for venture capital financing.

Selection of Time Period for Discounting

The analyst who uses a discounted future returns approach must determine *how far* into the future to project. The general answer is *as far as possible*, keeping in mind that the uncertainty of the estimates increases as they get further away. Because a business is usually assumed to be a *going concern*, returns are presumed to continue indefinitely. Thus one could assume that returns continue forever. Alternatively, the analyst could limit the analysis to a fixed time period, say 10 years. In this case, one makes specific annual projections for 10 years and estimates a **terminal value** of the business at the end of that period.

Although estimates of future returns, or of terminal value, become more speculative the further in the future they are, the effect of discounting mitigates the increased uncertainty. For example, at a discount rate of 20%, $1,000 in year 10 contributes only $161 to the present value, and $1,000 in year 20 contributes only $26 to the present value.

When we assume that future returns will continue forever in equal amounts, we have a **perpetuity**. The present value is given by:

Present value of ordinary perpetuity
   = Constant annual return/Discount rate

For a discount rate of 20%, the present value is five times the annual return ($5 = $1/0.2). As shown in Table 11.2, about 60% of the present value occurs in the first 5 years, and about 84% in the first 10 years. Returns in later years have relatively little impact on the present value.

Capitalized Earnings

Despite the conceptual soundness of the discounted future returns method, the subjectivity of future return estimates is a major deterrent to its use. Parties to the negotiations will likely disagree over the assumptions employed in arriving at the estimates. As a result, business valuation often employs a conceptually similar approach that appears to avoid future estimation. This approach is known as *capitalized earnings*.

We saw that the discounted future returns method computes a present value based on applying a *discount rate* to the estimated returns of a *number of future time periods*. The **capitalized earnings approach**, on the

Table 11.2. Impact of Time on Present Value

Period	Present Value of $1 at 20%	Cumulative Present Value	Percent of perpetuity value
1	0.833	0.8333	0.1667
2	0.6944	1.5278	0.3056
3	0.5787	2.1065	0.4213
4	0.4823	2.5887	0.5177
5	0.4019	2.9906	0.5981
6	0.3349	3.3255	0.6651
7	0.2791	3.6046	0.7209
8	0.2326	3.8372	0.7674
9	0.1938	4.0310	0.8062
10	0.1615	4.1925	0.8385
11	0.1346	4.3271	0.8654
12	0.1122	4.4392	0.8878
13	0.0935	4.5327	0.9065
14	0.0779	4.6106	0.9221
15	0.0649	4.6755	0.9351
16	0.0541	4.7296	0.9459
17	0.0451	4.7746	0.9549
18	0.0376	4.8122	0.9624
19	0.0313	4.8435	0.9687
20	0.0261	4.8696	0.9739

Note: Annual payments assumed to occur at the end of year.

other hand, computes a present value based on applying a *capitalization rate* to a *single amount of present or past returns*, as follows:

Present value = Amount of return to be capitalized/capitalization rate

This formula is equivalent to the present value of a perpetuity discussed above.

What *amount of return should be capitalized?* First, as discussed previously, any measure of return can be used—a cash flow measure, an income measure, or even revenues or dividends. Second, the return measure may be based on past, present, or even future data. Examples include the following:

- Return for the past 12 months or most recent fiscal year
- An average return, either simple or weighted, for some number of past years
- A *normalized* current or average return, excluding unusual or nonrecurring items
- A forecast for the current period or a future period.

Most commonly, the use of present returns, or an average of past returns, appears to avoid the estimation problem. But one cannot really avoid estimation. To base a present value on current or past returns implicitly assumes the continuation of such returns in the future.

The **capitalization rate** is the relevant discount rate, discussed above, minus the assumed rate of growth (or decline) in future returns. As an example, suppose last year's net income of $200,000 is the amount to be capitalized, that we decide on a relevant discount rate of 20%, and that we expect 3% earnings growth. The capitalized value of the company is:

Present value = Amount of return to be capitalized/capitalization rate
= $200,000/(0.20 − 0.03)
= $200,000/0.17
= $1,176,471

On the other hand, if we anticipate a 3% earnings *decline*, the capitalized value is:

Present value = Amount of return to be capitalized/capitalization rate
= $200,000/(0.20 + 0.03)
= $200,000/0.23
= $869,565

A capitalization rate for equity returns is the inverse of the familiar **P/E ratio** commonly cited for publicly traded companies, and thus is sometimes called an **earnings–price (E/P) ratio**. For example, a company selling at 17 times earnings has an effective capitalization rate of 5.88% (0.0588 = 1/17). In selecting a capitalization rate for a specific business, one could use E/P ratios of reasonably similar public companies as guides. However, when valuing small nonpublic companies, lower P/E ratios (higher E/P ratios and capitalization rates) are typically appropriate, to allow for increased risk. It is not uncommon for small nonpublic companies to sell for 3–10 times earnings.

Capitalizing Excess Earnings

A widely used variation of the capitalized earnings method is called the **capitalization of excess earnings**. This hybrid method reflects the concept that earnings derive from both the tangible assets and intangible assets of the business. Earnings from tangible assets are assumed to be relatively constant from one firm in an industry to another, whereas earnings from intangible assets may vary widely. The method proceeds as follows:

- Estimate the value of net tangible assets
- Estimate the earnings attributable to the tangible assets, perhaps by multiplying the value of the tangible assets by the average industry return
- Subtract this amount from total reported earnings; the difference is **excess earnings**, the amount above what is explained by the company's tangible assets
- Capitalize the excess earnings.

The value placed on the business has two components:

Business value = Net tangible assets
                 + Capitalized value of excess earnings

Because we tend to consider earnings attributable to intangibles to be more risky than earnings attributable to tangible assets, we tend to use high capitalization rates (low multiples).

Table 11.3. Capitalization of Excess Earnings ($)

Value of net tangible assets		350,000
Reported earnings of the company	50,000	
Earnings attributed to tangible assets = $350,000 × 0.10	35,000	
Excess earnings	15,000	
Capitalized value of excess earnings = $15,000/0.25		60,000
Estimated value of company		410,000

When we calculate negative excess earnings, the business is still presumed to be worth the value of its net tangible assets and we make no reduction for apparent negative intangibles.

For example, suppose a company reports earnings of $50,000 and net tangible assets of $350,000. Average industry earnings are 10% of net tangible assets, and we decide to capitalize excess earnings at 25%. The value estimate for the business is $410,000, as shown in Table 11.3.

The excess earnings method, like much of business valuation, has its foundation in materials promulgated by the Internal Revenue Service. Revenue Ruling 68–609 sets forth a so-called *formula method*, as follows:

> The question presented is whether the "formula" approach, the capitalization of earnings in excess of a fair rate of return on net tangible assets, may be used to determine the fair market value of the intangible assets of a business. The "formula" approach may be stated as follows:
>
> A percentage return on the average annual value of the tangible assets used in a business is determined, using a period of years (preferably not less than five) immediately prior to the valuation date. The amount of the percentage return on tangible assets, thus determined, is deducted from the average earnings of the business for such period and the remainder, if any, is considered to be the amount of the average annual earnings from the intangible assets of the business for the period. This amount

(considered as the average annual earnings from intangibles), capitalized at a percentage of, say 15 to 20 percent, is the value of the intangible assets determined under the "formula" approach.

The percentage of return on the average annual value of the tangible assets used should be the percentage prevailing in the industry involved at the date of valuation, or (when the industry percentage is not available) a percentage of 8 to 10 percent may be used.

The 8 percent rate of return and the 15 percent rate of capitalization are applied to tangibles and intangibles, respectively, of businesses with a small risk factor and stable and regular earnings; the 10 percent rate of return and 20 percent rate of capitalization are applied to businesses in which the hazards of business are relatively high.

The above rates are used as examples and are not appropriate in all cases....

The past earnings to which the formula is applied should fairly reflect the probable future earnings. Ordinarily, the period should not be less than five years, and abnormal years, whether above or below the average, should be eliminated. If the business is a sole proprietorship or partnership, there should be deducted from the earnings of the business a reasonable amount for services performed by the owner or partners engaged in the business....

The "formula" approach should not be used if there is better evidence available from which the value of intangibles can be determined....

Because of the extensive guidance given in Revenue Ruling 68–609, many business valuation analysts follow it closely, even though it contains many cautions and qualifications, especially in performing valuations for tax purposes. This approach has come to be known as the **Treasury Method.**[9]

Valuation Premiums and Discounts

After initially estimating the value of a business, that estimate may be adjusted upward (premium) or downward (discount) to reflect other factors related to the ownership interest in question. For example, a *controlling interest* in a business is worth more on a per-share basis than a *minority interest*, as the holder of a controlling interest has authority over business decisions, whereas the minority interest holder does not. This section briefly examines some common premiums and discounts.[10]

Business valuations typically begin with a *base value*, using techniques applicable to a broad range of businesses. A premium or discount is an upward or downward adjustment to this base value, to reflect some different characteristics of the particular business being considered. These characteristics are reflected in various ways. If one uses a discounted cash flow approach to valuation, a higher or lower discount rate could reflect the special characteristics. Alternatively, the analyst could adjust the initial valuation estimate upward or downward for specific features of the business. Knowing how to identify and quantify premiums and discounts is one of the specific skills of a business valuation expert. The following situations can increase or decrease the discount premium:

- *Control premium*: The buyer acquires a *controlling interest*— usually defined as more than 50% of the voting power—in the acquired company. Because of all the powers a controlling owner has, a controlling ownership interest is clearly worth more than a noncontrolling interest. These premiums can be in the 30–50% range.
- *Minority interest discount*: A minority interest discount, also known as a discount for lack of control, is the logical opposite of a control premium. If the ability to exercise control commands a premium, the lack of that ability is worth less.
- *Strategic acquisition premium*: Sometimes the acquisition of a business may be important from a strategic perspective. For example, an acquisition may complement the existing product line, broadening the geographic market, ensure a source of supply, or eliminate a key competitor, for a specific buyer.

- *Lack-of-marketability discount:* Publicly traded equity shares have a high degree of liquidity—they can be readily converted into cash at close to prevailing prices. Because investors value liquidity, a negative factor exists when the investor lacks the ability to sell on short notice at a market price. Studies report that thinly traded stocks realized a 30–50% price decline when the brokerage firm that was their sole market-maker went out of business.[11] Studies of restricted stock of public companies that itself cannot be publicly traded find discounts for the lack of marketability ranging from about 20% to 70%.[12] Ownership interests in nonpublic companies almost always are discounted for the lack of marketability.
- *Key person discount:* Some acquisitions include an arrangement for the key person(s) to join the new company for a period of time. In other cases, the key persons do not accompany the acquisition, perhaps due to death or retirement. When the key person does not continue with the business, attributes such as the loyalty of customers, suppliers, or employees may be lost, as well as the key person's particular business skills. Research studies and court cases find the key person discount to typically be in the range of 5–10% in public companies, and 10–25% in private companies.[13]

Discounts may be applied to base business valuations for factors other than those described earlier. One possibility is a **discount for contingent liabilities**, reflecting potential future claims resulting from past business activities that will become the responsibility of a buyer. Such contingent liabilities involve potential litigation such as product liability, potential environmental claims, or potential tax adjustments for prior years. Because these liabilities are situation-specific, the valuation analyst must look sharply for them!

The above discussion indicates that discounts are more frequent than premiums. After achieving a base valuation, the analyst considers adjustments for the various factors discussed above. Note that the impact of these factors can be incorporated into the base analysis—for example, by adjusting the estimates of future income or cash flows—or can be reflected as an adjustment to the base value calculation. However, incorporated into the business valuation analysis, discounts can have a large effect on the ultimate value.

Valuing Start-Up Businesses

Businesses that are yet to be undertaken, or are in the early stages of their development, are especially hard to value. Suppose an entrepreneur with a concept for a new business needs capital to launch the business. Because of the high risk of new businesses, traditional capital sources—banks and other institutional lenders, and the public equity markets—are usually not available. Most new businesses begin with capital raised from the founder's own resources, and perhaps from friends and family. Sometimes, an unrelated investor who believes in the concept, referred to as an "angel," also provides some seed capital. *Angels* are especially common in artistic ventures, such as movies or stage shows. As the business begins to develop, **VCs** often provide the next influx of capital. These investors take short-term ownership stakes in promising new businesses. Business valuations have a role to play in these situations as well as in the financing or purchase of established businesses.[14]

Approaches to Valuing a Start-Up

Because a new business has little to no history, and because it may be pursuing innovative products, services, or other business features, uncertainty about its future prospects is especially high. A capitalized earnings approach cannot be used, as new companies frequently report losses in the early years, and their present earnings (losses) may not be indicative of expected earnings. A discounted earnings or discounted cash flow approach is typically most appropriate. Many analysts favor using cash flows rather than earnings, because of the importance of cash management in start-up firms. Many start-ups fail because they quickly run out of cash. During the "dot. com" era, analysts often focused on the rate at which a start-up consumed cash, a phenomenon colorfully known as its **burn rate**.

When performing a discounted cash flow approach to valuing a new business, the analyst must decide on the estimate of cash flows to use. The entrepreneur's forecasts are likely to be highly optimistic, reflecting his or her vision of a successful future. When using an entrepreneur's forecasts, the analyst typically tries to neutralize the entrepreneur's optimism with a high discount rate. A high rate reflects both the degree of risk involved and the expectations of capital providers for high returns to compensate for the risk. VCs might seek rates of return of 50% or more during the seed capital stage and 30–50% at later stages.

VCs are not long-term investors. They seek to *cash out* after 3–5 years. Their investments often take the form of specialized equity, such as a preferred stock issue with a high dividend rate and mandatory redemption at a specified future time, either at a high cash price or at a generous conversion into common shares. The latter option is appealing when the VCs anticipate an **initial public offering** of the start-up's shares.

Venture capital investing is high risk. First-time start-ups have a 21% chance of succeeding. Even previously successful venture-capital-backed enterprise still only have a 30% chance of succeeding in the next venture.[15]

Multiscenario Approaches

In addition to using high discount rates for start-up companies, valuation analysts may use a multiscenario approach. One multiscenario approach begins by constructing alternative outcomes under different degrees of optimism about the future of the company. The approach next estimates a discounted cash flow value for each outcome, called a **conditional** value, and then weights each outcome according to a probability estimate of its likelihood of occurring. Often referred to as the **First Chicago Approach**,[16] this methodology frequently creates a table such as the one shown below, using the success percentages cited above:

Scenario	Conditional value ($)	Probability	Weighted value ($)
Very optimistic	150,000,000	0.02	3,000,000
Optimistic	80,000,000	0.08	6,400,000
Conservative	20,000,000	0.20	4,000,000
Break even	0	0.30	0
Pessimistic	(25,000,000)	0.40	(10,000,000)
Weighted Average			**$3,400,000**

Examples of Valuation

Many considerations and estimates enter into a business valuation. It is more art than science, with the skill and insight of the valuation expert playing an important role.

To illustrate some of the effects of the estimates and assumptions involved, consider a new business venture, Ron's Business Valuation Services, with the first-year cash flow estimates as shown in Table 11.4.

The first question is the expected growth of the business. Consider first an assumption of 6% annual growth. We assume that collections and all expenses will grow at that rate, though other assumptions could be made. A 5-year cash flow projection for Ron's Business Valuation Services, with 6% growth, would be as shown in Table 11.5.

A discount rate needs to be chosen. Since growth is already built into the cash flow assumptions, the discount rate reflects only the riskiness of this business. If we believed that the business had relatively little risk, we might choose a discount rate of 10%. This would give a present value for the 5 years of cash flow of $76,080. If we believed the risk was high, we might choose a discount rate of 30%, which would give a present value of $47,968. Clearly, the choice of discount rate has a major influence on the calculated present value.

Instead of estimating the cash flow of each of the first 5 years, suppose we simply estimated that the average annual cash flow over 5 years would be $20,293. This would not make a big difference in the present-value

Table 11.4. First-year Projected Cash Flow

Cash receipts ($)	
Cash collections from clients	200,000
Cash payments ($)	
Payroll	80,000
Marketing and customer service	16,000
Rent	30,000
Office supplies and equipment	20,000
Taxes and licenses	36,000
Total cash payments ($)	182,000
Net cash flow ($)	18,000

Table 11.5. Five-year Cash Flow Projection, 6% Growth Rate

	Year 1	Year 2	Year 3	Year 4	Year 5
Cash collections ($)	200,000	212,000	224,720	238,203	252,495
Cash payments ($)					
Payroll	80,000	84,800	89,888	95,281	100,998
Marketing and customer service	16,000	16,960	17,978	19,056	20,200
Rent	30,000	31,800	33,708	35,730	37,874
Office supplies and equipment	20,000	21,200	22,472	23,820	25,250
Taxes and licenses	36,000	38,160	40,450	42,877	45,449
Total cash payments ($)	182,000	192,920	204,496	216,764	229,771
Net cash flow ($)	18,000	19,080	20,224	21,439	22,724

calculations, giving $76,926 at a 10% discount rate and $49,425 at a 30% discount rate. These amounts are somewhat higher than shown earlier, because using an average in this case attributes somewhat higher cash flows to earlier years and somewhat lower cash flows to later years, thus increasing the present value.

This example considered only 5 years; what about subsequent years? One approach would be to continue the growth projections for more years, although the confidence in our estimates decreases as we go further out in time. At the other extreme, we could assign zero value beyond 5 years, on the basis that the survival of the business beyond that time is too uncertain. A third possibility is to assume that the average cash flows calculated above would continue indefinitely; the present value of that perpetuity would be $202,930 (=$20,293/0.10) at a 10% discount rate or $67,643 (=$20,293/0.30) at a 30% discount rate. As can be seen, the value of this business depends heavily upon the assumptions used in our calculations.

Consider next an assumption of 16% annual growth. Again, we assume that collections and all expenses will grow at that rate, though other assumptions could be made. A 5-year cash flow projection for Ron's Business Valuation Services, with 16% growth, would be as shown in Table 11.6.

Here the present value of the 5 years of projected cash flows is $91,244 at a 10% discount rate and $55,836 at a 30% discount rate. These present

Table 11.6. Five-year Cash Flow Projection, 16% Growth Rate

	Year 1	Year 2	Year 3	Year 4	Year 5
Cash collections ($)	200,000	232,000	269,120	312,179	362,128
Cash payments ($)					
Payroll	80,000	92,800	107,648	124,872	144,851
Marketing and customer service	16,000	18,560	21,530	24,974	28,970
Rent	30,000	34,800	40,368	46,827	54,319
Office supplies and equipment	20,000	23,200	26,912	31,218	36,213
Taxes and licenses	36,000	41,760	48,442	56,192	65,183
Total cash payments ($)	182,000	211,120	244,899	284,083	329,536
Net cash flow ($)	18,000	20,880	24,211	28,096	32,592

values are 20% and 16% higher, respectively, than those calculated under the 6% growth assumption. Average 5-year cash flow for this scenario is $24,758; the present value based on the 5-year average is $93,842 at 10%, and $60,300 at 30%, both 22% higher than the corresponding figures for the 6% growth scenario. Perpetuity values are $247,580 (=$24,578/0.10) at 10% and $81,927 (=$24,578/0.30) at 30%.

These comparisons represent the importance of **sensitivity analysis** in performing business valuation calculations. Sensitivity analysis addresses the question of how much difference in the outcome results from different assumptions. The more sensitive the outcome, the less confidence we should place in the result.

The Importance of Growth Rate on Firm Value

The growth rate of revenues can have a dramatic impact on the value of the business. As noted earlier, one way to determine the value of a business is to use the formula for the present value of perpetual annuity. The following formula was used.

Present Value of Ordinary Perpetuity
= Constant annual return/Discount rate

This formula can be slightly modified to include a growth in annual returns.

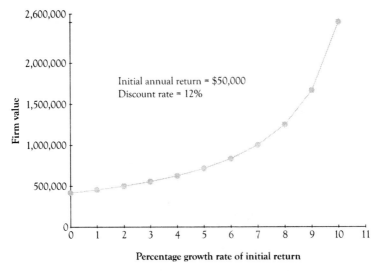

Figure 11.1. The influence of growth rate on firm value.

Firm Value = Initial Annual Return/(Discount Rate
                – Growth Rate of Initial Return)

If the initial annual return is $50,000 and the cost of capital is 8% and revenues are not expected to grow then the value of the firm would be $625,000. If the initial annual return is expected to grow at 2%, then the value of the firm would increase to $833,333.

Figure 11.1 presents a graph where the growth rate ranges from 0–10% with a discount rate of 12% and an initial annual return of $50,000. The present value of a firm with 0% growth rate is approximately $417,000. The present value of the firm with a 10% growth rate is $2,500,000. As the growth rate approaches the discount rate the present value of the firm increases exponentially. This in part illustrates why companies with very modest returns are sometimes valued very highly by potential investors. A firm with strong growth potential, even with small initial returns, is an attractive target for investors.

Conclusion

In this chapter, we have presented an overview of business valuation. The key points are the following:

- Business valuation is a complex and challenging field that offers several methods to choose from, and requires that many decisions be made when applying any method.
- These choices and decisions are typically guided by the purpose of the valuation, the nature of the business being valued, the availability of data, and the skill and expertise of the valuation professional.
- Multiple valuations based on different methods are likely to yield different results. Some analysts choose to average the values to arrive at a composite estimate. Others frame the valuation as a range of values defined by those outcomes that are reasonably consistent with one another, ignoring any outliers. There is considerably more *art* than *science* involved in this field.
- Once an initial valuation is completed, consideration should be given to any factors that may lead to an increase (premiums) or decrease (discounts) in the value of the business.
- Start-up or early-stage businesses are especially hard to value, due to the lack of a track record. Expected rates of return on investment are high at this stage, to compensate for the much higher risk that the endeavor will not be successful.

Business valuation for a start-up is often ignored because it is complex and because there is no historical financial patterns to turn to. It is, however, important because of the numerous stakeholders who are interested in the value of the business. It is also significant because it provides key insight into the overall financial structure and the firm's value proposition.

CHAPTER 12

Developing a Business Plan

The terms strategic planning and business plan are often used interchangeably, even though they are different. The strategic planning process is essentially the upfront activity related to generating a business model. It involves using the analytical strategic planning approaches discussed in chapter 8, such as value chain analysis, Porter's five-force model, the resource-based view of strategy, the technology life cycle, and SWOT analysis among others.[1] In chapter 9, we introduced an abbreviated approach to planning, called the Ten–Ten planning process that can be quickly implemented and assist in bringing focus and clarity to the entrepreneur's vision. You are encouraged to complete the FAD template, Organizational and Industry Analysis template, and the Business Plan Overview template and to also develop an executive summary using the material in earlier chapters before you develop a full-scale business plan. There are two reasons for this. The first reason is that the material developed during the Ten–Ten planning will be very useful in developing a focused, more complete, and better plan. The other reason for using the Ten–Ten process is that business models evolve very rapidly, and sometimes it is better to let the idea incubate and to also present the plan to a variety of audiences before committing and finalizing the full-blown plan.

In this section, we will present a more detailed approach for constructing a full-blown business plan. The expanded business plan provides additional focus by adding details on the what, why, how, when, and for whom a product or service will be produced. The business plan is an abbreviated description of the business model (see Table 12.1). The business plan is presented to the outside world through a business presentation and is accompanied by a business plan document.

Table 12.1. The Business Model: Important Business Model Decisions

What will the product features and product mix look like?
How will the firm acquire market share, define market segments, and market the product mix?
What type of pricing strategy will be used (menus, auctions, and bartering)?
Where will the organization build core competencies and capabilities?
With who, when, and why will partnerships and alliances be formed?
How and why are funding and resource decisions made?
How will the supply chain work? This involves the when, who, and how to tasks are performed.
Should supply chain tasks be outsourced, off-shored, or in-tasked?
How will employees be acquired and retained?
What will the information technology look like in terms of hardware, software, and networking?
How will product, process, and content innovation be carried out in terms of R&D?

Adapted from Afuah and Tucci.[2]

Purpose of the Business Plan

The business plan serves many purposes. The business plan presents a succinct overview of the what, how, when, and why of the business. First, it is used to communicate with investors. It provides investors with a concise overview of what the business is about and how investors can make money. In many ways, the business plan is a prototype of the business model. It is a scaled-down version that describes how the business will function. The business plan also serves as a platform for the business founders to communicate and it can be used as a blueprint for operating the business the first year.[3] It also helps mentors and consultants to identify weaknesses, missed opportunities, strange assumptions, and overly optimistic projections. Finally, the business plan also serves as a tool for educating new employees on how the business works and how they will fit into the business activities.

Approaches for Developing Business Plans

There are several approaches for developing a business plan. The first approach is to thoroughly develop the business plan and then make a presentation to investors, other entrepreneurs, interested parties, and family members. The feedback from the presentation is then used to rewrite and modify the business plan. The updated business plan is then presented to the relevant parties. The major criticism of this approach is that too much time is spent developing the business plan and not enough time on refining and streamlining the business model.

The second approach consists of writing an executive summary, or a business concept paper, and then to prepare a presentation and deliver it to the relevant parties without any modification from presentation feedback. We have used this approach for over 10 years. Guy Kawasaki uses a similar technique called the pitch and plan approach.[4]

Kawasaki believes that one purpose of the plan is to attract investors, but that the most important reason for developing a plan is to solidify the management team's objectives. He believes that the executive summary plays a critical role in attracting investors and creating focus for the management team. He recommends pitching the idea first and then developing a full-blown plan.

As noted above, we completely agree with that assertion and have used a similar approach for years. The FAD template, the Business Plan Overview template, the executive summary, the business presentation, and the full-blown business plan are in reality prototypes of the business. They are all abbreviated business models. They give the management team, the founders, and the investors an opportunity to focus on something that represents the actual business. How many times have you heard the following refrains?

They just don't understand our business model!
They just don't understand what we're doing!

One of the most important duties of the entrepreneur is to educate and facilitate the learning process of the management team, the founders, and investors. The objective should not be too obscure the way the business works, but rather to help interested parties understand why the business will work. The Ten–Ten planning approach coupled with the executive summary, the presentation, and the full-blown business plan should facilitate the learning process and lead to better communication. Better communication will in turn lead to an improved business model.

Prototyping the Product or Service

As noted throughout the book, a key activity for innovative activity is to engage in learning by doing. Learning by doing means that you make and build things, try experiments, and construct prototypes. Prototypes need to be constructed for tangible products and also for systems applications. If the product is a tangible product, then a generic mock-up of the product needs to be constructed as early as possible. If that is not possible, because of limited resources or an overly complex product, a handmade drawing with a graphics program or with CAD/CAM software or Google's free SketchUp application can be used to develop a prototype. If the product is a computer application, then a prototype can be constructed using a rapid prototyping language or with a presentation package such as PowerPoint. There are also many excellent applications available for the iPad to develop mock-ups of applications and drawings for product ideas.

One interesting way of presenting the idea behind the business is to tell a story about how the product or service solved a problem. Presenting a problem and solution scenario is a very effective way for communicating a business plan concept. One business plan presentation used a clipart in the form of a scenario comic book to communicate the business concept. It involved a consumer coming home to find the inside of the house flooded. The story then went on to describe how the consumer would use a new emergency repair network to find a reputable contractor via a competitive bidding process. It was a very convincing story and quite effective in illustrating how the service was much different than the competition's service. The goal of using a scenario is to get the readers to understand the details of what the business has to offer.

Business Plan Template

Table 12.2 presents an overview of a business plan. It should not be viewed as a checklist, to be filled in extensively with bullet points and narratives.

Table 12.2. Business Plan Template Part 1

1. Business pan title
   a. It should include the name of the business and the name of the founders.
2. Acknowledgements page
3. Table of contents
4. Executive summary (1–2 pages)
5. Business overview (2–3 pages)
   a. Description of products and services to be offered. If it is a complex product, provide a detailed description of the functions.
   b. Provide a prototype, a scenario, a picture, a diagram, or a mock-up of your product or service. Briefly discuss the prototype. It is often a good idea to illustrate your concept early if the product or service is complex or very unique.
   c. Describe how the product or service solves an important problem or presents an opportunity to fill an important market niche. Be sure to explain why the product or service is not just a good idea, but a sustainable source of revenue that can eventually generate a profit.
   d. Discuss how product is competitive compared with existing product or service offerings.
   e. Will you differentiate your product on price, quality, service, or all the three?
   f. Present a Strategy Canvas illustrating how your product or service compares to the competition.
   g. What is the size of the market you expect to enter?
   h. What is the growth potential of the market?
6. Industry, economic, and regulatory analysis (2–3 pages)
   a. Describe the current and potential competitors (substitute products). Be sure to discuss potential products and technologies that could make your offering irrelevant.
   b. How will the competition react to market entry?
   c. What are the barriers to entry in the marketplace?
   d. Are there any governmental or regulatory issues that should be considered?
   e. Economic issues?
7. Marketing strategy (1–3 pages)
   a. Exactly how will you price your product?
   b. What customer segments are you trying to reach?
   c. How will versions be matched to customer segments?
   d. How will you go about promoting your product?
   e. What techniques will be used to acquire customers?
   f. How will you answer inquiries about the product specifications, features, and functions?

(Continued)

Table 12.2. Business Plan Template Part 1 (Continued)

g. How will you retain and lock-in customers?

h. How will you interact and distribute your product to your customers?

8. Operations strategy (1–3 pages)

a. Who will design the product or service and where will product or service design take place?

b. Where will the product be made, who will make it and how will it be made?

c. What are the detailed variables and fixed costs for producing the product or service?

d. Are their important issues related to the supply of components and materials?

e. How will order fulfillment take place? Are there important issues related to the fulfillment of orders?

f. How will you provide customer service and support including tech support?

9. Human resource strategy (1–3 pages)

a. What kind of employees do we need to run the business?

b. Where will we recruit them from?

c. What kind of compensation incentives will be offered in terms of salary, stock options, and benefits?

d. How will employees be trained and developed?

e. How will employees be evaluated?

10. Financials and forecasts (1–3 pages)

a. Present a simple pro forma sources (cash inflows) and uses of funds cash outflows) for 3 years after launching.

   i. The sources of funds include starting cash, incoming cash from sales, investor funds, loans, and personal funds.

   ii. The uses of funds include payroll or salaries, rent, materials, supplies, land, office space, equipment, warehouse costs, transportation costs, maintenance, marketing, and other overhead.

   iii. Include ending cash balance for each year. Can also include net present value and internal rate of return calculations.

b. Present a simple pro forma income statement for 3 years after launching. Be sure to discuss assumptions for sales, expenses, and growth.

   i. Income should include total sales, less production costs or cost of goods sold, and net or gross margin.

   ii. Include operating expenses that have been somewhat aggregated and total expenses.

   iii. Bottom line should list net profit or loss.

c. Start-up and development costs needed before launch (see above). How will they be funded?

(Continued)

Table 12.2. Business Plan Template Part 1 (Continued)

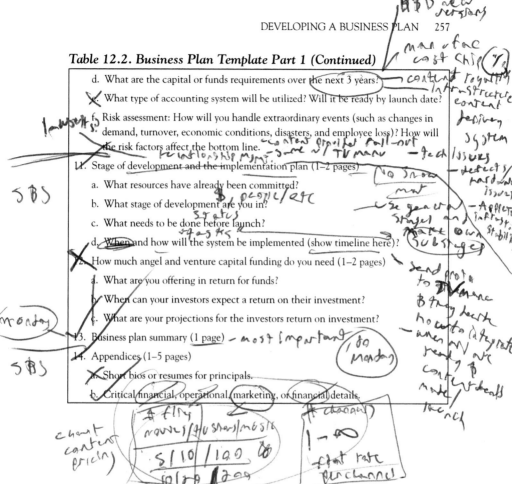

d. What are the capital or funds requirements over the next 3 years?

e. What type of accounting system will be utilized? Will it be ready by launch date?

f. Risk assessment: How will you handle extraordinary events (such as changes in demand, turnover, economic conditions, disasters, and employee loss)? How will the risk factors affect the bottom line.

11. Stage of development and the implementation plan (1–2 pages)

　　a. What resources have already been committed?

　　b. What stage of development are you in?

　　c. What needs to be done before launch?

　　d. When and how will the system be implemented (show timeline here)?

12. How much angel and venture capital funding do you need (1–2 pages)

　　a. What are you offering in return for funds?

　　b. When can your investors expect a return on their investment?

　　c. What are your projections for the investors return on investment?

13. Business plan summary (1 page)

14. Appendices (1–5 pages)

　　a. Short bios or resumes for principals.

　　b. Critical financial, operational, marketing, or financial details.

It should be viewed as a set of guidelines for constructing and developing a business model. Some of the subheadings for the sections may not even be addressed in the business plan and others may be addressed in great depth. It depends on the business context. A plan should typically be between 10 and 20 pages without appendices.

Writing, Organization, and Formatting: Helping the Reader to Read

Content is of course the king in all writing activities and this is also true for the business plan. However, the appearance and the look and feel of a document can often overcome minor deficiencies and sometimes hide major flaws. The most important element of the business plan is the "look." It must look clean. In general, the business plan should be between 10 and 20 pages.[5] Here are a few recommendations for preparing a business plan or an executive summary that will improve the way they look and read.

The first step in helping the reader to read is accomplished by having a document with the following features.

- *Use* good-quality paper.
- *Use* at least 1-inch document margins.
- *Always* double-space between lines. Never single space in the body of the business plan. You can single space tables, quotes, and the appendices.
- *Use* descriptive headings and subheadings to set off sections and to assist in transitions between content.
- *Use* a simple typeface, such as Arial, Calibri, Times-Roman, or Cambria or a related typeface that is easy to read. Use color to improve the appearance, but do not overuse.
- *Include* some figures and tables and refer to them in your discussion. Each figure and table should have a number and a caption. Make sure the figures, tables, and financial spreadsheets look attractive and are understandable. Use color to improve the appearance.
- *Never* present your business plan as a series of bullet points. The plan should have paragraphs and tell a story. It should **not** look like a presentation.

Simple fonts facilitate reading, understanding, and even the accomplishment of tasks. Psychologists at the University of Michigan conducted an experiment where they were trying to get 20-year-old college students to exercise.[6] They divided the students into two groups. One of the groups received instructions for a regular exercise routine in an Arial typeface and the other received the same instructions in a Brush typeface. The subjects who had read the exercise instructions in Arial indicated that they were more willing to exercise and they believed that the routine would be easier and take less time than those subjects reading the instructions in a decorative typeface. They conducted another test in which two groups of students read instructions in preparing sushi rolls in a simple typeface and a decorative typeface. The results were similar. The students using the simple typeface instructions were more willing to attempt making sushi rolls than those reading from instructions in a decorative typeface.

Reader fatigue is an important issue. Another way to reduce fatigue is by changing the lengths of your sentences. For example, have two short sentences and one long sentence and one short sentence followed by one long sentence and then one short sentence. The idea is to mix up the sentence structure and create interest. The second method that fatigues readers is of course having too much to read.[7] This is particularly true when the business plan involves difficult and unfamiliar material. Succinct and clear writing coupled with informative figures and tables will alleviate reader fatigue. This is the essence of pithy writing. The length of the business plan narrative should usually be between 10 and 20 pages and rarely if ever exceed 20 pages. You can also add between 4 and 6 pages of figure, tables, and appendices. Graphics and tables are also important elements for assisting in chronicling and presenting the business plan. Tables and figures should always have numbers and captions, and they should always be referred to by their figure number or table number in the text.

The last point is extremely important. "*Never* present your business plan as a series of bullet points." Remember, the goal of the business plan is to tell an interesting story. Bullet points need background and discussion. The business plan should **never** look like it was simply lifted from a presentation. This is a serious rookie mistake. Use bullet points sparingly and when you do use them, you need to discuss them, just as you would discuss a point during a presentation.

Finally, how can you cram all of this information into one business plan and not bore your readers. It requires hard work and constant refinement so that the core aspects of the business are communicated in less than 20 pages. Several trade-offs have to be made; some areas will expand and others will be reduced. Very few business plans look the same. They are highly differentiated. It is the role of the entrepreneur and the entrepreneurial team to educate and facilitate the learning process of the reader. The objective should not be too obscure the way the business works, but rather to help interested parties understand why the business will work.

Business Presentation

The business presentation is the dog and pony show. One of my students asked me whether the business presentation should be informational or a pitch. It should be both, and that is the ongoing dilemma for the presenters. Including the proper mix of information and creating excitement about the business is a difficult task. The presentation should have conveyed *approximately* the same content as the business plan, but in an abbreviated format (see Table 12.3). The goal is to maintain interest and communicate your ideas. The ideal number of slides for the presentation should be approximately one slide for each section. However, this can be increased if the slides are not too dense. This means that you will have to talk around the key concepts of each section. You do not want to

Table 12.3. Business Plan Presentation

General guidelines for business plan presentations
1. Introduction of team (30 seconds)
2. Company overview (4 minutes)
a. Description of products and services to be offered.
b. Presentation of your product, service, or system prototype. Could be a prototype, a scenario, a picture, a diagram, or a mock-up of your product, or service. Briefly discuss the prototype.
c. How does the product or service solve an important problem or present an opportunity to fill an important market niche
d. Discuss how product is competitive.
e. How do you intend to differentiate yourself (price, quality, or service)?
f. Present a Strategy Canvas illustrating how your product/service compares to the competition.
g. What is the size of the market you intend to enter?
h. What is the growth potential of your market?
3. Industry analysis (1 minute)
a. Description of current and potential competitors (substitute products).
b. How will competition react to market entry?
c. What are the barriers to entry?
d. Are there critical governmental or economic issues?

(Continued)

Table 12.3. Business Plan Presentation (Continued)

4. Marketing strategy (2 minutes)

   a. How will you price your product?

   b. What customer segments are you trying to reach? How will versions be matched to customer segments?

   c. How will you promote your product?

   d. What techniques will you use to acquire customers?

   e. How will you retain and lock-in customers?

   f. How will you distribute your product?

5. Operations strategy (2 minutes)

   a. Where will the product be made?

   b. How will it be made?

   c. Who will the product or service?

   d. What are the detailed variables and fixed costs for producing the product or service?

   e. Are their important issues related to the supply of components/materials?

   f. Are their important issues related to the fulfillment of orders?

6. Forecasts and financials (2 minutes)

   a. What do your projections show for sales, profit, expense, growth, and investment?

   b. Capital requirements over the next 3 years.

      i. Development costs

      ii. Advertising costs

      iii. Human resources

      iv. Sources of capital

7. Stage of development and the implementation plan (1–2 minutes)

   a. What resources have already been committed?

   b. What stage of development are you in?

   c. What needs to be done before launch?

   d. When and how will the system be implemented (show timeline here)?

8. How much venture capital funding do you need? (1 minute)

   a. What are you offering in return for funds?

   b. When can they obtain return?

   c. Return on investment expected?

9. Summary (30 seconds)

These are the restrictions I use: Questions (4 minutes): Total allowable time for presentation and questions is 19 minutes. Be sure to conduct a trial run of your presentation so that you will not go over the 15-minute presentation limit.

read your slides. Just have the key concepts on the slide and talk around them. The most important thing you can do is to practice your presentation and, if possible, memorize your notes. There are always limits on the length of the presentation and it is important to hit that mark within 30 seconds. Practice helps to convey the impression that you know what you are talking about and that you have the best product since sliced white bread. Guy Kawasaki suggests a 10/20/30 rule. That is 10 slides, for 20 minutes using a 30-point font. This is good advice, but it is sometimes necessary to extend the number of slides depending on the particular business context and the amount of content in each slide.

Be sure to illustrate a prototype or at least show an illustration of your product or service. The prototype could be an illustration, a picture, a diagram, an example report, a scenario, or a mock-up of your product or service. If you are developing a complex process that is hard to understand, then you should still try to convey the idea using some sort of flow diagram or business process diagram. The goal here is to try to get your audience to understand just what you are trying to sell and try to get them to buy your product or service. The goal is not to be vague or obscure. As noted earlier, the scenario is very effective tool for communicating the business concept. An actual or even a fictional scenario can be a powerful tool for explaining how the product or service works. Scenario presentations can include live acting, movie clips, storyboards using clipart and drawings, simulations and even the use of stick figure animation.

The business should be pitched and presented several times before the final plan is developed. The business plan presentation along with the executive summary will help to structure the business and make it more focused, clear, and understandable. It is all part of the learning process consisting of learning-about and learning-by-doing. It is important to have someone document all the questions that arise during the presentation and then to try to understand what the questions mean. It could be simply that the business model was not communicated effectively during the presentation, or a critical issue was not considered and that it needs to be addressed. Businesses are emergent; they take time to design, build, and to be successful; and the pitch and presentation is a critical part of the growth process.

Identifying Potential Investors

Investors invest in people and then they investigate the idea.[8] This is true even when your investors are your family and friends and when economic times are challenging. Superstars in music, cinema, and in baseball garner the accolades and ultimately the money because of their above-average expertise. Music and movie publishers and baseball general managers go to the superstars because they are a known commodity and have a track record for delivering hits. This is also true for start-ups. The investors look at the management team, the CIO, the VP's of marketing, operations, and finance, and the lawyers in terms of their reputation, education, job history, and previous experiences with start-ups.

Many start-ups have difficulty in getting funds.[9] There are a variety of avenues for generating additional funds that do not involve the professional investors. The first search for funds usually includes savings, credit cards, home equity loans, bank loans, and selling equity to family, friends, and selling personal assets. Bootstrapping is the process of starting a business from scratch with little or no outside capital. The goal of bootstrapping is to minimize expenditures and to reinvest the cash flow generated by the start-up back into the business.

Figure 12.1 illustrates the typical level of funds that can be generated as the business grows.[10] Figure 12.2 presents additional detail on where funds are generated as the business grows.[11]

Here is a list of additional sources of funds to keep the business going as it grows that the entrepreneur can turn to in lieu of professionally managing funds.

	Stage 0 pre-seed	Seed/start-up	Close to launch	Early	Later
Source	Founders friends and family	Individual angels	Angel groups	Venture funds	
Investment	$25,000 to $100,000	$100,000 to $500,000	$500K to $2M depending on region	$2M/ $5M and up	

Figure 12.1. Typical amount of funds generated during business development.

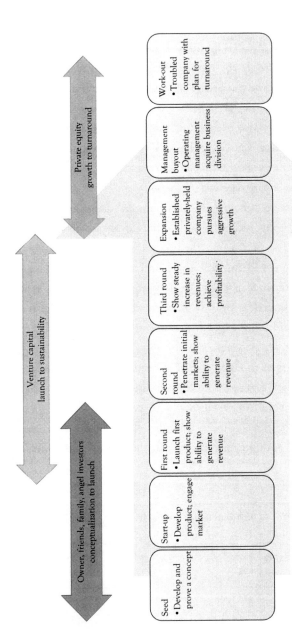

Figure 12.2. Funds generation as firm grows.

- *Trade credit*: Where a business sets up an account with another business and does not have to pay for the goods and services until a certain time period has elapsed (e.g., 30–90 days. Lumber and hardware companies often set up such accounts for contractors.
- *Asset-based loan*: A business will use its equipment, inventory, or facilities as collateral for a loan.
- *Factoring of accounts receivables*: A business sells its accounts receivables to the lender or factor. The lender usually handles most of the transactions that occur after the sale, such as sending out invoices and collecting the funds that are owed.
- *Loan*: Loan is given after the financial statements have been analyzed, a small business credit score is obtained, or both. Could be a bank or some other financial institution or individual. Sometimes involves collateral or assets such as inventory, facilities, or equipment or personal assets of the borrower.
- *Leasing*: The lender purchases the asset and then charges a monthly or some periodic fee for the lessor to use it (purchase of fixed assets by lessor).
- *Relationship lending*: This is the good buddy loan. The lender has dealt with the borrower in the past and grants a loan because of past success. There is often an ongoing advisory and guidance relationship between the lender and borrower. Could be a bank or some other financial institution or individual.

Sources of funds and their timing depend on the economic context, the type of business, and the capabilities and attitudes of the founders, and these figures reflect averages and processes that are forever changing.

Angel Investors

Angel investors are very early participants in funding start-ups. When the amount of financing required is <\$1 million, then the start-up should probably approach angel investors. The angel investors are usually not involved in managing the start-up. Angel investments range from $100K to $500K. Angel investors usually look for a 20–40% return on their investment after 3 years or somewhere between two and three times their original investment. For example, a $500K investment would return about $1M–$1.5M in three to 4 years with a 25% return. Not all of the investments by angel investors are successful (about 50%). A small percentage of the investments carry the load and subsidize the marginal and failed businesses.[12]

Venture Capital Funds and Venture Capitalists

Venture capital funds are professionally managed funds that provide high-potential start-ups with funds in exchange for management fees and equity or shares of stock in the start-up. Venture capitalists (VCs) invest between $1 and $20 million in a start-up, but it can vary. The venture capital funds are themselves funded by wealthy investors. The venture capital funds sometimes charge about 2–4% per year as a management fee. In addition, they charge 20–25% return (sometimes more) on their investment over the course of 5 years. So if a start-up borrows $5 million from the venture fund, then they may have to pay $100,000 in management fees per year (at 2%) and then pay out approximately $13.3 million in 5 years (at 20%) for the return on the VCs investment. The management fee is a kind of coaching or consulting fee. A typical fund can have 15–20 ventures with about half-generating returns. Only a few of the businesses are hits and the *hits* subsidize the failures and the marginally successful ventures.

Potential Problems with Venture Capital

There has been much criticism in the engineering community in reference to venture capital funds stifling innovation.[13] Some of it is related to investing in start-ups with superstar management and some of this is related to the tendency of VCs to pursue incremental innovations where there are lower levels of risk. VCs are not interested in technology; they are interested in adding a business to their portfolio that has a good chance of generating above-average returns. They know that some start-ups will fail, and they rely on their knowledge and expertise and portfolio diversification to deliver a few successful start-ups. The point is that it is hard for the new entrepreneur to make a splash because there are no previous splash patterns. Start-ups with little experience usually rely on the founder's money, family and friends, and a variety of other approaches to run the company (see http://brainz.org/startup-funding/ for an excellent overview of nonventure-capital fund sources). There are many opportunities to raise funds outside of professionally managed money and indeed that give the company's founder a degree of control and flexibility that may exceed the benefits of securing funds that reduce flexibility and control are accompanied by very high interest rates.

Importance of Market Potential to VCs

VCs are interested in firms that have the potential to acquire substantial market share in large markets.[14] They want to know whether the market is large, whether it is growing rapidly, and whether the start-up can capture some of that growth. They also want to know whether the business is scalable. A scalable business model means that the business can shrink or grow very quickly with minor changes in the cost structure. In the best situation, growth should not increase variable costs and fixed costs (perhaps even decrease variable costs). Ideally, growth should *not* incur large fluctuations in business processes as new customers are added. Remember, however, that scalable growth is usually scalable within a relatively narrow range.

The potential investors will also want to know whether the start-up can acquire customers and keep them. They will also be interested in the market forecast. Savvy investors will question market forecasts that indicate that the firm will garner either 1% or 10% of the market. The 10% share of the market usually means that the market is relatively small and the start-up needs 10% to break even. The 1% usually means that the market is huge and the start-up will be lucky to acquire even 1%. Market forecasts need to be based on realistic assumptions, rather than based on what makes for easy spreadsheet construction. There should be a strong rationale why the start-up will acquire 10% of the market the first year and increase that share by 20% in subsequent years.

Guy Kawasaki has several good ideas for developing market forecasts. His first idea is to develop a forecast from the bottom-up. In this approach, the start-up would try and identify the number of sales outlets and then estimate how many items might be sold at each outlet. Another example would consist of looking at the number of sales contacts each week for each salesperson and then estimate the percentage that will be successful. This approach, admittedly, also relies on percentages and, in some ways, is also seat-of-the-pants as is the 10% solution. The important point in developing forecasts is to examine and test assumptions and to constantly refine the forecasts.

Contingency Planning and Risk

Suppose you are developing a green or environmentally friendly product line that is particularly attractive because of a government tax credit. What if the government rolls back the tax credit? Or what would happen if a key member of the management team leaves the company? What if interest rates sky rocket? What if a key employee deletes the design specifications of a new product? What if a disgruntled employee destroys the social networking application and backup files? It is impossible to have a fall-back plan for every situation. But if there are key people and key assumptions that will determine business success, then a contingency plan is essential.

Risk is the probability that some adverse event will happen that will have a negative impact on the start-up's ability to survive. Risk management is an attempt to identify the adverse events within a company and in the external organizational environment, and in turn develop strategies to deal with the consequences. Many of the internal risks to the start-up are related to the critical assumptions involving the tenure of the management team, the ability to attract key personnel, the ability to set up key organizational systems such as operations and marketing, the ability to manage cash flows, and the ability to adapt untested technologies. There are also external industry-related risks related to the ability to forecast market growth, and the risks related to unforeseen competitors and unforeseen emerging technologies that might affect profitability. There are also external risks related to economic downturns, interest rates, government intervention, political movements, and even changes related to social norms. Risk assessment also has to be made in terms of the impact of adverse weather conditions, earthquakes, and other natural disasters.

As noted earlier, there is some danger in pointing out weaknesses and threats, but they need to be addressed in a surreptitious manner. This can be accomplished by presenting alternative scenarios and focusing on the probability of their occurrence. Contingency planning and risk assessment should be addressed in the business plan or at least informally documented and communicated among the founders of the business and key management employees.

Due Diligence

Professional investors such as angels and VCs, potential employees, and family members use a variety of criteria for evaluating a business plan. The process of evaluating the plan is referred to as due diligence. The Merriam Webster dictionary defines due diligence as:

1. The care that a reasonable person exercises under the circumstances to avoid harm to other persons or their property;
2. Research and analysis of a company or organization done in preparation for a business transaction (as a corporate merger or purchase of securities).

Due diligence can be evaluated in terms of how careful investors are in evaluating a business plan and how diligent the founders are in preparing the business plan. There is evidence that when the investor is duly diligent, the business will have a greater chance of succeeding.[15] We also believe that due diligence becomes very important as the business emerges from the conceptualization stage and is being built. Due diligence becomes important when the shoe meets the pavement or rather when the entrepreneur starts interacting with the investor. Here are the modified definitions of due diligence:

1. How wise and careful did the entrepreneur put together the business plan?
2. How wise and careful did the investor examine the business plan?

We usually read about 20–40 business plans per year. We evaluate the plans in terms of organization and format of the plan, writing, and content. All three areas are interrelated, and it is our experience that hard work usually leads to a great format, good writing, and strong content. Table 12.4 presents an overview of the major due diligence questions asked by investor, founders, and potential employees. It is one checklist that needs to be checked off. Some of the questions are more important to one group than to another. Just go through them before submitting the final plan. One thing is clear, if the writing style is poor and the plan is poorly organized, then it will be very difficult to sell your ideas. At least 2 or 3 people outside of the founding group should be sought to provide editorial support for the plan format and the content to insure that the plan makes sense.

Table 12.4. Due Diligence Checklist Questions Asked by Investors, Founders, and Employees

• Could such a business make money?	☐Yes ☐No ☐Maybe ☐NA ☐Needs Work
• Solves a problem or presents unique opportunity?	☐Yes ☐No ☐Maybe ☐NA ☐Needs Work
• Is the business concept scalable?	☐Yes ☐No ☐Maybe ☐NA ☐Needs Work
• Is the market large and expanding?	☐Yes ☐No ☐Maybe ☐NA ☐Needs Work
• Has the target market been adequately identified?	☐Yes ☐No ☐Maybe ☐NA ☐Needs Work
• Is the product or service differentiable?	☐Yes ☐No ☐Maybe ☐NA ☐Needs Work
• Can customers be acquired at a reasonable cost?	☐Yes ☐No ☐Maybe ☐NA ☐Needs Work
• Can customers be locked-in?	☐Yes ☐No ☐Maybe ☐NA ☐Needs Work
• Is pricing addressed adequately?	☐Yes ☐No ☐Maybe ☐NA ☐Needs Work
• Are current and potential competitors identified?	☐Yes ☐No ☐Maybe ☐NA ☐Needs Work
• Addresses competition's reaction to market entry?	☐Yes ☐No ☐Maybe ☐NA ☐Needs Work
• Is the marketing plan adequate and executable?	☐Yes ☐No ☐Maybe ☐NA ☐Needs Work
• Is the operation's plan adequate and executable?	☐Yes ☐No ☐Maybe ☐NA ☐Needs Work
• Is the implementation plan adequate/ executable?	☐Yes ☐No ☐Maybe ☐NA ☐Needs Work
• Are the projected financial statements reasonable?	☐Yes ☐No ☐Maybe ☐NA ☐Needs Work

(Continued)

Table 12.4. Due Diligence Checklist Questions Asked by Investors, Founders, and Employees (Continued)

• Can the key management personnel get the job done?	☐Yes ☐No ☐Maybe ☐NA ☐Needs Work
• Can the business be built and fulfill promises?	☐Yes ☐No ☐Maybe ☐NA ☐Needs Work
• Any hidden traps, oversights, oversimplifications?	☐Yes ☐No ☐Maybe ☐NA ☐Needs Work
• Is there contingency planning and risk assessments?	☐Yes ☐No ☐Maybe ☐NA ☐Needs Work

Legal Issues

Since we are on the topic of due diligence, this is a nice segue into the importance of attorneys in developing a business. Guy Kawasaki has identified a number of difficulties that arise when dealing with lawyers.[16] But Kawasaki also believes that lawyers are critical for the success of business start-ups.[17] Lawyers and entrepreneurs often have trouble interacting because lawyers focus on what can go wrong and the entrepreneur is the eternal optimist and focuses on getting things done. Entrepreneurs tend to embrace risk and focus on the prize, whereas lawyers tend to be risk averse and focus on what can go wrong. Entrepreneurial enthusiasm tempered with a bit of lawyerly caution that can alleviate many hazards on the road to building the business. Lawyers can assist with the following activities:

- They can help in selecting the appropriate form of business incorporation such as a sole proprietorship, a corporation, or a limited liability corporation.
- They can provide guidance on whether you can leave a company and start a business in the same industry.
- They can provide insight and counsel on protecting intellectual property in using copyright, patents, and trademarks.
- They can assist with real estate and rental transactions.
- They can check employee benefits and employment contracts.
- They can provide legal expertise on venture and angel investment funds.
- They can assist in selling the business and going public with the issuance of stock.

A good starting place for information on the selection of legal counsel, working with accountants, and incorporating companies can be found at http://www.entrepreneur.com and http://www.sba.gov/. You probably do not have to include the lawyering and legal issues in the business plan, but you need to be aware that there are numerous legal issues and accounting issues that are looming. Professional expertise is expensive, but in some instances their advice is critical for successfully navigating through the legal and financial systems.

Conclusion

In this chapter, we have illustrated the process and the elements that are used to develop a full-blown business plan. The key points are the following:

- The FAD template, the Organizational and Industry Analysis template, and the Business Plan Overview template and executive plan are used as the basis for developing the full-blown business plan.
- The business plan serves many purposes including serving as a communication tool for investors; it is a scaled-down version of how the business will function and it is used as a platform for communications among the founders, employees, consultants, and mentors; and finally, it can be used as a blueprint for operating the business the first year.
- A business plan template is presented that illustrates the typical sections that are contained in the business plan.
- The writing style, the organization and the formatting are just as important as the content for communicating the essence of the business model.
- It is important to pitch and present the business plan before finalizing the full-blown plan. This will help to bring focus and clarity on the emergent business.
- In many instance, investors invest in the management as much as in the idea.
- Many investors are interested in market potential in terms of the growth of the market and the total size of the market.

- Contingency planning and risk assessment should be addressed in the business plan or at least informally among the founders of the business and key management employees.
- Time, hard work, and attention to details will lead to better business plans.
- Legal counsel and accounting expertise are essential for incorporating the business and providing guidance through the legal and financial systems.

The business plan is presented to the outside world through a business presentation and the presentation leads to the development of a short business plan document. An important part of developing the business plan is the learning-by-doing process. It is important that the emerging company make and build things, try experiments, and construct prototypes. Prototypes need to be constructed as early as possible for tangible products and also for systems applications. As illustrated in Figure 12.3, the process is iterative and ends only after the business is not in existence.

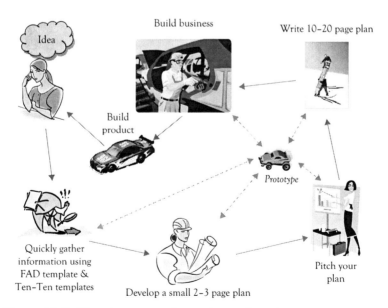

Figure 12.3. Planning process is ongoing an iterative.

The most important element of the business plan and the business presentation is the "look and feel." The plan and the presentation should look clean and streamlined. The development of a business model and plan begins with the moment that the entrepreneur has the original *aha* experience; this is followed with a very brief strategic planning process (we recommend the Ten–Ten approach coupled with a FAD analysis) and this is in turn followed by the development of the executive summary.

CHAPTER 13

Project Management for New Products and Services Development

As discussed throughout the book, there is an overarching business life cycle involving several key development points. These points are primarily under the control of the entrepreneur, the founders, or executive management. They are the initial conceptualization of the business through some form of business plan, the development of the initial business processes using some form of project management, the business launch, the addition of additional controls and structure as the business grows, and finally the re-conceptualization of the business as it begins to decline (Figure 13.1).

Once the business model has been created and the business plan has been developed, the hard work begins. In most situations, everything is new and needs to be built up from scratch. The entire supply chain has to be built and tested to insure that orders for products and services can be accepted, filled, and supported. This is the *Building-the-Business* phase and it is vital to a successful business launch. As illustrated in Table 13.1, several key business questions must be answered before launching the business.

The hard part is to install initial processes or systems to make the business work, and that is where project management is essential. We use the term *project management system* loosely, since in many instances the system can be self-contained and organized in the mind of the entrepreneur. Nevertheless, the hard part involves building the business to produce the product and deliver the service. This requires project management. Even if you have plans for manufacturing, marketing, and distributing the product, you still need to have a process to accomplish or execute the plan.

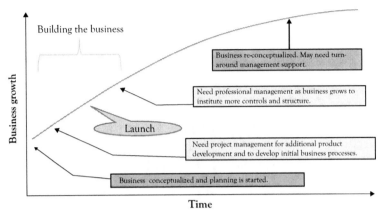

Figure 13.1. Key management activities during the business life cycle.

Table 13.1. Key Business Questions Before Launch

a. Where will the product or service be made?
b. Who will make the product?
c. How will it be made?
d. How will orders be tracked?
e. With who, when, and why will partnerships and alliances be formed?
f. What will the supply chain look like and how will dependencies work?
g. Should supply chain tasks be outsourced, off-shored, or in-tasked?
h. What will the information technology look like in terms of hardware, software, and networking?
i. Are there important issues related to the supply of components/materials?
j. How will order fulfillment work?
k. Are there important issues related to the fulfillment of orders?
l. Where will the organization build core competencies and capabilities?
m. How will employees be acquired and retained?
n. How will business and accounting transactions be handled?

In many instances, entrepreneurs turn to turnkey systems for accounting and inventory management. Turnkey systems are ready-to-go-software, ready-to-go-processes, or both for running a business. Time and effort is still needed to identify the turnkey solution and then more time and effort is required to actually implement it. Some sort of mechanism is necessary for determining what solution fits the business, how the system will be implemented, who will operate the system, and how it fits in with the other business activities. Even if the so-called turnkey solutions have been identified for accounting and inventory management, additional planning is needed for implementing and creating business processes for installing and running the system.

Project management is the tool for executing the plan and installing the business processes. It helps to detail what tasks will be accomplished, who will be involved in completing the tasks, and when tasks should start and finish. The minimal tasks that need to be accomplished for a business to start or launch include *marketing and sales, production and operations, staffing,* and *accounting.* In addition, some sort of research and development (R&D) process needs to be initiated soon after launch in order to re-prime the pump. These are the first steps in designing organizations for the long term.

Organizational design involves the simultaneous integration of the tasks that need to be completed by overlaying some type of organizational structure that uses a blend of technology and people to fulfill the organizational mission.[1] Here are the *Building-the-Business* functions and critical questions that need to be in place before or soon after launch:

Need a marketing function or system:

- How will you promote your product or service?
- What techniques will you use to acquire customers?
- How will you retain and lock-in customers?
- How will you distribute and sell your product?
- How will you support your customers and maintain an ongoing relationship?
- How will you track customer satisfaction?

Need an operations or production function or system:

- Who will design the product/service and where will product/ service design take place?
- Where will the product be made and who will make it?
- How will it be made?
- Who will supply the components and materials?

- How will the company keep track of finished goods inventory, components, and raw materials and track the production process?
- How will order fulfillment take place?

Need a human resource function or system:

- What kind of and how many employees are needed to run the business?
- Where will we recruit employees?
- What criteria will be used to select employees?
- How will performance be evaluated and rewarded?
- What kind of compensation incentives will be offered (salary, stock options, and benefits)?
- How will employees be trained and developed?

Need an accounting function or system:

- How will you keep track of business transactions?
- How will you track business performance?
- How will the company handle accounts payable, accounts receivables, general ledger, purchase orders, and payroll?

Need an R&D function or system (immediately after launch):

- What organizational functions will be involved in product development and deployment?
- Who, where, and how will R&D (learning-about and learning-by-doing) be conducted?
- How will product and service development and deployment be evaluated?
- How will scientific, product, and organizational knowledge be retained and utilized (knowledge management)?

Need legal counsel and assistance:

- Assist in selecting appropriate form of business.
- Assist with real estate and rental transactions.

- Assist in developing contracts for employee benefits and employment contracts.
- Provide legal expertise on venture and angel investment funds and with initial public offerings of stock and related financial funding issues.
- Assist in protecting intellectual property in the form of copyrights, patents, and trademarks.

Even the simplest start-up company has to accomplish the functions described above in some capacity. These systems may be in the mind of the entrepreneur and also executed by the entrepreneur, but they are still necessary for survival. There are other system processes that need to be in place as illustrated in Figure 13.2. These systems or functions typically emerge and evolve as the business grows and prospers. A good way to consider the complexity of a large business is to think about the components

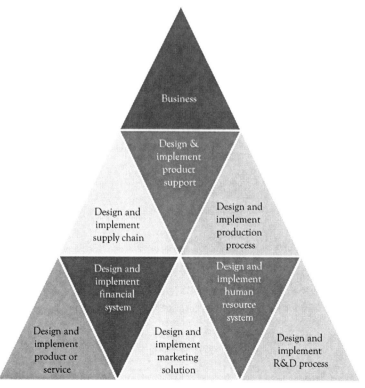

Figure 13.2. Systems emerging over time.

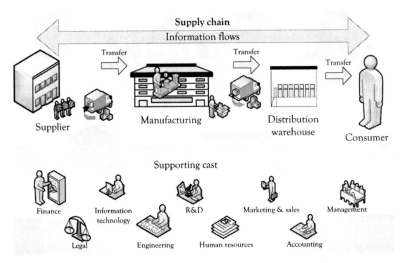

Figure 13.3. Large organizations need many systems and structures.

of the supply chain. This is again illustrated in Figure 13.3 where a number of critical processes need to be in place for a large and growing supply chain. In larger organizations, these activities are part of a more formal approach. The formal approach is project management. If a business only has one employee, the entrepreneur, then all the systems will be conceptualized and executed by the entrepreneur. However, even in a small, one-person operation, understanding and implementing some type of project management is necessary in order to deal with the complexity of the start-up process. Just having a checklist of things to do and things that have been accomplished will help in dealing with the overwhelming complexity of launching a start-up.

Why Project Management is Beneficial

Project management involves time and effort, but it can also be a friend of the start-up. There are two reasons that project management is important. First, project management assists in dealing with complexity and time pressure. Many organizational tasks are difficult, and from the perspective of the entrepreneur, they are close to rocket science because the number of hands for completing tasks are so few. Project management is structured problem solving and it assists with problem decomposition and with managing the risk inherent in product and service development. Even though the focus of this book has been on product differentiation, many products and services also suffer from too much differentiation and feature creep.

Features are critical for maintaining an edge over the competition in the context of monopolistic competition, but there is some point where products need to be delivered and specifications stabilized. Project management is there to assist in converging on a satisfactory solution to problems related to delivering products and services by freezing the specifications. The specs are not frozen for long; perhaps a couple of weeks, a month, or even two, until it is time to renew the innovation process and develop an upgraded product.

Another important feature of project management is that it is very useful in developing and maintaining localized managerial and scientific knowledge related to core competencies and know-how. Project management assists in formalizing the learn-by-doing and learning-about processes into the genetic foundations of the emerging organization.

What is a Project?

The Project Management Institute, an organization that sets industry standards in project and portfolio management, conducts research and provides education, certification, and professional exchange opportunities for project managers, defines a project as: "a temporary endeavor taken to create a unique product, service, or result."[2] Temporary means the project has a definite beginning and end. This applies to the project, and not necessarily to the product, service, or result. All the systems that need to be built by the entrepreneur and his or her partners are basically projects.

Typically, projects progress in steps or incremental stages. The goal of a project is to reach a stated objective, and then terminate, passing results to ongoing operations. Initiation of projects is usually due to a market, customer, or organization demand, a technological advance, or a legal

Figure 13.4. Project management.

requirement. Figure 13.4 presents an overview of the project management process.[3] It is sometimes referred to as a waterfall process because the process is typically sequential or linear.

In many instances, project management can be carried out in a linear fashion. Linear projects follow the waterfall approach to project management. That is, the activities for completing the project are sequential and each separate activity follows in a more-or-less precise order. In general, the linear approach is amenable to very straightforward projects. Many of the activities related to setting up accounting systems, human resource systems, and many inventory management systems could be handled using the linear approach to project management.

There are instances where the project to be accomplished cannot be solved using a linear project management approach. Some projects are very complicated, with very loose specifications, and the final outcome in terms of success and features of the product are unpredictable. For example, new product development in the nanotechnology area where there are few products with similar features and the territory is largely uncharted needs a different approach to project management. Many of the emerging software applications involving social networking and game development also need a different approach. Agile project management is suitable in situations where learning-by-doing plays a more dominate role in product development. Discovery is the key as new territory is charted and the solution to the problem unfolds. Scrum development is one example of an iterative and agile approach to project management.[4] The key difference from the traditional, waterfall process is that the agile process will be iterative and occur many times.

Regardless of the process, there are several tools that may be used to help manage a project and to communicate to the project team. There are of course sophisticated approaches and tools to managing the process as well as software tools for tracking projects. The simplest of tools includes a diary that can be used to track the amount of time that is spent on project activities. Exhibit 1 is a sample Project Management Individual Diary for the initiation of a new business, as outlined earlier in the chapter. This diary outlines the tasks or activities needed to complete the project or subproject. Exhibit 2 presents the Project Management Summary Diary, an aggregation of the individual project tasks used to manage projects.

Another useful tool is the work breakdown structure (WBS). The WBS is always based on the project deliverables, rather than the tasks needed to create those deliverables, and is built from the top-down. It is constructed through decomposition. Deliverables are broken down into progressively smaller pieces. The result is a graphical, hierarchical chart, logically organized from top to bottom. Figure 13.5 represents a portion of a simple WBS.

A Gantt chart is another very useful tool for understanding where a project has been, where it is going, what tasks need to be completed, and the tasks that have already been completed. Bar charts, or Gantt charts, show activities represented as horizontal bars and have a calendar along the horizontal axis. The length of the bar corresponds to

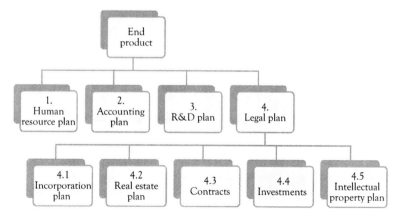

Figure 13.5. Work breakdown structure.

Task	Planned		Actual			Show Gantt chart for:											
	Start	Duration	Start	Duration	% Done	Jun-10	Jul-10	Aug-10	Sep-10	Oct-10	Nov-10	Dec-10	Jan-11	Feb-11	Mar-11	Apr-11	May-11
						1	2	3	4	5	6	7	8	9	10	11	12
Human resources																	
Resource estimates	11-Jul	20															
Employee recruitment plan	11-Jul	5															
Performance measurement plan	11-Aug	5															
Compensation and incentive plan	11-Aug	5															
Training and development plan	18-Aug	10															
Recruitment	1-Sep	60															
Accounting																	
Accounting management plan	11-Jul	5															
Performance measurement plan	18-Jul	5															
Functional plan (AP, AR, GL, POS, Payroll)	25-Jul	20															
Research & development																	
R&D resource plan	11-Jul	15															
Development plan	4-Aug	60															
Evaluation plan	4-Aug	10															
Knowledge management plan	4-Aug	5															
Development	27-Oct	120															
Legal																	
Business incorporation assessment	11-Jul	15															
Real estate/rental plan	11-Jul	15															
Employee contracts	24-Sep	10															
Funding and investments	11-Jul	60															
Intellectual property	8-Dec	90															

Highlight month: 2   Planned

Figure 13.6. Gantt chart.

the length of time the activity should require. A bar chart can be easily modified to show percentage complete (usually by shading all or part of the horizontal bar). It is considered to be a good tool to use to communicate with management because it is easy to understand at a glance. A typical Gantt chart for a project is illustrated in Figure 13.6.

Launching the Business or Project

There is extensive literature by academics and practitioners on why businesses and projects fail. There is some agreement that management commitment and participation, along with involvement of employees, are the key success and failure factors, but after that the literature is somewhat confusing and inconclusive.[5] Table 13.2 presents a few of the areas that can cause problems and perhaps even cause the project to fail. These issues should be treated as watch outs.

Risk is inherent in all businesses and projects. It is virtually impossible to make everything perfect and deliver a perfect product or service. Guy Kawasaki in *Reality Check* is very aggressive in his view of launching a new product or service.[6] He states "Don't worry, be crappy" and thinks that it is acceptable to ship a version of a product with elements of crappiness. He believes that the crappiness can be subsequently fixed in version 2.1

Table 13.2. Watch Outs During Project Management

Management did not spend enough time and resources on the project and/or business.
The employees that were to use a system were not sufficiently involved in the development.
Insufficient resources were allocated to the project. This includes money, technology, time, and staff and others.
The function or process was not developed to match the tasks that were to be accomplished.
The system interfaces were poorly designed.
Not enough time to complete the project and too many competing commitments.
Too many changes were made to the original specifications of the project.
An emerging and immature technology was not ready for prime time.
There was no demand for the business or the project.
There was little if any project management.

Table 13.3. Kawasaki Insights

"Innovation had better create wealth because it is so damn hard to do."
Build something that you want to use. Don't look towards the "visionary entrepreneurs" (that is a "crock of bull shitake"). People start companies because they want to use the products or services they create.
Make meaning. Great innovations enable people to do something better or permit people to do things they never wanted to do. For example, the iPad, iPod, iPhone, the Frisbee, and auto global positioning system.
Jump to the next curve. Most companies spend all of their time duking it out on the same demand curve. True innovation occurs when companies jump to the next demand curve. We do not need icehouses and landline phones anymore.
Don't worry be crappy. It is ok to ship an innovation with elements of crappiness. First versions are seldom perfect and you will never ship if you wait till it is perfect.
Churn, baby churn. It is all right to ship with elements of crappiness, but you should not stay crappy. You need versions 1.5, 1.9, 2.0, and so forth. Employees do not want to hear about product complaints during launch. They just want to ship. "Innovation is not an event it is a process."
Don't be afraid to polarize people. Deliver great products and do not worry if your product does not appeal to every demographic, socioeconomic, and geographic location. You want to incite passion in the marketplace.
Break down barriers. It takes a long time to gain acceptance in the marketplace. Do not become flustered when acceptance is slow. You need to keep on chugging and get people to test drive your innovation.
Let a hundred flowers blossom. Be flexible in how people use your products. People used Apple for desktop publishing rather than use it for the spreadsheet, word-processing, and so forth. Recall that Avon Skin-So-Soft was also used as a bug repellent.
Think digital act analog. Use all of the technology to deliver innovation, but remember it is the happy people and not the coolness of the technology that is important.
Never ask people to do what you wouldn't want to do. If the product solves a great problem and it is hard to use, then it will not stick.
Don't let the bozos grind you down. Do not let influential people outside of the company influence you. Stick to your knitting.

of the product. Kawasaki has a number of very insightful views on the innovation process as illustrated in Table 13.3.

Launch Date

There comes a time when a decision has to be made when to launch the business or project. Problems inevitably arise as the launch date approaches and the question whether to continue with the launch date or delay it looms its ugly head. Delaying a launch after the date has been announced

- Will our company and the entire supply chain process be able to successfully complete most tasks, such as fulfillment, at launch given expected demand?

- Will our company and the entire supply chain process be able to successfully complete most tasks at launch even with above average demand?

- Will product design defects at launch adversely affect our customers and our reputation?

- Did we have a successful dry run and adequate testing before launch.

- Do most of our employees have confidence in the products and the processes that are being launched?

- Is there a backup plan and are there processes available if problems occur at launch.

- Will competitors launch and gain critical market share and gain first mover advantages if we do not launch?

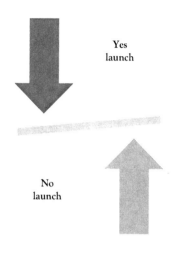

Yes
launch

No
launch

Figure 13.7. To launch or not to launch: these are the questions.

can adversely impact the employees of a start-up and create a negative view of the business by consumers and the media. We have developed a very simple set of questions that can be used to ascertain if the launch should go as scheduled.[7] The questions are outlined in Figure 13.7.

There is no simple answer regarding the decision to launch, even in the face of numerous deficiencies and potential problems. Sometimes it only takes a negative answer to only one question and the launch should be delayed. If a new online banking service is being launched, then any hint of problems should preclude launching. In some instances, there can be numerous problems with a product and downloading software patches can alleviate them. Online gaming developers are notorious for launching software with numerous bugs. It is a very contextual decision and dependent on the product features and what the product will be used for.

Growing Up and Professional Management

Growing pains are an inevitable part of life for the start-up and they begin to emerge soon after launch (see Figure 13.1). They are impossible to avoid because the world is not stagnant. The entrepreneur may not be looking for stability and consistency in the face of market dynamics and change, but the organization and the employees are looking for stability and consistency. Organizations and organizational members seek control in the form of standardized, coordinated business processes and systems; they want well-defined, enriched, and specialized jobs; and they also want salaries and benefits with the potential to grow. Small companies with astute founders can manage and perhaps even perform these tasks admirably. As the business grows, there may be a need to hire professional managers with the knowledge and skills to implement better practices.

Growing up does not mean that the founder should be ostracized or relegated to honorary duties. This may in fact put the organization at risk. The founder may have a certain entrepreneurial mojo that cannot be replaced. Steve Jobs had an almost magical power to guide Apple in the right direction and the company. The company certainly performed better under his leadership than when he was away. Identifying professional managers is itself a project, requiring project management. Deciding on how to manage and guide the growth of the business is a key decision for survival.

Growing up also means that there are more groups that are trying to protect their own turf with somewhat unique objectives. This includes operations, managerial accounting, marketing, human resources, and product design groups. The six hats approach discussed in a previous chapter can help to reconcile conflicts during meetings, but a new organizational process for product development may be necessary in order to reconcile the inevitable differences that will occur when the functional silos begin to emerge. Concurrent engineering may be a solution for organizations as they become larger and more complex.

Concurrent engineering is the simultaneous design and development of a product and the manufacturing process for building a product.[8] An important part of concurrent engineering is the use of multifunctional teams. Concurrent engineering design teams are typically very comprehensive. They could include customers, suppliers, workers, dealers, regulators, design and manufacturing engineers, purchasing, materials managers, marketing managers, customer support, and financial and accounting representatives, among others. The objective of assembling such teams is to instill the diversity of opinion into the design and manu-facturing process. Using such teams also forges trust among the parties and can also help to develop organizational knowledge that can be used to reduce development times for new products.

Conclusion

In this chapter, we have illustrated that the business cycle for a new ven-ture involves several development points, mostly under control of the entrepreneur. The key takeaways include the following:

- Project management is the primary tool for executing the business plan, installing the businesses processes, and achieving the strategic ambitions of the entrepreneur.
- Project management helps to detail what tasks will be accomplished, who will be involved in completing the tasks, and when tasks should start and finish.
- Typically, projects progress in steps or incremental stages; however, other approaches for rapid, interactive project management are also widely used.
- Several tools can be used to manage the project and communicate timing and status, including task diaries, WBSs, and Gantt charts.
- Projects fail for many reasons. It is management's responsibility to determine whether the inherent risks in the project can be accepted and the project can be launched, or whether the project be delayed.

Project management is not a panacea, but rather a critical tool in the never-ending process of growth and renewal of the business. It allows the entrepreneur to minimize and mitigate inherent risks and increase the potential for success of the launch and the ongoing operations.

EXHIBIT 1

Project Management Individual Diary (This is Used by an Individual to Track How Much Time is Spent on Project Activities)

Group Number and Group Name	Project Description	Individual(s) Preparing	Review Date
Legal Team	Project Firestorm	Norma Gleeson	4/1/11

Task or subtask	Date	Hours worked	What's going well? What's not going well? Additional resources (people, technology) required? Are users and management participating?
Needs assessment conducted	2/12/11	8	Cross-functional team, including management. Need documented and agreed upon.
Name search conducted, name approved	2/14/11	4	No issues.
Real estate search conducted	2/19/11	40	Various properties researched and visited.

(Continued)

Task or subtask	Date	Hours worked	What's going well? What's not going well? Additional resources (people, technology) required? Are users and management participating?
Rental contract signed	2/21/11	4	Ahead of plan.
Incorporation paperwork completed and filed	2/21/11	40	No issues.
Incorporation status completed.	3/3/11	16	On target with plan.
Investors contacted for funding opportunities	3/31/11	36	In process.

EXHIBIT 2

Project Management Summary Diary (This Diary is an Aggregation of the Individual Project Diaries)

Group Number and Group Name	Project Description	Individual(s) Preparing	Preparation Date	Review Date
PMO	Project Firestorm	James Xu	2/11/11	4/1/11

Task or subtask	Assigned to	Due Date	Hours scheduled	Hours accumulated	Percent completed	What's going well? What's not going well? Additional resources (people, technology) required? Are users and management participating?
Requirements gathered	James Xu	2/16/11	40	32	100	
Team development and project planning	James Xu	2/16/11	8	8	100	
Legal plans	Norma Gleeson	3/3/11	240	240	100	
R&D plans	Garry Hall	3/10/11	480	540	100	Over budget due to expanded scope.
Accounting plans	Michel Bulan	3/24/11	240	240	100	On budget and on plan.
HR plans	Davis Wilson	3/31/11	440	420	100	Completed on budget and ahead of plan.
Funding and investments	Norma Gleeson	5/5/11	480	240	50	
Employee recruitment	Davis Wilson	6/23/11	480	0	0	
Employee contracts	Davis Wilson	7/7/11	80	0	0	
Development	Garry Hall	11/10/11	960	0	0	
IP (patents)	Norma Gleeson	11/10/11	730	0	0	

CHAPTER 14

Re-priming the Business Using Real Options Concepts

It does not matter how innovative or how much money the current business is making. There is a life cycle for products and technologies, and eventually, the business will decline unless it can find new opportunities. The business needs to be constantly re-primed with new products and services or it will fade and dissolve (see Figure 14.1). Critical in re-priming a business is scalability of the business. Scalability means that the business can shrink or grow very quickly with minor changes in the cost structure. Ideally, the ability to grow will not require a large change in variable costs, perhaps even decreasing variable costs and little increase in fixed costs. In addition, a scalable business should be able to handle a large influx of new customers and still be able to handle them without having to drastically change business processes. However, scalability cannot be achieved without investing money and time in stepping stones for future business that provide the business with options. For this reason, real options concepts can be used as the catalyst for differentiation and to re-prime the business pump. This chapter will focus on how real options concepts can be used as the foundation for continually reinventing the business.

Investment Decisions

Making the right investment decision on the right projects and the right products at the right time is a combination of having the right information, intuition, and luck. As Figure 14.1 illustrates if there is a

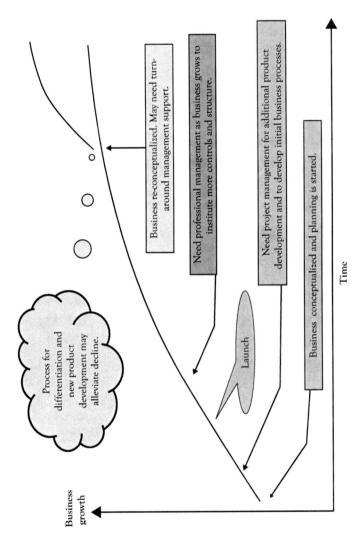

Figure 14.1. Critical organizational activities during business life cycle.

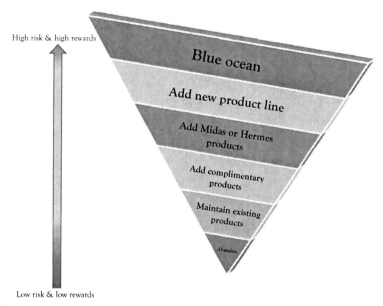

High risk & high rewards

Blue ocean

Add new product line

Add Midas or Hermes products

Add complimentary products

Maintain existing products

Abandon

Low risk & low rewards

Figure 14.2. Risk is inherent as you get closer to the top.

process in place for differentiation and new product development, then the decline of the business may be alleviated. There are choices and decisions to be made related to populating the product and project portfolio. These are the critical investment decisions that the entrepreneur has to make. Figure 14.2 illustrates that the potential profitability is greater as you climb up the inverted pyramid, but there are also greater levels of risk and uncertainty toward the top. All businesses face the following investment decisions while climbing the reward pyramid:

Maintenance decision: They can maintain their current investment in products, projects, machines, and technologies. This also takes into account investment to deal with depreciation. This is the maintain option. The goal of the maintain strategy is to keep current customers with existing products and services. Learning-about and learn-by-doing are maintained at current levels.

Growth decision: They have the option to invest a little or a lot in new products, projects, machines, and technologies. There is a step-up in learning-about and learning-by-doing. This is the growth option and it includes a number of approaches:

- Differentiate by scaling-up existing product line. Scaling up your investment and investing even more. For example, adding features for Midas customers and acquiring new Hermes customers on the existing demand curve.
- Differentiate by scoping-up and developing complementary products for existing product line.
- Differentiate by scoping-up and developing new products that are not part of the existing demand curve.
- Differentiate by switching-up the growth path. A switching-up decision incorporates both growth and abandonment options. When a company makes a switch-up decision, it may discard previous investments and take a different path for growth based on the capabilities accumulated from the previous investments. It typically concerns a switch of input, output, or location. For example, instead of using technology A, a firm may use technology B to produce the same thing. Instead of using the current machine to produce product X, a firm may produce product Y (cf. flexible manufacturing system). A company can switch among locations for research and development, manufacturing, distribution, and so forth.
- Develop new Blue Ocean market. This involves scaling-up, scoping-up, and switching-up. This can be a substitute product that competes with an existing line.

Abandon decision: They have the option to abandon investing in new or existing products, projects, machines, and technologies. The abandon strategy relates to the inadequacy of the current business model and the need to bail.

Postpone decision: They can defer investing in a product or a technology until a later date. Some investment might occur in the form of monitoring and very early exploratory work. The major investment includes learning-about in the form of search and synthesis.

There are three primary approaches for evaluating investment decisions. They are payback, discounted cash flow analysis, and real options analysis. We discussed the discounted cash flow techniques in the last chapter. The focus of this chapter is on real options analysis.

Real Options

Amazon was incorporated in July of 1994.[1] Amazon reported its first-ever profits of $5 million (a penny a share at a $12.60 closing price) in the fourth quarter 2001 over 7 years after selling its first book.[2] I doubt that most investors using net present value (NPV) and internal rate of return (IRR) analysis would have been willing to wait so long to receive such a modest return. Profits in the fourth quarter of 2009 were $384 million (85 cents a share).[3] As Jeff Bezos noted in his articulation of Amazon's strategy:

> We start with the customer and we work backward. We learn whatever skills we need to service the customer. We build whatever technology we need to service the customer. The second thing is, we are inventors, so you won't see us focusing on "me too" areas. We like to go down unexplored alleys and see what's at the end. Sometimes they're dead ends. Sometimes they open up into broad avenues and we find something really exciting. And then the third thing is, we're willing to be long-term-oriented, which I think is one of the rarest characteristics.[4]

NPV, IRR, and payback approaches may not be suitable for pursuing projects that will provide a competitive edge. The benefits of new technologies sometimes result in very strange NPV calculations that are either very high or very low. They are difficult to apply in situations involving emerging technologies where some level of investment is required in order to examine their long-run potential. There are inherent difficulties in data collection, decision analysis, and risk assessment when new and emerging technologies are involved. To put it bluntly, it is very difficult to apply discounted cash flow techniques for analyzing Blue Ocean markets. Real options can play an important role in developing a diversified product and technology portfolio for competing in dynamic environments.

The Role of Real Options in Investment Decisions

A real option is a decision or choice to invest a little or a lot in a product, a technology, or a project. They are called *real* options because they are investments in tangible assets, products, processes, and services rather than financial instruments such as stocks. For financial investments, option-pricing techniques are heavily used to take into account the flexibility issue. The most popular is the Black–Scholes option-pricing model where the option value is determined by five input values of the exercise price of an option, the time to exercise date, the current price of the asset, the variance per period of rate of return on asset, and the risk-free rate of interest. If you plug all these values into the Black–Scholes option-pricing model, you would get a positive value (do not forget all options have a positive value). This is the option value. This value would be added to the NPV analysis. So, what is initially a negative NPV would become a positive NPV once the project's option value is incorporated. This calculation looks very simple. However, investments in technology differ from those in financial assets in terms of priceability and tradability of the underlying asset. Contrary to financial investments, in technology investment situations, the price of an underlying asset is hard to know, and the underlying asset cannot be traded easily.

The purpose of a real option is to explore the potential of a product or new technology. Car manufacturers are constantly making small investments (from their perspective) in emerging technologies. They purchase real options in fuel technologies, engine technologies, drive-by-wire technologies, steering and braking technologies, advanced construction materials, and design. Sometimes they invest a little money and just search for information and try to understand whether a technology is applicable and cost-effective. Sometimes they invest a lot of money and develop full-blown prototypes using a variety of technologies and showcase the technologies in the so-called concept cars. Sometimes they decide to go whole-hog and develop a fresh line with modern features and technologies. Sometimes they just abandon a product or a technology completely.

Amazon did not just settle into the production of the Kindle e-book. They explored various technologies such as the screen technologies, the book delivery mechanism, and the file format for storing the books as well as if consumers would be interested in reading e-books.

The following example illustrates how a real options analysis can be conducted.

Jin Beans Tonic Elixirs

Jin Beans Tonic Elixirs produces exotic health drinks containing a combination of vitamins, herbs, fruit extracts, and supplements.[5] The competition is fearless and they compete with a number of highly competitive vitamin water, energy drink, and sports drink and boutique water industry. They are known for delivering healthy drinks in unique high-quality safe plastic biodegradable containers. The super high quality of their ingredients, the design of their bottles, as well as the design of their labels set them apart from the competition.

Most of their bottles are being produced overseas and because they change the design of the bottles every 2 months, the cost of design, development, and delivery is very high. They are exploring the idea of manufacturing the bottles at each of their five bottling centers in the USA. This will require the purchasing of injection blow molding equipment (see Figures 14.3, for an overview of the blow molding process).

Jin Beans Real Option Decision

The president of Jin Bean's assembled a group of financial analysts; the marketing department and the operations department conducted a study to ascertain the cost of switching bottle production in-house. They determined that it would cost the company an additional $1 million per year to purchase the machines, hire staff, and maintain the machines over what they are currently paying to import their bottles. Each machine costs $250,000 and will involve personnel costs and maintenance costs exceeding $100,000. No matter how they put the numbers together, they could not generate a positive NPV. Even though the figures did not

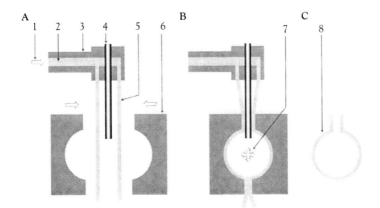

Steps in the creation of plastic blow-molded product.

1. Plastic is fed from the extruder.
2. The plastic (yellow) is melted and passed through the extruder pipe.
3. The extruder head (green) separates the plastic into two pipes (see 5).
4. The air tube (silver/black) is used to blow air into the mold.
5. This is the tubular shape of the hot plastic.
6. This is the mold.
7. Air pressure expands the plastic in the mold.
8. The end product.

Figure 14.3. Blow injection molding diagram. Developed by Laurens van Lieshout, available under Creative Commons Attribution share license.[6]

look good, the presidents of Jin Bean decided to go ahead and purchase one machine and install it in Florida. The decision of Jin Bean's president was based on her knowledge of real options analysis. By purchasing and using one machine, they were able to learn and conduct an economic experiment. The company could obtain insight and also acquire the flexibility to expand in the future as the effect of the investment on the bottom-line gets clearer and knowledge about the use of the machine is accumulated.

The result of this experiment and installation was enlightening. Jin Bean was able to generate more sales with the new injection molding machine and they were also able to provide external consulting to other businesses and to sell specialized plastic containers at a premium price. Jin Bean also used the injection machine to experiment with new bottle designs and product ingredients. In the past, it would take them a year to introduce a new bottle to the market and several months to understand the sales results. Now they were able to deliver a new product in less than a year. They were able to increase their market share and became very responsive to market demands because of their increased flexibility. The data they were able to gather by experimenting with one machine was then used to conduct an NPV and IRR analysis and resulted in a very attractive return for their investment (see Figure 14.4). Jin Bean subsequently decided to obtain four additional machines because they have the confidence to further pursue a growth option and invest in more injection molding machines.

			Projected cash flows before investing			
Cash receipts		Year 0	Year 1	Year 2	Year 3	Year 4
Additional cash sales			$150,000	$ 165,000	$181,500	$199,650
Total cash in			$150,000	$ 165,000	$181,500	$199,650
Cash out						
Payroll expenses			$ 60,000	$ 66,000	$ 72,600	$ 79,860
Maintenance			$ 15,000	$ 16,500	$ 18,150	$ 19,965
Training			$ 15,000	$ 16,500	$ 18,150	$ 19,965
Mechine cost		$ 250,000				
Startup costs		$ 15,000				
Total cash out		$265,000	$90,000	$99,000	$108,900	$119,790
Net cash flow (in - out)		$ (265,000)	$ 60,000	$ 66,000	$ 72,600	$ 79,860
Discount rate	12.00%					
NPV	$ (50,345)					
IRR	2%					
			Projected cash flows after investing			
Cash receipts		Year 0	Year 1	Year 2	Year 3	Year 4
Additional cash sales			$ 260,000	$ 299,000	$ 343,850	$ 395,428
Consulting revenues			$ 100,000	$ 115,000	$ 132,250	$ 152,088
Total cash in			$ 260,000	$ 299,000	$343,850	$395,428
Cash out						
Payroll expenses			$104,000	$ 119,600	$137,540	$158,171
Maintenance			$ 26,000	$ 29,900	$ 34,385	$ 39,543
Training			$ 26,000	$ 29,900	$ 34,385	$ 39,543
Machine cost		$ 250,000				
Startup costs		$ 15,000				
Total cash out		$265,000	$156,000	$179,400	$206,310	$237,257
Net cash flow (in - out)		$ (265,000)	$104,000	$ 119,600	$137,540	$158,171
Discount rate	12.00%					
NPV	$ 108,590					
IRR	31%					

Figure 14.4. Financial analysis before and after installing one machine.

Many real-world investment decisions are not easily analyzed with NPV and IRR analysis. Investing in a new technology can take the firm down many different paths as the organization learns about and learns by doing and experimenting with new technology and products. If you look at most of the Blue Ocean markets, for example, Cirque du Soleil, social networking services, and global positioning system products, they come about as a result of experimentation and the progression of little *ahas* that turn into the big *aha*. It is basically a learning and adaptation strategy that is focused on product and process differentiation.

> Business conditions are fraught with uncertainty and risks. These uncertainties hold with them valuable information. When uncertainty becomes resolved through the passage of time, actions and events, managers can make the appropriate mid-course corrections through a change in business decisions and strategies. Real options incorporates this learning model, it is akin to having a strategic road map, while traditional analyses that neglect managerial flexibility will grossly undervalue certain projects and strategies.[7]

Real options analysis can be very technical, requiring a significant amount of financial and technical scrutiny. However, we believe that using complicated calculations is overkill for small- and medium-sized businesses. Real options concepts are nevertheless important. The takeaway from the perspective of the entrepreneur is that you need to experiment and also need to diversify your portfolio of products and projects under consideration. This does not mean that you have to actually buy machinery, make products, and constantly modify your business processes, but it does mean that you should learn-about many products and technologies related to your business and learn-by-doing and experimenting when an opportunity looks promising.

There are two important considerations related to real options that companies should consider before making large investment decisions. The first important consideration is how will the investment interact with current investments, and the second important consideration is how will the competition respond to an investment decision.[8]

The influence of Interaction Effects on Investment Decisions

New investments can interact positively or negatively with existing assets of the firm. For example, when Amazon started offering electronic books (Kindle) and electronic audio (Audible), there was an obvious and natural synergy with existing content and their core competencies. These investments improved Amazon's firm performance because they complemented existing company assets. When Amazon began adding tools and a variety of other home improvement products and then started selling groceries in certain markets and branched out into cloud computing, there were concerns related to synergy. Part of the answer relates to Amazon's core competencies. Amazon is good at online retailing and it is very good at maintaining a very scalable and robust server and processing infrastructure. They had core competencies that were transferable to those businesses.

There are numerous examples where an investment lacked synergy with existing assets. Many believed that eBay's acquisition of Skype was ill conceived because there did not appear to be any positive synergies between the businesses.[9] The businesses did not appear to mesh and the executives at both eBay and Skype were constantly fighting. eBay eventually sold Skype at what was considered a very modest amount. In some ways, eBay's competitive advantage was undermined because of the relationship. The interaction effects between eBay's assets and Skype's assets were negative.

The Influence of Competitor's Response on Investment Decisions

A new investment may force competitors to think about their existing investments and engage in counterinvestments to compete with a new investment. These competitor reactions or counterinvestments made by competitors can affect the revenue base and cost structure of a firm in the long term. This is part of the reason that first-mover advantages are transient. If a move appears to be threatening, then competitors may invest substantially more in the technology or product in order to catch up and perhaps even surpass the first mover's investment. The net effect is that the new entrant can dilute earnings and performance. An investment that is projected to produce profits can prompt the competition to overreact and invest at even higher than expected. These types of responses are common in the consumer electronics marketplace and, in general, are found in many types of markets.

When Amazon entered the cloud-computing market in 2006 with the introduction of Amazon Web Services, there was a definite reaction by many companies, some of them were competitors and others were just interested. Data storage vendors, CPU and hardware manufacturers, infrastructure companies, operating systems companies, service providers, consulting companies, ERP vendors, and all sort of applications software developers took note. Many of these companies responded by investing more and more money in cloud computing. Amazon's continued pursuit of the growth option in cloud computing was in turn answered with many other companies pursuing a growth option in cloud computing. Dell, for example, invested more than a billion dollars in cloud computing.

The Strategic Actions Model: Combining Interaction Effects and Competitor Response

Figure 14.5 illustrates how these two dimensions can be combined to provide guidance into the investment decision process. The implication is that when there are positive interactions with existing capabilities, then growth options should be pursued. If competitor reactions are low, then an aggressive growth option should be pursued. When competitor reactions are high, then a switching-up option should be pursued. The point is if there are strong competitor reactions, a company may want to change its future investment for growth, even if the interaction effects are high.

Risk enters in the framework when the synergies between existing competencies are low and competitors are not responding. The implication is that the technology may not be important and there is little reason to pursue it if the market is not responding accordingly. The other

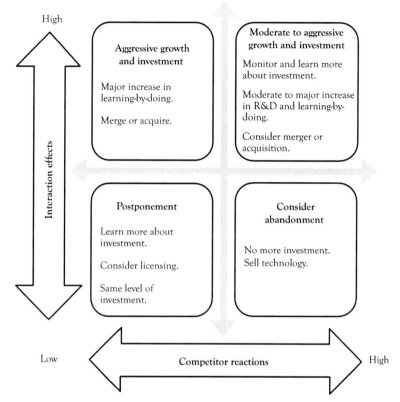

Figure 14.5. Strategic action framework (modified from Kim and Sanders).

tricky quadrant occurs in the instance where there is a competency and interaction effects and competitors are not signaling that it is important. In that instance, the product or technology may need to be monitored closely.

The Project Selection Model: Considering Risk and Reward

After a company decides a strategic action to pursue based on the strategic action model, it needs to decide how it will proceed with the action, that is, what kind of project it will launch to implement the action, how much of risk it can bare, and how much of reward it wants to gain. Most companies want to minimize risk and maximize reward in launching a project. O'Sullivan and Dooley[10] have categorized projects in terms of their risk and reward as being pearls, oysters, bread and butter projects, and white elephants (see Figure 14.6). It would be nice if all investments translated into pearls and a few ended up being successful oysters, but that is not possible. Therefore, when selecting a project, companies take into account the strategic action they will pursue. For example, if the strategic action chosen is aggressive growth, it may want to develop a project falling into the category of pearls. If the strategic action chosen is switching-up growth, it may want to develop a project falling into the category of oysters. On the other hand, if the strategic action selected is postponement, it may want to play with a bread and butter project, a small, simple, low-risk project, and wait for additional information.

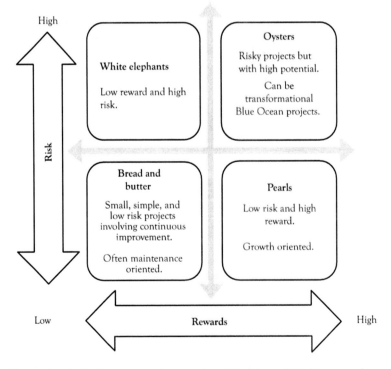

Figure 14.6. Project categorization (modified from O'Sullivan and Dooley).

Conclusion

In this chapter, we have discussed real option concepts and strategic action framework. The key points are the following:

- It is often difficult, if not impossible, to use the financial techniques including discounted cash flow, NPV, and economic value added to justify an investment in certain projects, "exploratory" or "experimenting" or learning projects in particular. The "Jin Beans Tonic Elixirs" case nicely illustrates this very point.
- Firms should keep options open under the conditions of uncertainty and irreversibility and develop a portfolio of investment opportunities. Firms can defer "commitment" under uncertainty and irreversibility. This way of thinking can make a big difference for firms' strategy, including portfolio decisions, mergers and acquisition decisions, governance choice, technology adoption decisions, and so forth.
- To develop a portfolio of investment opportunities, firms need to keep monitoring risk, assessing market trends, and trying new things on a small basis of experimentation.

Investment decisions are never easy. Cash flows, whether they are positive or negative, are fraught with uncertainty. Selecting the appropriate discount rate is never easy, but it has a dramatic influence on the go/no-go decision. Technical analysis using discounted cash flow techniques does not alleviate the uncertainty and does not permit hunches and intuition. One student noted that his presentation in another class was marked down because he had a hunch that a company should invest in a project, even though the NPV analysis was unfavorable. After discussing the issue for a short time, I let him in on the great secret that was revealed to me by one of my mentors after I had spent days trying to justify a modest expenditure using return on investment calculations. He told me to tinker with the numbers until they fit the desired outcome. Investment in emerging technologies and a new product line rarely result in positive NPVs unless the data have been cooked. Real options when combined with the development of a product and project portfolio can bring truth, beauty, and enlightenment into the investment process.

Real options concepts can be applied in a variety of ways. Smaller organizations can focus on learning-about by investing in education, reading high-tech magazines and trade publications, attending trade shows, and attending research conferences. Larger organizations can use real options as the basis for learning-about as well as investing in basic research and using learning-by doing strategies to develop prototypes. The important point is to keep ones options open and to develop a portfolio of investment opportunities. Important activities included in the development of the portfolio include monitoring risk and frequent monitoring and assessment of the product and project portfolio by a cross-functional team of key personnel who understand and are aligned with the business mission.

CHAPTER 15

Wrap-Up

Carol Roth[1] is convinced that most people are not right for entrepreneurship. Some people try to become entrepreneurs because they want to be the boss; but they end up working for more people. They end up working for investors, lenders, landlords, customers, suppliers, and even their employees. Some people think that if they start a business involving their favorite hobby, they will have more time to spend working on the hobby that they love. The reality is that they end up spending less time on the hobby and more time running the business. Baking cakes is different than running a bakery.

The business of the entrepreneur is primarily about designing and maintaining business systems.[2] As illustrated in the project management chapter, there are at least 30 main activities and systems that have to be attended before launch date and very few involve cake baking and decorating. After one of my students filled out the Ten–Ten business template, she told me that her life-long desire to own a florist shop was gone. The two templates can be filled out very quickly, but they also highlight the numerous details that eventually need to be dealt with before launching the business. Filling out the simple templates and preparing an executive summary is a good check on reality.

Roth's other contention is that most of the great ideas for businesses are already taken. And she argues that the value of a business is not in the idea, but in the execution. We agree, in part. The best execution of an outdated idea can surely lead to failure. Where are the old icons of the music industry, how about telegraphy, where are desktop PCs headed, and what about those old persimmon woods? The key for survival is product differentiation coupled with improving execution and driving down costs. The key is the dynamic tension created from developing Midas and Hermes versions of products and services.

Ideas for products do not seem to be diminishing, but rather increasing. Compared with the approximately 49,000 patents granted in 1963, there were over 244,000 patents granted in 2010.[3] Knowledge development and the ensuing products and services are the result of the cumulative progression of ideas over years, decades, and even centuries.[4] The foundational knowledge for a simple digital voice recorder are the results of discovering the properties of metals, research in physics on ferromagnetic theory, and the development of electronics components such as vacuum tubes in the late 18th century and earlier. The world of today is truly built on the shoulders of ancient ideas.

I am constantly amazed at the diversity of products and services students developed for term project in my class. They include a robotic surgical simulator, a 100-amp cable dispenser, an online animated user manual development system, an organic chemistry tutorial system, a penny auctioning site where anyone could offer a penny auction, various smartphone apps, numerous shopping assistance applications, a franchise system for asphalt sealing, generic mentoring software, home, pet and child monitoring systems, home improvement and emergency repair services, a variety of health monitoring and health-related products, adult pajamas with footies, an atomic scale measuring device, different types of cloud-computing systems, and many others. Because of my ongoing interest in global positioning system technology, there have been several products related to bus scheduling, tracking assets, and social networking. I am still amused by the Smell-Me-Up-Clock that produces smells, such as coffee brewing, to wake a person up. I am also bemused by the Rent-a-Friend. It was funny and provided a poignant commentary on contemporary society.

Several projects have been or in the process of being patented, including a technology that isolates atoms and molecules and then measures the effect of electrical and mechanical stimulus on atoms and molecules. Then there was the hockey puck that had radio-frequency identification (RFID) chips embedded in the puck that could be used to determine when a gala was scored. The prototype for the puck was developed using 3D printing technology. Another interesting product was the improved lightning arrestor device used by utility companies that would last longer and perform better.

The point is that there are many new opportunities for new businesses, but there are also many good ideas for improving existing companies. Many of the projects developed in the class are related to improving existing businesses and improving existing versions of products and services. Monopolistic competition is relentless. If a business does not make little and sometimes big tweaks to products and services, it will become a business footnote. The ideas and concepts presented in this book will not guarantee success, but they can be used to confront and sometimes even ignore the competition. Ignoring the competition is achieved by focusing on the development of new opportunities rather than meeting the checklists of product features touted by the competition. A definition of entrepreneurship was presented in the beginning of the book:

Entrepreneurship is a risky endeavor involving the continuous creation and re-creation of a new enterprise, a new product, or a new idea.

The traditional concept of the entrepreneur is that the entrepreneur starting the business absorbs most of the risk. In today's climate, however, businesses need to be entrepreneurial. Businesses must absorb and deal with the risk of product development and enhancement. In today's climate, the individual has to be entrepreneurial in terms of their career path. Knowledge and skills have transitory value that can be in demand today and out next year. Differentiation of the individual can only be achieved by continuous leaning-about and learning-by-doing.

As noted in the beginning of the book, entrepreneurship is currently being viewed as a set of skills that are part of a rational and logical process for identifying and creating opportunities. The skills have been likened to learning how to read, write, calculate, and conduct scientific reasoning. Entrepreneurship requires insight and knowledge of problem solving, strategic planning, new product development, project management, and portfolio management among others. Participation in entrepreneurial activity leads to the creation of opportunities for individuals, businesses, and countries.

Entrepreneurs are made though life experiences and a willingness to work hard and become totally immersed in a goal. Being an entrepreneur is the goal of the entrepreneur. The research on the personal and demographic factors contributing to the entrepreneurial activity supports the idea that the entrepreneur cannot be identified by any single demographic characteristic. There are demographic tendencies, but in reality entrepreneurs can be young or old, male or female, and from wealthy or disadvantaged backgrounds. The key is participation and self-motivation and, most importantly, continuous learning and adaptation. It is hoped that this book will put you on the right path to becoming an entrepreneur on your own or as an intrapreneur in an existing organization.

Notes

Preface

1. We do not believe that technology and new product development should be pursued with abandon and without analysis. We do believe that bandwagon effects can occur and that unbridled enthusiasm can lead to faulty business models and major mistakes. A sound planning process can alleviate many of these issues.
2. Cohen and Levinthal (1990), p. 128.
3. Grove (2010).
4. Pisano and Shih (2009).
5. Pisano and Shih (2009).
6. Sims (2011).

Chapter 1

1. By the way, I detest pop quizzes. They may work to force people to read the material, but they make learning miserable.
2. Brakman and Heijdra (2004).
3. An oligopoly is a special case of a monopoly. There are a small number of firms (e.g., 2–8) and they control more than 50% of the market. An oligopolistic market is characterized by low levels of product differentiation and very high fixed costs of entry, where competition is often based on price with elements of both price taking and price leadership. Sample sectors include steel, copper, autos, breakfast cereals, tires, some appliances, and home-care equipment. See McConnell, Brue, and Campbell (2004).
4. Kirzner (1973).
5. Sarasvathy and Venkataraman (2008).
6. Arora et al. (2008).
7. Miller (2010, November 28).
8. Kawasaki (2008).
9. Patent Technology Monitoring Team (n.d.).
10. Moore (n.d.).
11. Spence (1981).
12. Gartner (n.d.).
13. Moore (1999).

14. VC MIKE (2010).
15. Liebowitz and Margolis (1994).
16. Liebowitz and Margolis (1994).
17. Matheson and Matheson (1998).
18. Annacchino (2006).
19. Schmoch (2007).
20. Goldenberg and Mazursky (2002).
21. Madsen (2007).
22. Laursen and Salter (2006).
23. Laursen and Salter (2006).
24. Laursen and Salter (2006).
25. Laursen and Salter (2006).
26. Cohen and Levinthal (1990).
27. Schank and Cleary (1995), p. 74.
28. Cohen and Levinthal (1990).
29. In general, the terms value chain and supply chain can be used interchangeably, although the value chain is rooted in the strategic planning literature whereas the supply chain is linked to the work in the operations management area.

Chapter 2

1. Shapiro and Varian (1998); Varian (1996).
2. Lipsey and Chrystal (2007).
3. One of my colleagues says that 2 is the perfect number because many consumers will delay purchase when there are more than two choices because of the excess demands on cognitive processing.
4. Schwartz (2003).
5. Phillips (2005).
6. Federal Trade Commission (n.d-a.).
7. Federal Trade Commission (n.d-b.).
8. Anderson (2008).
9. Research on cattle using global positioning system devices has shown that water is a more powerful draw than salt in attracting cattle to new grazing ground. See Ganskopp (2006).
10. Becerra (2009).

Chapter 3

1. Varian (1996).
2. Prahalad (2006).

3. Traditional marketing analysis techniques such as focus groups can still be used to identify features. However, they are just part of the input used to identify product versions.

4. As noted in the last reading, the terms price discrimination and price differentiation can, in general, be treated as synonymous. Companies use price discrimination to differentiate prices.

5. Varian (1996).

6. It is ironic that some of the ill will that was directed at cable companies is now being directed at satellite TV carriers. The lesson is that quality customer service and perception management are never-ending processes.

7. Wolverton (2000).

8. See the Research and Innovative Technology Administration Bureau of Statistics site at: http://www.bts.gov/programs/economics_and_finance/air_travel_price_index/html/annual_table.html

9. The "I" is Sanders.

10. I eventually got the bongos as a Christmas gift from my grandmother. She bought them from JC Penney's for a substantially lower price.

11. See the following Web site for a good discussion of the Law of Demand: http://www.investopedia.com/terms/l/lawofdemand.asp

12. Oz Shy (2008).

Chapter 4

1. Adamson (2006).

2. Kim and Mauborgne (2005). A related concept in the marketing literature, called lateral marketing, was developed by Kotler and de Bes (2003).

3. Shapiro and Varian (1998).

4. Shapiro and Varian (1998).

5. Nalebuff and Ayres (2003), also see *Why not? About the book.* Also visit Wikipedia.

6. Bertini and Wathieu (2010).

7. I realize that there are many patrons for this large segment of humanity. The goal is to have a question for the bottom of the pyramid. Please see Prahalad (2006) and many others who have been committed to this group.

8. Athreye and Kapur (2009).

9. *Dynamic Tension* was an exercise approach developed by Charles Atlas, but it also works here.

10. Prahalad (2006).

11. See the discussion at the end of this chapter on Pareto Economics, Welfare, and Efficiency.

12. Jain (2000).

13. Shapiro and Varian (1998).

14. Heracleous and Wirtz (2010)

15. Sugden (1984).

Chapter 5

1. Slavin (2008).

2. This section has been adapted from a paper by Gopal and Sanders (2000).

3. Ihnatko (2009).

4. Borden (2009).

5. Markoff (2008).

6. Lieberman (2003).

7. A special note of thanks is extended to Emily Wester, consultant and owner of Magic City Media, for providing insight into the material used in this section.

8. American Cancer Society (2010).

9. Sahlman and Flaherty (2010).

10. The students analyzed the case by first using the FAD (features, attributes, and design) template and the Ten–Ten planning templates. In general, the case analyses were superlative and several creative solutions for versioning were identified.

11. Grueber and Studt (2011).

Chapter 6

1. Cf. Hülsheger, Anderson, and Salgado (2009).

2. The classic four-stage model of creativity was published by Wallas in 1926. The art of thought. New York: Harcourt Brace Jovanovich.. See Lubart (2001), for an overview of the various approaches for modeling creativity. The updated model used in this book has been adapted and extrapolated from the following papers: An, Hunt, and Sanders (1993); Cerveny, Garrity, & Sanders (1990).

3. In large organizations, this information may be put into complex knowledge management repositories and is referred to as knowledge management. A significant amount of knowledge is actually maintained in the largest knowledge repository of all, the World Wide Web.

4. Sims (2011).

5. Varian (1997), pp. 2–3.

6. Varian (1997).

7. Gardner (1994).

8. See, for example, Highfield and Carter (1993); Isaacson (2008); Ohanian (2008).

9. For an overview of convergent and divergent thinking and questions related to these typologies and the psychological, sociological, and biological theories related to creativity, see Runco (2006).

10. Dyer, Gregersen, and Christensen (2009).

11. Sawyer (2006).

12. Cf. Hülsheger et al. (2009).

13. Sawyer (2006).

14. Amabile, Hadley, and Kramer (2002).

15. Goldenberg and Mazursky (2002).

16. Nalebuff and Ayres (2003).

17. Michalko (2006).

18. Wang and Chern (2008).

19. Amabile et al. (2002).

20. Donovan (2010).

21. Lupien, McEwen, Gunnar, and Heim (2009).

22. c.f. Michalko (2006).

23. Michalko (2006).

24. Nalebuff and Ayres (2003).

25. Nalebuff and Ayres (2003).

26. Choate (2005).

27. Nalebuff and Ayres (2003).

28. Nalebuff and Ayres (2003).

29. This idea has been attributed to Alan Kay, one of the pioneers behind object-oriented programming and the graphical user interface, when he was a scientist at Xerox's Palo Alto Research Corporation in the 1970s.

30. Rose (2002).

31. Hofstede and Hofstede (2004).

32. Gladwell (2008).

33. Selling (2009).

34. de Bono (1999).

35. Han, Kim, and Srivastava (1998).

Chapter 7

1. Software developers often use a technique referred to as user-centered design or participative design that has elements of UDD and MDD. In user-centered design, there is an iterative process of building the application and having the user continuously validate software solution.

2. As noted in an earlier chapter. A Blue Ocean market is a market that is not in existence. A Blue Ocean product is a new product that is radically differentiated from existing products that are being offered.

3. Cf. Verganti (2009).

4. Lyons (2010b, September 1).

5. Verganti (2009).

6. Bitner, Ostrom, and Morgan (2008).

7. Adamson (2006).

8. Cf. Jo, Moon, Garrity, and Sanders (2007).

9. Heckhausen and Schulz (1995); Skinner (1996).

10. Jo et al. (2011).

11. Pierce, Kostovab, and Dirks (2003).

12. Schwartz (2003).

13. Iyer and Muncy (2005); Keller, Sternthal, and Tybout (2002); Keller and Tybout (2002); Kim and Mauborgne (2005); McGrath and MacMillan (2000); Tybout and Sternthal (2005).

14. Adamson (2006).

15. Bitner et al. (2008).

16. This notion is discussed in the chapter on innovation and is also the result of several research projects I have been involved with. See in particular Cerveny, Garrity, and Sanders (1986).

17. The Printed World (2011).

18. In 2011, the 3D printers start at around $10,000 (just search for "3D printers" to see what is currently available.). There are hobbyists versions of 3D printers in the $1,000 range.

19. Search for "wine aging" at the U.S. patent office and with any search engine.

20. Kim and Mauborgne (2005).

21. Kotler and de Bes (2003).

22. Malhotra and Birks (2009).

23. Cavusgil, Knight, Riesenberger, and Yaprak (2009).

24. http://www.wengerna.com/giant-knife-16999#

25. Manjoo (2010).

Chapter 8

1. Michael Porter originally identified three generic strategies. He noted that a business can also focus on a market that is not very competitive. Most people consider this to be a special case of the other two strategies. See Porter (1980).

2. Adapted from May (2010).

3. Porter (1985).
4. Coase (1937).
5. Williamson (1985).
6. Porter (2008).
7. This is in part the reason that outsourcing and off-shoring started to increase so dramatically.
8. Prahalad and Hamel (1990).
9. Barney (1991).
10. Henry (2007).
11. Grant (2007).
12. Cf. Kaplan and Norton (1996, January–February, 2003b) and visit http://www.balancedscorecard.org/BSCResources/AbouttheBalancedScorecard/tabid/55/Default.aspx
13. Nørreklit (2000).
14. Nørreklit (2000).
15. Nørreklit (2000).
16. Kim and Mauborgne (2005).
17. Burke, Stel, and Thurik (2009).
18. Before he died in 2005, Humphrey wrote a brief history of SWOT development. He indicated that it was initiated in 1960 because long-range planning approaches were not working properly. The research team interviewed 1,100 organizations and had 5,000 executives complete a 250-item questionnaire. The approach was originally called SOFT (Satisfactory, Opportunity, Fault, and Threat) but after subsequent adaptations by a number of consultants and academics, it evolved into SWOT. There are devotees of SWOT that believe it originated at Harvard Business School under the guise of Albert Smith, Roland Christensen, and Kenneth Andrew. See Humphrey (2005); Panagiotou (2003).
19. Panagiotou (2003).

Chapter 9

1. See Horan (2007). This is an alternative approach to Horan's approach developing a brief plan. One deficiency of the Horan approach is that it does not integrate the key ideas found in the major planning approaches. The deficiency in all of the other planning approaches discussed in chapter 8 is they take too much time and, yet, they are not comprehensive enough because they do not include and build on other approaches. The Ten–Ten approach attempts to reconcile speed with comprehensiveness.
2. Porter (1998).

3. Barney (1991).
4. Prahalad and Hamel (1990).
5. Kim and Mauborgne (2005).
6. Kawasaki (2008).
7. See the Appendix at the end of the chapter for an example of an actual business where the templates have been filled in.
8. http://www.wineinstitute.org/files/PerCapitaWineConsumptionCountries.pdf
9. http://www.winemarketcouncil.com/research_slideview.asp?position=9

Chapter 10

1. Arthur (1989).
2. Shapiro and Varian (1998).
3. Liebowitz and Margolis (1994).
4. Burnham, Frels, and Mahajan (2003).
5. This section is based on Kaplan and Norton (2003a, September 15); Shapiro and Varian (1998).
6. Jo, Moon, Garrity, and Sanders (2007).
7. Raustiala and Sprigman (2006), p. 1719.
8. Raustiala and Sprigman (2006).
9. Fitzpatrick and Lueck (2010).
10. Belcourt (2006), pp. 269–279.
11. Lenskold (2003).
12. Reichheld and Schefter (2000).

Chapter 11

1. This chapter is adapted from material originally appearing in Huefner, Largay, and Hamlen (2005 and 2007, Thomson Custom Publishing; used by permission of the copyright holders).
2. Jones and Van Dyke (1998).
3. The first two digits in a Revenue Ruling number signify the year of issue. Thus, Revenue Ruling 59–60 was issued in 1959.
4. Pratt (2001).
5. This listing is drawn from American Institute of Certified Public Accountants (2003).
6. See Cornell (1993).
7. The payback approach is related to the hyperbolic discounting phenomena. There appears to be psychological as well as economic reasons behind the fact that people prefers a reward today rather than wait for a substantial

reward. Studies have found that people sometimes use average annual discount rates of over 300% over the course of 1 month and over 100% over a 1-year horizon. They ask people whether they prefer $100 today rather than $200 next month. See Noor (2009).

8. See Slee and Paglia (2010).

9. See Pratt et al. (1993) for an expanded discussion of the excess earnings method.

10. For an extended discussion of premiums and discounts, see Pratt (2001).

11. Pratt (2001), p. 79.

12. Pratt (2001), chapters 5–9.

13. Pratt (2001), chapter 12.

14. For an expanded discussion of valuation of startup companies, see Abrams (2001), especially chapter 12, and Evans and Bishop (2001), especially chapter 15.

15. Gompers, Kovner, Lerner, and Scharfstein (2010).

16. Abrams (2001), pp. 410–413.

Chapter 12

1. The SWOT analysis is rarely part of the business plan and is usually not part of the business presentation. The purpose of a SWOT analysis is to assist the founders in understating what the business is all about and where it is heading. The strengths and opportunities will of course be woven into the business plan and the business plan presentation. But there is little to be gained from focusing on the threats and the weaknesses. Indeed, a significant part of the business plan and presentation involves developing strategies for dealing with weaknesses and threats.

2. Afuah and Tucci (2001).

3. Sahlman (1997, July-August).

4. Kawasaki (2008).

5. An interesting book on the details of writing a business plan was published by Chambers (2007).

6. Herbert (2009).

7. Guy Kawasaki posits that for every 10 pages over 20 you reduce reading and funding probability by 25%.

8. Sahlman (1997, July-August).

9. See the following Web sites for an overview of funding issues and general entrepreneurial concepts:
   http://www.sba.gov/
   http://www.entrepreneur.com/
   http://www.nvca.org/

10. Applegate, Simpson, White, and McDonald (2010).
11. Applegate et al. (2010).
12. Applegate et al. (2010).
13. Stuck and Weingarten (2005).
14. Sahlman (1997).
15. Applegate et al. (2010).
16. http://blog.guykawasaki.com/2007/09/the-top-ten-six. html#axzz18O5LrqfG
17. http://blog.guykawasaki.com/2007/10/ten-questions-1.html #axzz18OGNAE1M and http://blog.guykawasaki.com/2007/06/482413_ for_lega.html#axzz18OGadUe2

Chapter 13

1. Adapted from Leavitt (1965).
2. Project Management Institute (2004).
3. IPS Associates (1997).
4. Cf. Takeuchi and Nonaka (1986).
5. We have been involved in several research papers on the subject including Garrity, Glassberg, Kim, Sanders, and Shin (2005) and Garrity and Sanders (1998).
6. Kawasaki (2008).
7. Varianini and Vaturi (2000).
8. Anderson (2010).

Chapter 14

1. http://phx.corporate-ir.net/phoenix.zhtml?c=97664&p=irol-faq
2. http://news.cnet.com/2100-1017-819688.html
3. http://online.wsj.com/article/SB10001424052748704878904575031504 159206726.html
4. Lyons (2010a, January 4).
5. The company used in the example is fictitious. Jin Bean is a compendium of numerous examples of actual companies that have decided to go ahead with an investment in the face of negative values for NPV. See Mauboussin (1999); Mun (2005); Trigeorgis (1996), for additional examples that also include financial calculations.
6. "Permission is granted to copy, distribute and/or modify this document under the terms of the GNU Free Documentation License, Version 1.2 or any later version published by the Free Software Foundation; with no

Invariant Sections, no Front-Cover Texts, and no Back-Cover Texts. A copy of the license is included in the section entitled GNU Free Documentation License." http://commons.wikimedia.org/wiki/File:Blow_molding.png

7. Mun (2005), p. 16.
8. This section is based on an article by Kim and Sanders (2002).
9. http://dealbook.blogs.nytimes.com/2010/03/15/skype-poised-for-a-big-initial-stock-offering/
10. O'Sullivan and Dooley (2008).

Chapter 15

1. Roth (2011).
2. Gerby (1995).
3. Visit the U.S. Patent Office at http://www.uspto.gov/web/offices/ac/ido/oeip/taf/us_stat.htm
4. Cf. Garud and Nayyar (1994).

References

Abrams, J. B. (2001). *Quantitative business valuation: A mathematical approach for today's professional.* New York, NY: McGraw-Hill.

Adamson, A. P. (2006). *BrandSimple: How the best brands keep it simple and succeed* (1st ed.). New York, NY: Palgrave Macmillan.

Afuah, A., & Tucci, C. L. (2001). *Internet Business Models and Strategies.* Boston: McGraw-Hill.

Amabile, T. M., Hadley, C. N., & Kramer, S. J. (2002, August). Creativity under the gun. *Harvard Business Review.*

American Cancer Society. (2010). *Cancer Facts & Figures 2010.* Retrieved August 17, 2011, from American Cancer Society Web site: http://www.cancer.org/Research/CancerFactsFigures/CancerFactsFigures/cancer-facts-and-figures-2010

American Institute of Certified Public Accountants. (2003). Exposure Draft of the AICPA Practice Aid, *Valuation of privately-held-company equity securities issued in other than a business combination* (pp. 20–26). New York, NY: AICPA.

An, J. M., Hunt, R. G., & Sanders, G. L. (1993). The role of domain coverage and consensus in a network of learning and problem solving systems. In R. Blanning & D. King (Eds.), *Current research in decision support technology* (pp. 227–240). Los Alamitos, CA: IEEE Computer Society Press.

Anderson, D. M. (2010). *Design for manufacturability & concurrent engineering: How to design for low cost, design in high quality, design for lean manufacture, and design quickly for fast production.* Cambria, CA: CIM Press.

Anderson, S. P. (2008). Product differentiation. In S. N. Durlauf & L. E. Blume (2nd ed.), *The New Palgrave Dictionary of Economics.* Gordonsville, VA: Palgrave Macmillan.

Annacchino, M. A. (2006). *The pursuit of new product development: The business development process.* Burlington, MA: Butterworth-Heinemann.

Applegate, L. M., Simpson, K. A., White, M., & McDonald, C. (2010). *CommonAngels.* Boston, MA: Harvard Business Publishing.

Arora, N., Dreze, X., Ghose, A., Hess, J. D., Iyengar, R., Jing, B., Joshi, Y., Kumar, V., Lurie, N., Neslin, S., Sajeesh, S., Su, M., Syam, N. B., Thomas, J., & Zhang, Z. J. (2008). Putting one-to-one marketing to work: Personalization, customization and choice. *Marketing Letters 19,* 305–321.

Arthur, W. B. (1989). Competing technologies, increasing returns, and lock-in by historical events. *The Economic Journal 99*(394), 116–131.

Athreye, S., & Kapur, S. (2009). Introduction: The internationalization of Chinese and Indian firms—Trends, motivations and strategy. *Industrial and Corporate Change 18*, 209–221.

Barney, J. (1991). Firm resources and sustained competitive advantage. *Journal of Management Information Systems 17*(1), 99–120.

Becerra, M. (2009). *Theory of the firm for strategic management: Economic value analysis.* Cambridge, UK: Cambridge University Press.

Belcourt, M. (2006). Outsourcing—The benefits and the risks. *Human Resource Management Review 16*(2), 269–279.

Bertini, M., & Wathieu, L. (2010). How to stop customers from fixating on price. *Harvard Business Review 88*, 84–91.

Bitner, M. J., Ostrom, A. L., & Morgan, F. N. (2008). Service blueprinting: A practical technique for service innovation. *California Management Review 50*(3).

Borden, M. (2009, September). Nokia rocks the world: The phone king's plan to redefine its business. *Fast Company.*

Brakman, S., & Heijdra, B. J. (2004). *The monopolistic competition revolution in retrospect.* Cambridge, UK: Cambridge University Press.

Brooks, D. (2011). *The social animal: the hidden sources of love, character, and achievement.* Random House.

Burke, A., van Stel, A., & Thurik, R. (2009). *Blue Ocean versus competitive strategy: Theory and evidence.* ERIM Report Series (ERS-2009-030-ORG.), Rotterdam, Netherlands: Erasmus Research Institute of Management

Burnham, T. A., Frels, J. K., & Mahajan, V. (2003). Consumer switching costs: A typology, antecedents, and consequences. *Journal of the Academy of Marketing Science 31*(2), 109–126.

Cavusgil, S. T., Knight, G., Riesenberger, J., & Yaprak, A. (2009). *Conducting market research for international business.* New York, NY: Business Experts Press.

Cerveny, R., Garrity, E., & Sanders, G. L. (1986). The Application of prototyping to systems development: A rationale and model. *Journal of Management Information Systems 3*(2), 52–62.

Cerveny, R., Garrity, E., & Sanders, G. L. (1990). A problem solving perspective on systems development. *Journal of Management Information Systems 6*(4), 103–122.

Chambers, K. D. (2007). *The entrepreneur's guide to writing business plans and proposals.* Westport, CT Greenwood Publishing Group.

Choate, P. (2005). *Hot property: The stealing of ideas in an age of globalization.* New York, NY:Knopf Doubleday Publishing Group.

Coase, R. H. (1937). The nature of the firm. *Economica 4*(16), 386–405.

Cohen, W. M., & Levinthal, D. A. (1990). Absorptive capacity: A new perspective on learning and innovation. *Administrative Science Quarterly 35*, 125–152.

Cornell, B. (1993). *Corporate valuation: Tools for effective appraisal and decision-making,* Homewood, IL: Business One Irwin.

de Bono, E. (1999). *Six thinking hats* (2nd ed.). New York, NY: Back Bay Books.

Delmar, F., & Davidsson, P. (2000). Where do they come from? Prevalence and characteristics of nascent entrepreneurs. *Entrepreneurship & Regional Development 12,* 1–23.

Donovan, P. (2010, October). *Some adversity makes us stronger.* Retrieved August 17, 2011, from SUNY Buffalo Web site: http://www.buffalo.edu/ubreporter/2010_10_21/seery_adversity

Dyer, J. H., Gregersen, H. B., & Christensen, C. M. (2009, December). The innovator's DNA. *Harvard Business Review.*

Evans, F. C., & Bishop, D. M. (2001). *Valuation for M&A: Building value in private companies,* New York, NY: John Wiley & Sons.

Federal Trade Commission. (n.d.-a). *Exclusionary or predatory acts: Predatory pricing.* Retrieved August 17, 2011, from Federal Trade Commission Web site: http://www.ftc.gov/bc/antitrust/predatory_pricing.shtm

Federal Trade Commission. (n.d.-b). *Price discrimination among buyers: Robinson-Patman violations.* Retrieved August 17, 2011, from Federal Trade Commission Web site: http://www.ftc.gov/bc/antitrust/price_discrimination.shtm

Fitzpatrick, B. W., & Lueck, J. J. (2010). The case against data lock-in. *Communications of the ACM 53*(11), 42–46.

Ganskopp, D. C. (2006). Altering beef cattle distribution within rangeland pastures with salt and water. *Eastern Oregon Agricultural Research Center SR1057,* 61–63.

Gardner, H. (1994). *Creating minds: An anatomy of creativity seen through the lives of Freud, Einstein, Picasso, Stravinsky, Eliot, Graham, and Gandhi.* New York, NY: Basic Books.

Garrity, E., & Sanders, G. L. (Eds. and contributors). (1998). *Information systems success measurement.* Hershey, PA: Idea Group Publishing, now IGI Global.

Garrity, E., Glassberg, B., Kim, Y. J., Sanders, G. L., & Shin, S. K., (2005). An experimental investigation of electronic commerce success factors for web-based information systems. *Decision Support Systems 39*(3), 485–503.

Gartner. (n.d.). *Gartner hype cycle.* Retrieved August 17, 2011, from Gartner Web site: http://www.gartner.com/pages/story.php.id.8795.s.8.jsp

Garud, R., & Nayyar, P. (1994). Transformative capacity: Continual structuring by inter-temporal technology transfer, *Strategic Management Journal 15*(4), 365–385.

Gerby, M. (1995). *The E-myth revisited: Why most small businesses don't work and what to do about it.* New York, NY: HarperCollins.

Gladwell, M. (2008). *Outliers: The story of success.* New York, NY: Little, Brown and Company.

Goldenberg, J., & Mazursky, D. (2002). *Creativity in product innovation* (1st ed.). Cambridge, UK: Cambridge University Press.

Gompers, P., Kovner, A., Lerner, J., & Scharfstein, D. (2010, April). Performance persistence in entrepreneurship. *Journal of Financial Economics 96*(1), 18–32.

Gopal, R., & Sanders, G. L. (2000). Global software piracy: You can't get blood out of a turnip. *Communications of the ACM 43*(9), 82–89.

Grant, R. M. (2007). *Contemporary strategy analysis: Concepts, techniques, applications* (6th ed.). Malden: MA Wiley-Blackwell.

Grove, A. (2010, July 5). How America can create jobs. *Bloomberg Business Week.*

Grueber, M., & Studt, T. (2011, December). 2011 Global R&D funding forecast—Industrial R&D: Life sciences. *R&D Magazine.*

Han, J., Kim, N., & Srivastava, R. K. (1998). Market orientation and organizational performance: Is innovation the missing link? *The Journal of Marketing 62*(4), 30–45.

Heckhausen, J., & Schulz, R. (1995). A life-span theory of control. *Psychological Review 102*(2), 284–304.

Henry, A. (2007). *Understanding strategic management.* New York, NY: Oxford University Press.

Heracleous, L., & Wirtz, J. (2010, July–August). Singapore Airlines balancing act. *Harvard Business Review.*

Herbert, W. (2009, February). A recipe for motivation: Easy to read, easy to do. *Scientific American.*

Highfield, R., & Carter, P. (1993). *The private lives of Albert Einstein.* London: Faber and Faber.

Hofstede, G., & Hofstede, G.-J. (2004). *Cultures and organizations: Software of the mind.* New York, NY: McGraw-Hill.

Horan, J. (2007). *The one-page business plan.* Berkeley: The One Page Business Plan Company.

Huefner, R. J., Largay, J. A., III, and Hamlen, S. S. (2005). *Advanced financial accounting* (9th ed.). Mason, OH: Thomson Custom Publishing.

Huefner, R. J., Largay, J. A., III, and Hamlen, S. S. (2007). *Advanced financial accounting* (10th ed.). Mason, OH: Thomson Custom Publishing.

Hülsheger, U. R., Anderson, N., & Salgado, J. F. (2009). Team-level predictors of innovation at work: A comprehensive meta-analysis spanning three decades of research. *Journal of Applied Psychology 94*(5), 1128–1145.

Humphrey, A. S. (2005, December). SWOT analysis for management consulting. *SRI Alumni Association Newsletter.*

Ihnatko, A. (2009, January 22). Microsoft opens Windows 7, shuts door on Vista. *Chicago Sun Times.*

IPS Associates. (1997). *Project management manual,* developed by, Harvard Business School, October 6.

Isaacson, W. (2008). *Einstein: His life and universe.* New York, NY: Simon & Schuster.

Iyer, R., & Muncy, J. A. (2005). The role of brand parity in developing loyal customers. *Journal of Advertising Research 45*(2), 222–228.

Jain, S. C. (2000). *Marketing planning & strategy* (6th ed.). Cincinnati, OH: South-Western Publishing.

Jo, S., Moon, J., Garrity, E. J., & Sanders, G. L. (2007). Massively Multiplayer Online Role-Playing Games (MMORPGs) and commitment behavior: An integrated model, *AMCIS 2007 Proceedings.* Paper 70.

Jones, G. E., & Van Dyke, D. (1998). *The business of business valuation* (p. 1). New York, NY: McGraw-Hill, 1998.

Kaplan, R. S., & Norton, D. P. (1996, January–February). Using the balanced scorecard as a strategic management system. *Harvard Business Review*, 75–85.

Kaplan, R. S., & Norton, D. P. (2003a, September 15). Lock-in strategies: A new value proposition. *Harvard Business Review 5*(5).

Kaplan, R. S., & Norton, D. P. (2003b). *Strategy maps: Converting intangible assets into tangible outcomes.* Boston, MA: Harvard Business Publishing.

Kawasaki, G. (2008). *Reality check: The irreverent guide to outsmarting, outmanaging and outmarketing your competition* (1st ed.). New York, NY: Penguin Group.

Keller, K. L., & Tybout, A. (2002). The principle of positioning. *Market Leader 19 Winter.*

Keller, K. L., Sternthal, B., & Tybout, A. (2002, September). Three questions to ask about your brand. *Harvard Business Review*, 80–89.

Kim, W. C., & Mauborgne, R. (2005). *Blue ocean strategy: How to create uncontested market space and make competition irrelevant.* Boston, MA: Harvard Business School Press.

Kim, Y. J., & Sanders, G. L. (2002). Strategic actions in information technology investments based on real option theory. *Decision Support Systems 33*, 1–11.

Kirzner, I. M. (1973). *Competition and entrepreneurship* (1st ed.). Chicago, IL: University of Chicago Press.

Kotler, P., & de Bes, F. T. (2003). *Lateral marketing: New techniques for finding breakthrough ideas.* Hoboken, NJ: John Wiley and Sons.

Laursen, K., & Salter, A. (2006). Open for innovation: The role of openness in explaining innovation performance among U.K. manufacturing firms. *Strategic Management Journal 27*, 131–150.

Leavitt, H. J. (1965). Applying organizational change in industry: Structural, technological, and humanistic approaches. In J. G. March (Ed.), *Handbook of organizations.* Chicago: Rand-McNally.

Lenskold, J. (2003). *Marketing ROI: The path to campaign, customer, and corporate profitability.* New York, NY: McGraw-Hill Professional.

Lieberman, D. (2003, January 29). Turner quits as AOL loss hits $99B. *USA Today.*

Liebowitz, S. J., & Margolis, S. E. (1994). Network externality: An uncommon tragedy. *Journal of Economic Perspectives 8*, 133–150.

Lipsey, R. G., & Chrystal, K. A. (2007). *Economics* (11th ed.). New York, NY: Oxford Press.

Lubart, T. I. (2001). Models of the creative process. *Creativity Research Journal 13*(3&4), 295–308.

Lupien, S. J., McEwen, B. S., Gunnar, M. R., & Heim, C. (2009). Effects of stress throughout the lifespan on the brain, behavior and cognition. *Nature Reviews Neuroscience 10*, 434–445.

Lyons, D. (2010a, January 4). The customer is always right. *Newsweek*.

Lyons, D. (2010b, September 1). Apple's shuffle: No one innovates better. *Newsweek*.

Madsen, J. B. (2007). Are there diminishing returns to R&D? *Economics Letters 95*, 161–166.

Malhotra, N. K., & Birks, D. F. (2009). *Marketing research: An applied orientation* (6th ed.). Lebanon, Indiana, IN: Prentice Hall.

Manjoo, F. (2010, July/August). Apple nation. *Fast Company*.

Markoff, J. (2008, January 15). The passion of Steve Jobs. *New York Times*. Retrieved August 17, 2011, from New York Times Web site: http://bits.blogs.nytimes.com/2008/01/15/the-passion-of-steve-jobs/

Matheson, J., & Matheson, D. (1998). *The smart organization: Creating value through strategic R&D*. Boston, MA: Harvard Business School Press.

Mauboussin, M. (1999). *Get real*. New York, NY: Credit Suisse First Boston.

May, G. L. (2010). *Strategic planning fundamentals for small business*. New York, NY: Business Experts Press.

McConnell, C. R., Brue, S. L., & Campbell, R. R. (2004). *Microeconomics: Principles, problems, and policies* (16th ed.). New York, NY: McGraw-Hill Professional.

McGrath, R. G., & MacMillan, I. (2000). *The entrepreneurial mindset*. Boston, MA: Harvard Business School Press.

Michalko, M. (2006). *Thinkertoys: A handbook of creative-thinking techniques* (2nd ed.). Berkeley, CA: Ten Speed Press.

Miller, C. C. (2010, November 28). Google grows, and works to retain nimble minds. *New York Times*, p. A1.

Moore, G. E. (1999). *Crossing the chasm: Marketing and selling high-tech products to mainstream customers*. Boston, MA: Harvard Business School Press.

Moore, G. E. (n.d.). *Intel executive biographies*. Retrieved August 17, 2011, from Intel Web site: http://www.intel.com/pressroom/kits/bios/moore.htm

Mun, J. (2005). *Real options analysis: Tools and techniques for valuing strategic investment and decisions*. Hoboken, NJ: John Wiley & Sons, Inc.

Nalebuff, B., & Ayres, I. (2003). *Why not? How to use everyday ingenuity to solve problems big and small*. Boston, MA: Harvard Business Press.

Noor, J. (2009). Hyperbolic discounting and the standard model: Eliciting discount functions. *Journal of Economic Theory 144*(5), 2077–2083.

Nørreklit, H. (2000). The balance on the balanced scorecard: Critical analysis of some of its assumptions. *Management Accounting Research 11*, 65–88.

O'Sullivan, D., & Dooley, L. (2008). *Applying innovation*. Oaks, CA: Sage Publications.

Ohanian, H. C. (2008). *Einstein's mistakes*. New York, NY: W.W. Norton & Co.

Oz Shy, C. F. (2008). *How to price: A guide to pricing techniques and yield management*. Cambridge, UK: Cambridge University Press.

Panagiotou, G. (2003). Bringing SWOT into focus. *Business Strategy Review 14*(2), 8–10.

Patent Technology Monitoring Team. (n.d.). *U.S. Patent Statistics Chart Calendar Years 1963–2010*. Retrieved August 17, 2011, from U.S. Patent and Trademark Office Web site: http://www.uspto.gov/web/offices/ac/ido/oeip/taf/us_stat.htm

Phillips, R. (2005). *Pricing and revenue optimization* (11th ed.). Stanford, CA: Stanford University Press.

Pierce, J. L., Kostovab, T., & Dirks, K. T. (2003). The state of psychological ownership: Integrating and extending a century of research. *Review of General Psychology 7*(1), 84–107.

Pisano, G. P., & Shih, W. C. (2009). Restoring American competitiveness. *Harvard Business Review 87*, 114–125.

Porter, M. E. (1980). *Competitive strategy*. New York, NY: The Free Press.

Porter, M. E. (1985). *Competitive advantage*. New York, NY: The: Free Press.

Porter, M. E. (1998). *Competitive advantage: Creating and sustaining superior performance*. New York, NY: Free Press.

Porter, M. E. (2008). The five competitive forces that shape strategy. *Harvard Business Review, 86*(1).

Prahalad, C. K. (2006). *The fortune at the bottom of the pyramid: Eradicating poverty through profits*. Upper Saddle River, NJ: Wharton School Publishing.

Prahalad, C. K., & Hamel, G. (1990). The core competence of the corporation. *Harvard Business Review, 68*(3).

Pratt, S. P. (2001). *Business valuation: Discounts and premiums* (pp. 20, 79). New York, NY: John Wiley & Sons, Inc.

Pratt, S. P., Reilly, R. F., & Schweihs, R. P. (1993). *Valuing small businesses and professional practices*. Homewood, IL: Business One Irwin.

Project Management Institute. (2004). A guide to the project management body of knowledge. Newtown Square, PA: Project Management Institute, Inc.

Raustiala, K., & Sprigman, C. (2006). The piracy paradox: Innovation and intellectual property in fashion design. *Virginia Law Review 92*(8), p. 1719.

Reichheld, F. F., & Schefter, P. (2000). E-loyalty your secret weapon on the web.

Harvard Business Review 78(4), 105–115.

Rose, F. (2002, March). The father of creative destruction. *Wired 10*.

Roth, C. (2011). *The entrepreneur equation: Evaluating the realities, risks, and rewards of having your own business*. Dallas, TX: BenBella Books.

Runco, M. A. (2006). *Creativity theories and themes: Research, development and practice*. Burlington, MA: Elsevier Academic Press.

Sahlman, W. A. (1997, July-August). How to write a great business plan. Boston, MA: *Harvard Business Review*, 98–108.

Sahlman, W. A., & Flaherty, S. G. (2010). NovaCure Ltd., Boston, MA: Harvard Business School Publishing.

Sarasvathy, S. D., & Venkataraman, S. (2008). *Ought to can: Questions for an entrepreneurial future*. Included in ten papers selected for the first World Entrepreneurship Forum held under the aegis of French President Nicolas Sarkozy in Evian, November 13–15,.

Sawyer, R. K. (2006). *Explaining creativity: The science of human innovation*. New York, NY: Oxford University Press.

Schank, R., & Cleary, C. (1995). *Engines for education*. Hillsdale, NJ: Lawrence Erlbaum Associates.

Schmoch, U. (2007). Double-boom cycles and the comeback of science-push and market-pull. *Research Policy 36*, 1000–1015.

Schwartz, B. (2003). *The paradox of choice* (1st ed.). New York, NY: HarperCollins Press.

Selling, T. (2009, February 10). *High "power distance" at the SEC: Why madoff was allowed to take investors down with him*. Retrieved August 17, 2011, from The Accounting Onion Web site: http://accountingonion.typepad.com/theaccountingonion/2009/02/high-power-dist.html

Shapiro, C., & Varian, H. R. (1998). *Information rules: A strategic guide to the network economy*. Boston, MA: Harvard Business School Press.

Sims, P. (2011). *Little bets: How breakthrough ideas emerge from small discoveries*. New York, NY: Free Press.

Skinner, E. A. (1996). A guide to constructs of control. *Journal of Personality and Social Psychology 71*(3), 549–570.

Slavin, S. (2008). *Microeconomics* (8th ed.). New York, NY: Irwin/ McGraw-Hill.

Slee, R., & Paglia, J. (2010, March/April). *The Value Examiner*. Retrieved August 17, 2011, from Pepperdine University Web site: http://bschool.pepperdine.edu/privatecapital

Spence, M. (1981). The learning curve and competition. *The Bell Journal of Economics 12*, 49–70.

Stuck, B., & Weingarten, M. (2005). How venture capital thwarts innovation. *IEEE Spectrum 42*(4), 50–55.

Sugden, R. (1984). Is fairness good? A critique of Varian's theory of fairness. *Nous 18*, 505–551.

Takeuchi, H., & Nonaka, I. (1986, January). New product development game. *Harvard Business Review.*

The Printed World. (2011, February 10). Three-dimensional printing from digital designs will transform manufacturing and allow more people to start making things. *The Economist.*

Trigeorgis, L. (1996). *Real options: Managerial flexibility and strategy in resource allocation.* The MIT Press.

Tybout, A. M., & Sternthal, B. (2005). Brand positioning. In A. Tybout & T. Calkins (Eds.), *Kellogg on branding* (pp. 11–26). John Wiley & Sons.

Varian, H. R. (1996). Differential pricing and efficiency. *First Monday 1.*

Varian, H. R. (1997). How to build an economic model in your spare time. In M. Szenberg (Ed.), *Passion and craft: Economists at work.* Ann Arbor, MI: University of Michigan Press.

Varianini, V., & Vaturi, D. (2000). Marketing lessons from E-failures. *McKinsey Quarterly 4*, 86–97.

VC MIKE. (2010). *Guest blogger Bob Metcalfe: Metcalfe's law recurses down the long tail of social networks.* Retrieved August 17, 2011, from VCMIKE's Blog : http://vcmike.wordpress.com/2006/08/18/metcalfe-social-networks/

Verganti, R. (2009). *Design driven innovation: Changing the rules of competition by radically innovating what things mean.* Boston, MA: Harvard Business Press.

Wang, S. C., & Chern, J. Y. (2008). The "Night Owl" learning style of art students: Creativity and daily rhythm. *International Journal of Art & Design Education 27*(2), 202–209.

Wallas, G. (1926). *The art of thought.* New York, NY: Harcourt Brace Jovanovich.

Why not? About the book. Retrieved August 17, 2011, from Why Not Web site: http://www.whynot.net/main/about_book.php

Wikepedia. *Croesus.* Retrieved August 17, 2011, from Wikipedia Web site: http://en.wikipedia.org/wiki/Croesus

Williamson, O. E. (1985). *The economic institutions of capitalism.* New York, NY: The Free Press.

Wolverton, T. (2000). *Amazon backs away from test prices.* Retrieved August 17, 2011, from cnet NEWS Web site: http://news.cnet.com/2100-1017-245631.html

Index

The italicized *f* and *t* following page numbers refer to figures and tables, respectively.

Announcing the Business Expert Press Digital Library

Concise E-books Business Students Need for Classroom and Research

This book can also be purchased in an e-book collection by your library as

- a one-time purchase,
- that is owned forever,
- allows for simultaneous readers,
- has no restrictions on printing, and
- can be downloaded as PDFs from within the library community.

Our digital library collections are a great solution to beat the rising cost of textbooks. e-books can be loaded into their course management systems or onto student's e-book readers.

The **Business Expert Press** digital libraries are very affordable, with no obligation to buy in future years.

For more information, please visit **www.businessexpert.com/libraries**. To set up a trial in the United States, please contact **Sheri Dean** at *sheri.dean@globalpress.com*; for all other regions, contact **Nicole Lee** at *nicole.lee@igroupnet.com*.

Marketing Research
Collection Editor: **Naresh Malhotra**

Developing New Products and Services: Learning, Differentiation, and Innovation
by G. Lawrence Sanders

CPSIA information can be obtained at www.ICGtesting.com
Printed in the USA
BVOW070058081111

275507BV00005B/5/P